The Guns Of The Gunfighters

Lawmen, Outlaws & Hollywood Cowboys

Doc O'Meara

Published by

krause publications
An F&W Publications Company

700 East State Street • Iola, WI 54990-0001
715-445-2214 • 888-457-2873
www.krause.com

Please call or write for our free catalog of publications.
Our toll-free number to place an order or obtain a free catalog is 800-258-0929
or please use our regular business telephone 715-445-2214.

Library of Congress Catalog Number: 2002107609
ISBN: 0-87349-433-4

Printed in the United States of America

DEDICATION

This book is written in memory of "Sidewinder Pete" Martin, who understood the meaning of "The Cowboy Way," and the many brothers and sisters with whom he perished in the effort to save others on that horrible September morning. Of their selfless heroism their city and their nation is proud and grateful.

ACKNOWLEDGMENTS

The author wishes to thank the following persons and institutions for their generous assistance in the preparation of this book: Wayne Allwine, Bobbi Jean Bell, William A. Dascher, John Dowming, Tom Eiben, Scott Hughes Mayerly, James Nottage, Richard Rattenbury, Roy "Dusty" Rogers, Jr., Peter J. Stebbins, John Taffin, Russi Taylor, The Autry Museum of Western Heritage, The J.M. Davis Museum, The National Cowboy & Western Heritage Museum, The Roy Rogers & Dale Evans Museum

FOREWORD

From the time explorers and colonists first set foot upon the New World an inexorable move toward the west began. When, in 1803, Thomas Jefferson negotiated the Louisiana Purchase from France, the United States expanded its territory across the entire continent. Reports from the Lewis and Clark expedition that had explored the new territory set the mountain men to scouring the Rocky Mountains for furs. In the course of their explorations, mountain passes were discovered that permitted overland settlement to the fertile valleys and rich coastal waters of Oregon. From there Americans migrated north to Washington and south to California. In between, however, was a land of vast prairies and rugged mountains almost ignored by settlers until the coming of the transcontinental railroads in 1868.

In the half-century or so that followed the American Civil War the United States experienced its greatest period of expansion. It was a time of adventure, exploration, settlement and, sometimes, lawlessness, during which was defined much of the national character. Recent attempts at revisionist history notwithstanding, this nation was, indeed, born and raised with a gun in its hand. The very first battle of the Revolutionary War was fought in response to British efforts to disarm individual colonists and to confiscate their militia arms. From that time on, the heroic exploits and legendary marksmanship of men like Daniel Boone, Simon Butler, Davy Crockett and Kit Carson were told around campfires, in the newspapers and pulp fiction novels of their time.

As the nation continued its move west following the Civil War new heroes and villains came to the stage of public attention. The common denominator was skill at arms. In some instances the individuals really were possessed of an awesome level of marksmanship. Others won their fame, not so much for the ability to hit that at which they aimed, but for their determination to stand their ground and keep fighting, in spite of the lead being sent their way by adversaries. More often than not, such steadfastness allowed them to prevail and their legends to grow. There were also those whose self-aggrandizement far outshone their physical abilities. Often they were their own best public relations promoters and the media of the time were willing accomplices.

Skill with firearms was also much admired in the sporting world. During the last quarter of the 19th century the exploits of local, state and national shooting teams and their champions were the frequent subject of news accounts. Shooting matches were popular spectator events. Circuses, fairs and Wild West shows almost always provided performers who demonstrated feats of extraordinary skill with rifle, shotgun or handgun. Female performers, such as Annie Oakley and, later, Plinky Topperwein, were especially popular.

During the 20th century motion pictures and television provided new heroes, many based upon the historical characters portrayed in them. Other characters were purely fictional, but were usually provided with a historically appealing, if not necessarily accurate, setting for what came to be a uniquely American variant of the morality play.

The firearms used by the true-to-life gunmen on both sides of the law, and the actors and trick-shot artists who performed before cameras and live audiences, run the gamut from plain to ornate. Many of the real lawmen and outlaws were not averse to sporting highly decorated arms, some of which were custom-crafted or had features that improved their performance, at least in the hands of their owners.

Among the professional marksmen, who required top-notch performance from their firearms, high quality arms prevail, though not always the brands usually expected. However, among the firearms used by movie and television actors many were, although visually appealing on screen, virtually worthless for any real-life application. As well, a considerable number that appear to be highly decorated on screen are actually poorly embellished and look much less impressive when seen close up. Still, as long as the firing pin hit the primer of the blank cartridge, the director reckoned it was good enough to print the take.

In the pages that follow we will examine some of the guns actually owned or used by many of the best known gunfighters of the Old West, some of the modern era, and the performers who portrayed the real and fictional gunfighters depicted by the entertainment industry. In a few instances we will also see guns owned by people who were neither gunfighters nor performers, but whose skills and contributions have left an indelible mark upon the martial art that is shooting.

Along the way, we will also debunk some popular myths and point out some realities. One of which we may as well consider immediately; that is that professional lawmen or outlaws had any special fondness for the particular firearms they used. Although they may often have shown a preference for a particular make, model or caliber of firearm, rarely was there any sentimentality demonstrated for the particular guns. They were usually regarded as nothing more than tools of the trade, as demonstrated by the frequency with which some changed from one to another. Still, they were generally cared for meticulously so that they would perform as they

should when called upon to do so. Outside appearance meant little, but internal mechanisms were well kept. To keep a firearm in such a condition was not mere fastidiousness; it was a matter of survival.

Gimmick guns were used in the entertainment industry, particularly in the television series of the 1950s and 1960s, and in a few movies. These are pieces modified in some distinctive fashion to draw particular attention to the hero of the show. The premise is that with this cleverly modified, or in some instances ridiculously contrived arm, perhaps combined with the purity of his heart, our hero is somehow capable of vanquishing his enemies in circumstances under which lesser men would surely fail. As well, there is the matter of speed. Characters were depicted as having a speed of draw so fast that a mere blink of the eye would cause the observer to miss the act, and with this speed the protagonist's unerring aim allowed him to place his shots with near surgical precision. Actually, some rare individuals really do have such talents. However, people like Ed McGivern, Thell Reed and Bob Munden are very rare. Many of the actors in those screenplays had significant assistance by means of stop-action photography and by skilled film editors. Still, they were entertaining and sometimes amusing to watch, and that was the whole idea.

So, let's examine some of the guns of the gunfighters - in the real world of fact and the fantasy world of the entertainment industry. They take us to a place we remember well.

"Doc" O'Meara
2002

"My heroes have always been cowboys".......
Willy Nelson

TABLE OF CONTENTS

Part One: The Real Gunfighters

Part Two: The Reel Gunfighters

Part One
THE REAL GUNFIGHTERS

Billy The Kid

THERE ARE MORE stories about the early life of Billy the Kid than The Kid had aliases. Best known to history as Billy the Kid, his aliases included several variations of family names. Starting with his probable given name, Henry McCarty, he also called himself Henry Antrim, William Antrim, Kid Antrim and William Bonney. Among the Mexican community he was referred to as El Chivato (The Kid).

Most biographies say he was born in New York City. Some even narrow it down to the borough of Brooklyn. There are those, however, who insist that he came from Indiana. The former seems more likely. Most sources put the year of his birth at 1859 or 1860 and list his father's name as either Patrick Henry McCarty or William Bonney and his mother as Catherine McCarty or Katherine Bonney-McCarty. Regardless of the man's name, Billy the Kid's father appears to have died at some time around the end of the Civil War and Billy, his mother and elder brother, Joe, moved to Indiana. There, in about 1873, she married William Antrim and the family moved to New Mexico, where they took up residence in Silver City. Antrim died in 1874, leaving Billy's twice widowed mother to fend for herself and her children. Sadly, she suffered from tuberculosis and later that same year she, too, died.

Legend has it that he claimed to have killed 21 men; one for each year of his life, the more probable number is six. Some speculate that he was really a decent sort; misunderstood and picked on, who fell victim to circumstances. His last legitimate employer, and supposed mentor, the rancher John Tunstall, had taken the young man under his wing. Under his influence and tutelage reformation seemed possible. Yet modern lawmen and criminal psychologists would very likely consider the appearance of reform to be manipulative behavior.

When Tunstall was murdered, Billy the Kid set out to avenge his death. Whether his reaction was the result of genuine grief and a desire for some measure of justice, or anger because his plans for taking advantage of Tunstall's possibly misplaced generosity is a matter of conjecture. Worth considering, however, is that Pat Garrett knew Billy the Kid well. If Garrett regarded Billy as salvageable, it seems likely he would not have shot The Kid dead with no attempt to take him alive.

Until a previously unknown photographic portrait alleged to be that of Billy the Kid in his mid-teen years surfaced in the 1970s, the only image known was that of him standing with a revolver of indeterminate make on his left hip, a cocky expression on his face, leaning on a Model 1873 Winchester held by the muzzle in his outstretched right hand. Based on that old picture it had, for nearly a century, been believed that The Kid was left-handed. Then, some sharp-eyed observer realized that the loading gate on the Winchester was on the wrong side. At some point early on the negative had been reversed and in subsequent publications of it the error continued. It turns out he was right-handed all along. It should be noted that the subject in the photo in question has been disputed, probably for good reason. The young man depicted in that old tintype does not fit the more attractive physical descriptions some contemporaries have given of him.

Historical accounts indicate that Billy the Kid's preferred handgun was a Colt SAA, chambered to match his .44-40 rifle. Yet, legend would have that the Colt Model 1877 .41 Long Colt Thunderer revolver was his favorite. The young man killed by Pat Garrett at Pete Maxwell's house in Ft. Sumner, New Mexico, on the night of July 13, 1881, is said to have been armed with such a revolver; an ejectorless version with a 4-inch barrel, with ivory stocks and the name, "Billy," professionally inscribed across the top of the left panel.

There really isn't anything particularly contradictory here. Many young shooters of today gravitate toward the Glock and Sig semi-auto pistols, eschewing the tried and true 20th century six-shot revolvers by Colt, S&W and Ruger. In 1881 the self-cocker was new, innovative and controversial. When or how he may have come by it no one knows, but his having such a firearm is perfectly reasonable.

On the other hand, there is some reason to doubt that Pat Garrett killed Billy the Kid that fateful night. The coroner's jury that, by the way, had neither coroner nor

It's this photo, which generations of Western history buffs have believed to be of Billy the Kid that caused some to claim he was left-handed. It took a sharp-eyed individual who knew something about the Model 1873 Winchester to realize that for all that time the photo had been seen in reverse. One matter is clearly obvious and that is the holster was not designed to facilitate a fast draw.

If this studio portrait really is of the teen-aged Billy the Kid, as alleged, it offers no explanation for contemporary reports that women found him handsome and charming. He looks more like a sulking child who would rather be anywhere else but sitting in front of the camera wearing that stiff collar.

any medical testimony, consisted entirely of individuals of Mexican lineage. One of the key witnesses was a woman known as "Tia" de Luvina, Pete Maxwell's housekeeper. She testified at the inquest that it had been Billy that was killed, but later said that she and the other witnesses had lied, so that Billy the Kid could escape. She claimed it was another young man who had come to her for a meal and taken a butcher knife from the kitchen to cut some meat from a side of beef hanging on Maxwell's porch. While none of Garrett's deputies knew The Kid, the Sheriff certainly did and would have had to be in on the conspiracy for it to work. Moreover, he would have had to murder an innocent man in the process, or at the very least, to kill him by mistake, then

conspired in a cover-up. That is unlikely, but certainly possible.

One firearm associated with Billy the Kid, the provenance of which is undisputed, is a Whitney-Kennedy .44-40 rifle that he surrendered to Deputy U.S. Marshal Eugene van Patten, when he was captured at Stinking Springs, New Mexico. This model was made from 1879 to 1886, so it must have been fairly new when The Kid handed it over on December 23, 1880. The piece shows evidence of considerable wear, so in all likelihood it was used extensively for a time after coming into van Patten's possession.

Aside from the suspect 1877 Colt Thunderer, there are several other guns associated with Billy the Kid. One is a Single Action Army revolver that became a part of the per-

Governor Lew Wallace is said to have met secretly with Billy the Kid in Lincoln, New Mexico, to promise him aid, and possibly amnesty, if he would turn himself in. Whether he reneged or was simply unable to provide the help The Kid sought is a matter of conjecture. What is known is that The Kid surrendered four days later and was indicted for murder. Facing a hangman's rope, he and his co-defendant, Tom O'Folliard, escaped custody and returned to their old ways.

Among the most enduring actors in Western films, Bob Steel's career spanned more than 40 years. He was one of many who played the role of Billy the Kid, but he portrayed him as a misunderstood hero, rather than the vicious delinquent history records. Note that there's no front sight on the revolver he's holding. Often, if a revolver's barrel was longer than desired, studio prop personnel simply took a hacksaw to it. Many fine collectibles were ruined that way.

sonal collection of the silent screen star, William S. Hart. It is suspect, because the serial number of the .44-40 in question indicates manufacture late in the year of The Kid's death. A Model 1873 Winchester carbine, said to have been among the possessions inventoried after his death, may have actually been his. The 10-gauge double-barreled shotgun he used to kill Bob Olinger during his escape from the Lincoln County Courthouse wasn't his. It belonged to Olinger and was only briefly in The Kid's hands. Considering the number of firearms claimed to have association with Billy the Kid, it seems almost as if he changed guns even more frequently than he changed his name.

Billy the Kid's .44-40 Whitney-Kennedy was nearly new when he surrendered it to Marshal van Patten at Stinking Springs, New Mexico. It was obviously subjected to quite a lot of use in the years that followed. (Courtesy The Autry Museum of Western Heritage)

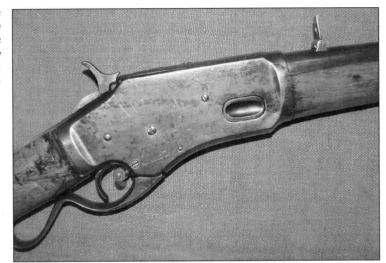

Charles Bolton

(Black Bart, The PO8)

IN THE EIGHT years Charles Bolton made his living behind a gun, robbing at least 27 Wells Fargo stagecoaches, he was never known to have shot anyone. For all that time his identity was a mystery, but he was the subject of grudging admiration for his ability to ply his trade without gratuitous violence and for the sense of humor he displayed by leaving short pieces of verse he composed himself. Perhaps the best known of these is the following:

I've labored long and hard for bread,
For honor and for riches,
But on my toes too long you've tred,
You fine-haired sons-of-bitches.
BLACK BART, the PO8

From the tone of that little ditty it would seem that he had some personal animosity toward Wells Fargo, but the precise nature of his grievance is lost to history. Bolton's success might have continued had a shot aimed in his direction by a guard not startled him into leaving behind some evidence that led to his capture. As he was concluding a robbery near Copperopolis, California, Bolton dropped a handkerchief. James B. Hume, the Wells Fargo investigator assigned to the case, noted that it had a laundry mark. A Chinese laundry service, one of about 90 that were checked, led Hume to his man. Bolton was arrested without incident, was tried and sent to prison for a term of six years. He served four; was released early for good behavior and was never to be heard from again. It was rumored, however, that Wells Fargo made a generous donation to his "retirement" fund, to assure that he would not go back to his old trade.

In order to give the impression that he was not alone, Bolton would place a revolver where the stagecoach crew could see it, concealed in the foliage of a tree. One, believed to have been his, was found years later, badly rusted from exposure to the elements and with part of the branch where it had rested, grown up around it. It might be interesting to know why it was never retrieved.

The shotgun used so judiciously by Bolton in his persona as Black Bart was a 12-gauge double-barreled Lumas, IXC #15, probably made in Belgium. Wells Fargo displayed it as part of their exhibit at the Chicago World's Fair in 1893.

Charles Bolton appeared to the world to be a refined gentleman of advanced middle years, but his mode of earning a living was among Wells Fargo's most troublesome problems. During the eight years he plied the trade of highwayman, he relieved Wells Fargo of stagecoach strong boxes at least 27 times. Dogged detective work brought him to justice, but it was rumored that Wells Fargo financed his retirement in order to keep him from returning to his old trade upon release from prison.

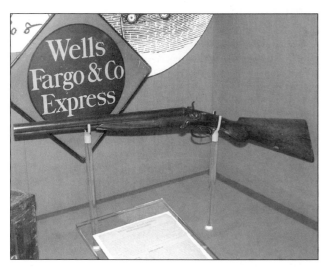

Black Bart used this Belgian-made Lumas shotgun during some of his robberies. Taken into custody as evidence following his arrest, it became a favorite part of the Wells Fargo exhibit during the 1893 Chicago World's Fair. (Courtesy The Autry Museum of Western Heritage)

REWARD!

WELLS, FARGO & Co.'s EXPRESS BOX, on Chinese and Copperopolis Stage, was ROBBED this morning, by one man about two miles from **Burns Ferry.** (Ruplee's Bridge,) Tuolumne county side, of $600 in coin and gold dust.

For arrest and conviction of the Robber, we will pay $300, and one-fourth of any portion of treasure recovered.

ROBBER described as follows: A Mexican, lightish complexion, rather short and thick set; weight about 150 lbs.; had a moustache and short growth of beard.

JOHN J. VALENTINE,

San Francisco, Dec. 1, 1875.   General Superintendent.

This poster, published early in his career, indicates that Wells Fargo seemed to regard Black Bart as little more than an annoyance. It also appears from the description of the robber that he tried to disguise his voice to make victims think he was Mexican.

William Frederick Cody

(Buffalo Bill)

STUDENTS OF HISTORY recognize him readily by his given name, but throughout the world, the nickname he earned providing meat for the hungry crews laying track for the Kansas-Pacific Railroad followed "Buffalo Bill" forever. The sensational pulp fiction stories about him, in what were called "dime novels," were certainly fabrications. However, there was more than enough real adventure in his life to satisfy the imagination of the most fanciful historian. Cody's biography reflects in many ways all the stages of the transition from the grand adventure that was the Old West, to the settled place of commerce, industry and normalcy that it had become by the end of his days.

William Frederick Cody was born on February 26, 1846, to Isaac and Mary Ann Cody in Le Claire, Scott County, Iowa. The fourth child among seven, his early years were typical of one growing up in the sparsely settled plains. When he was six, the family moved to Kansas, settling on a farm near Ft. Leavenworth. In 1857 his father died, following a long illness that resulted from a stab wound received when someone took offense at his expressing his abolitionist views. Just 11 years of age at the time, the youngster was burdened with man-size responsibilities. He obtained work as a mounted messenger and horse wrangler for a freight company. Two years later, the lure of the Pike's Peak gold rush beckoned, but he didn't strike it rich.

It was an incident during his term of employment as a rider for Russell, Majors and Wadell's Pony Express mail service that first brought the young Bill Cody to public attention. The Pony Express involved a series of 190 relay stations and ferries that were established over the more than 1,800 miles between St. Joseph, Missouri, and San Francisco, California. The object was to reduce the time required for communications between the East and the West coasts. By normal transport it took three weeks or more to get a message to California. Pony Express riders reduced that time to 10 days. It was a dangerous ride, over rough terrain, often in foul weather, with hostile Indians and outlaws to evade. For their skilled horsemanship and perilous journey riders were paid well, earning $125 a month at a time when one fifth of that amount was the norm for the average working man.

The killing of a relief rider left the 15-year-old Cody with the responsibility to carry on. Using 21 different horses, he rode at the gallop the 322 miles from the station at Red Buttes to the one at Rocky Ridge in just 21 hours. It was a remarkable feat of endurance and determination, especially for one so young.

With the completion of the transcontinental telegraph the Pony Express was no longer necessary, so it was disbanded after only 18 months. Cody went home to help his ailing mother to run the boarding house she owned. When she died two years later, Bill Cody was just 17 years old. The Civil War was raging, so

he enlisted in the 7th Kansas Cavalry, where he served as a dispatch rider. After Lee surrendered at Appomattox, Cody took a job as a stagecoach driver, which brought him to St. Louis. There he met Louisa Frederici, the young woman who would, two years later, become his bride.

George Armstrong Custer was posted at Ft. Larned, Kansas, and Cody became his scout. Part of Custer's assignment was to provide protection for the railway crews building the line ever westward. Hundreds of laborers were required for that job and their hard work developed healthy appetites. There was plenty of food on the hoof in the form of buffalo. Those hired to provide it were making a good living. With his skills and experience, Cody found that work ideally suited to his talents. During the 17 months he held the job he is said by some sources to have killed 2,928 bison. Cody's own tally came to 4,280 of the shaggy beasts.

Cody's years as a frontiersman were over by the time he was in his late 20s. From then until nearly the end of his life he was a showman. Trading-in on his early exploits and the exaggerated stories of them, Cody created an entertaining spectacle and won audiences throughout the United States and Europe, and made himself a wealthy man.

As Buffalo Bill grew old he began making poor and sometimes foolish investments. His fortune dissipated, he was nearly penniless at the time of his death. He remained, nevertheless, a national hero. Thousands of mourners attended his funeral.

A co-worker by the name of Bill Comstock took to calling himself "Buffalo Bill" and Cody, too, had used that moniker. They decided to have a contest to determine which of them would get the exclusive right to use it. On the day of the competition each was to shoot as many buffalo as he could in eight hours. When the last shot was fired Comstock had accounted for 46 and Cody had beaten him soundly by taking 69, winning officially the right to use the name by which he has been known throughout the world ever since.

By 1868 transcontinental railway construction was ending. Construction crews were reduced to maintenance crews, so there was no longer a need for the quantity of food Buffalo Bill and his co-workers had been providing. Cody went back to work for the army, serving as chief of scouts for the Fifth Cavalry, under Lt. General Philip H. Sheridan. During his four years in that capacity he fought in 16 battles. The most significant of those, from a historical viewpoint, was the 1869 engagement at Summit Springs, Colorado, from which the defeated Cheyenne were never able to fully recover.

Writer Edward Zane Carroll Judson, better known as Ned Buntline, was wandering the West in the summer of 1869 in search of new subjects for his sensationalist stories when he encountered Buffalo Bill. By some accounts Cody was nursing a severe hangover at the time of their meeting. Before the end of the year, "Buffalo Bill, King of the Border Men," the first of a long series of fanciful tales, appeared in *The New York Weekly.* Cody's fame spread rapidly. Throughout the nation his name became associated with the romance and adventure of the Wild West. No doubt, much of the publicity thus engendered influenced the congressional action that led to his being awarded the Medal of Honor on May 22,

1872, for bravery in action the month previous. Ironically, it was revoked in 1916, because Cody was not a member of the armed forces, but as a scout was a civilian employee at the time of the conflict for which it was presented. It was posthumously restored 73 years later, in 1989.

Later in 1872 Cody went to New York. Judson was producing a play about him and talked him into taking the stage to portray himself. Buffalo Bill was no actor, but audiences enjoyed the self-deprecating humor with which he presented himself. It's difficult to say whether the local press references to him as "Bison William" were simply snooty or a poor effort at snide humor. In either event, at $500 a week, the 26-year-old Cody was suddenly making more money that he ever dreamed of and certainly liked the fact that he didn't have to risk his scalp to do it. For the rest of his life, show business was his business.

There were a couple of brief periods during which he returned to action on the frontier. The first came about when the nation was horrified to learn that Custer and his troops had been slaughtered at the Little Big Horn on June 25, 1876. Cody vowed revenge and was engaged to scout for Col. Wesley Merritt. Less than three weeks after the killing on the Greasy Grass, near War Bonnet Creek, Nebraska, a force of 800 Cheyenne warriors on their way to join the Sioux were stopped by Merritt's troops and, during the fight, a war chief called Yellow Hair (often mistakenly called Yellow Hand) was killed. Some say Cody shot him. Others say the two met in hand-to-hand combat. Another account has it that Yellow Hair fell to an unknown hand, but that, when the fighting was done, Cody took credit. One thing is for certain: Cody lifted Yellow Hair's scalp when the fight was over.

A 12-gauge side-by-side shotgun, by Thomas, of Chicago and a .44-40 Colt Burgess rifle, embellished by the meistergraver, Cuno Helfricht, were among the guns Cody used in his Wild West Show. (Courtesy The Autry Museum of Western Heritage)

Again, in 1890, the army called upon Buffalo Bill to help restore the peace after the massacre at Wounded Knee. There, he and some of the Indians in his troupe were instrumental in calming matters. In between those events Cody had expanded from the stage to organize Buffalo Bill's Wild West and Rocky Mountain and Prairie Exhibition in 1883. An outdoor extravaganza, it featured cowboys, Indians, sharpshooters and mini representations of such stock-in-trade Western clichés as stagecoach robberies, buffalo hunts and the Indian Wars. There was also a generous measure of circus-style performances. After the short-lived Spanish-American War, the title of the troupe was changed to Buffalo Bill's Wild West and Congress of Rough Riders of the World. The show played throughout the United States and in many European nations making Cody a wealthy man.

For personal defense, Cody relied on a pair of Henry Deringer's pocket pistols early in his career

Soon after the turn of the century there began a long slide to ruin. With the death of his business partner, Nate Salsbury, and his daughter, Arta, in 1902, Cody's fortunes changed. Bad investments left him heavily in debt and his health was failing, too. Although he managed to carry on until very nearly the end of his time, he was never able to restore his fortunes and died broke. Still, he remained an American icon and was remembered so fondly that his funeral procession included more than 3,000 cars.

Partly because he endorsed Winchester's Model 1873 rifles commercially, it is often supposed that he used one during his buffalo hunting days, but the rifle wasn't made until those hunts had ceased. It was a .50-caliber rifle with which he fed the railroad crews. Cody did, however, use a handsomely engraved Model 1873 rifle regularly as part of his Wild West show. He also used a 12-gauge side-by-side shotgun done by E. Thomas Jr., of Chicago. His Colt Burgess rifle, a .44-40 exquisitely engraved by Cuno Helfricht, was among the finest firearms he owned.

For personal defense, Cody relied on a pair of Henry Deringer's pocket pistols early in his career, but substituted a nickel-plated and engraved .41 Rimfire Remington double-barreled derringer with ivory stocks, later in life. He certainly owned larger handguns over the course of his career, but like many of his contemporaries, when it came time to fight, his first choice was a rifle, not a handgun.

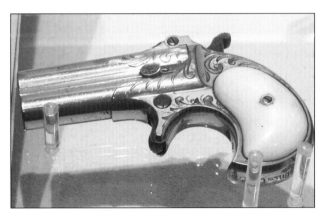

In later years Buffalo Bill carried this diminutive nickel-plated and engraved .41 Rimfire Remington derringer for personal protection. The stocks are elephant ivory. (Courtesy The Cody Firearms Museum)

Colt's Model 1878 Double Action Army revolver typically has a rather stiff trigger, but this .45 caliber piece with its 7-1/2-inch barrel was Capt. Jack Crawford's choice for trick shooting with a handgun. (Courtesy The Autry Museum of Western Heritage)

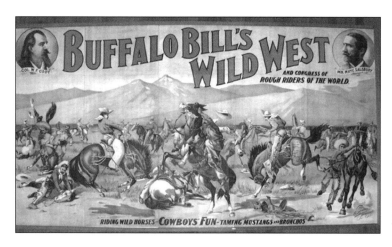

Banner advertisements such as this, for Buffalo Bill's Wild West and Congress of Rough Riders of the World, promised audiences the excitement and adventure of the frontier life while they remained safe in their own hometowns. (Courtesy The Cody Firearms Museum)

Gordon C. Lillie was better known as Pawnee Bill. Lillie was another genuine frontiersman, whose career began a couple of decades after Cody's, who became a showman. He was fluent in Pawnee and several other Indian languages and acted as an interpreter for the U.S. Government during tribal negotiations. In 1888 he opened a Wild West Show of his own. The Model 1892 Winchester .44-40 shown here was made as a smoothbore and used by Lillie in his act. Toward the end of their careers, Cody and Lillie combined their shows. (Courtesy The Autry Museum of Western Heritage)

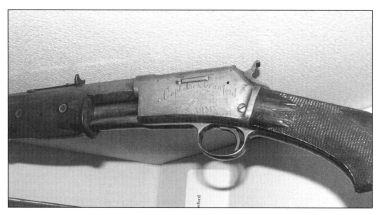

Army Captain Jack Crawford was one of the premier exhibition shooters of the late 19th century. The engraved Colt Lightning .44-40 that he used in his act is a slide-action design, which is much faster to use than the lever-actions that were available. This made it possible for Crawford to effectively engage several aerial targets at once, thrilling audiences with his speed and accuracy. (Courtesy The Autry Museum of Western Heritage)

Numerous motion pictures have presented Buffalo Bill as a central or peripheral character over the years. Paul Newman wore this extravagantly decorated sixgun rig playing the role of Cody in the film, Buffalo Bill and the Indians. *The revolver is a prop dummy, not a real SAA Colt.* (Courtesy The Autry Museum of Western Heritage)

This revolver was destined for Buffalo Bill's Wild West Show, which was touring Europe in the 1880s, but was diverted when it arrived in England. Chambered for the .45 Colt cartridge, the barrel is a smoothbore, made for use with shotshells for trick shooting exhibitions. It left Hartford with a blued and case-hardened colored finish, but was nickel-plated immediately after being subjected to British proof testing. Then, it was displayed at the Paris Exhibition. It remains unfired and in new condition. (Courtesy Rick DiTocco Collection, Kastle Keep Arms, Largo, FL)

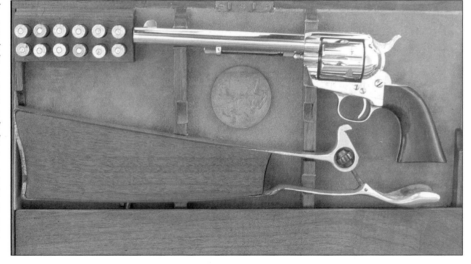

Emmett Dalton

EMMETT DALTON WAS the lone survivor of one of the boldest attempted robberies in Western history. That was when Emmett, some of his brothers and the rest of the Dalton gang, tried to rob two banks at once in Coffeyville, Kansas, on October 5, 1892. The plan may have worked, but an alert citizen recognized the gang and passed the word among the other townspeople. When the robbers tried to make their escape, they were all gunned down, as were several of the locals, in one of the wildest gunfights in Western history. Emmett survived his wounds and was sent to prison. His life sentence was suspended when he was granted a pardon in 1907. He spent the rest of his life in peaceable pursuits, first as a building contractor and real estate agent, then as a writer, technical advisor and sometime actor for the movies. He also lectured against crime and for prison reform.

The Dalton Gang was among the most successful of its kind, specializing in train robbery, as well as banks. It may be that the success was partially owing to several of the brothers having formerly been lawmen, thus knowing how the opposition would think and react. For them, robbery was a business and, like other businessmen, they were inclined to take an occasional vacation in order to savor the rewards of their labors.

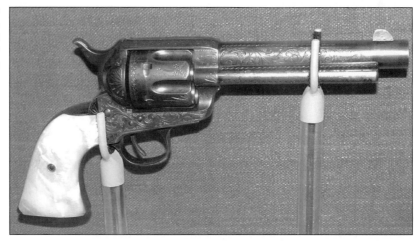

Emmett purchased this Single Action Army Colt at Simmons Hardware, in St. Louis. He and the rest of the Dalton gang purchased 10 of them, all alike, featuring mother-of pearl stocks and what was then known as "two-dollar engraving." (Courtesy The Autry Museum of Western Heritage)

On one such occasion they spent some time in St. Louis, seeing the sights and enjoying the amenities to be found in such a large city. One of the highlights of that holiday was a visit the gang made to Simmons Hardware, one of the premier agents for Colt firearms. There, the gang found 10 identical Helfricht-engraved SAA Colt .45s, each with a 5-1/2-inch barrel and mother-of-pearl stocks, two pairs of which had consecutive serial numbers. They bought all of the revolvers and those that Emmett kept for himself were among the consecutively numbered pairs. He lost them at Coffeyville.

Jug-eared and steely eyed, Emmett Dalton turned to crime for the money, not for any high-minded pretence. He and his brothers, Robert and Gratton, had been lawmen, but preferred the paydays associated with armed robbery.

After doing a 14-year stretch in prison for his crimes, a reformed Emmett Dalton found honest work. Eventually he wrote scripts and acted in some Western movies, also serving as a technical advisor.

Wyatt Earp

ONE OF THE most controversial figures of the Old West, Wyatt Berry Strapp Earp, has been lionized as a heroic lawman and condemned as an accused swindler, horse thief, gambler and pimp, among numerous other unsavory activities. Modern historians tend to agree that Earp was by no means a pillar of the law-enforcement community. On the other hand, he is known to have worn the badges of at least four frontier towns (more than once, it seems, in Dodge City) and is believed to have served briefly as a Deputy U.S. Marshal while in Tombstone. He also worked as a guard and messenger for banks and courier services, such as Wells Fargo.

Earp was born in Monmouth, Illinois, in 1848, the son of Mexican War veteran, Nicholas Porter Earp, and Virginia Ann Cooksey Earp. He was named in honor of Captain Wyatt Berry Strapp, his father's wartime company commander.

Among the more significant controversies surrounding Earp is the matter of the Buntline Special. Alleged to have been one of five given as gifts from Edward C.Z. Judson, a pulp fiction writer, also known as Ned Buntline, to Earp and the four other members of the, so-called, "Dodge City Peace Commission."

The Buntline Special has been described as having a 12-inch barrel; or an 18-inch barrel that Earp had cut to the more manageable foot-long length. Some say his compatriots cut

theirs to more conventional configurations, each to suit his own preference. Much ink has been used both to prove the existence of such a revolver and to deny it. Earp alleged that someone to whom he'd loaned it threw his revolver overboard from a mail boat caught in rough seas off the coast of Alaska in order to lighten its load during a storm.

The only documented historical reference to Wyatt Earp's use of a revolver with an especially long barrel was the testimony of a witness at the inquest following the shootout at the O.K. Corral. The man described Earp as having used a revolver with a barrel that appeared to be a foot long. To one unfamiliar with firearms, a Colt Single Action Army revolver with a 7-1/2-inch barrel — with the longest of the standard lengths offered — might seem substantially longer; especially in the excitement and confusion of such a moment. It has also been a matter of conjecture that the revolver he used during that notorious confrontation might have been a .44 caliber Smith & Wesson Model Number 3 American, which had an 8-inch barrel. Some speculate Earp borrowed the revolver from John Clum, editor of the *Tombstone Epitaph* newspaper.

That the Buntline gift revolvers ever existed is doubtful. Colt's records are silent on the matter. The most telling factor indicating that the story is fictional is a complete lack of mention of the alleged presentation by Judson, who, it seems logical, would have done so in grand terms, if the story were true. Nor is there any mention whatsoever of the supposed unusually lengthy revolvers by any other member of the Peace Commission.

The only gun we were able to provide here that is confirmed as having direct association with Wyatt Earp is a well-used 5-1/2-inch SAA Colt he reportedly used while employed as a Wells Fargo guard during his time in Tombstone. It has been identified as the sixgun with which Earp killed Curly Bill Brocius. Officially, that confrontation had to do with a robbery of the Wells Fargo office, but Earp seems to have had a personal matter at stake. Among the items taken in the robbery of the office was an engraved and silver- and gold-plated Single Action Army Colt revolver that a group of Chinese residents of Tombstone had presented to Earp. A rifle of unknown make and model was also taken. The highly decorated revolver was

confiscated some time later, when Sheriff John Slaughter arrested Brocius' partner in the robbery, Johnny Ringo. The revolver that Earp used to get Brocius found its way into the personal collection of Wells Fargo Chief Special Officer Fred W. Dodge, where it remained for many years.

Contemporary assessments of Earp's character and the numerous accounts of his involvement in con games and brawls, not to mention frequent association with women of loose morals and men of doubtful repute, leads the modern observer to conclude that he was no hero. On the contrary, he seems to often have used the badges he wore as a means of intimidation while he surrounded himself with people of a similar bent, including his own brothers. Nevertheless, he comes to us through the mists of history as one of the most adept of the gunfighters of the Old West.

Wyatt Earp had a reputation as a tough no-nonsense lawman, but there is credible evidence that he was corrupt and often misused his badge for financial gain. In his early years he was accused of horse-theft and in his later years he's said to be a swindler and a confidence man. Of his abilities with a sixgun there seems to be agreement that he was among the best.

These were some of the baddest hombres ever to pack a badge and a six-shooter. The lawmen of Dodge City during the heyday of the cattle drives included W.H. Harris, Luke Short, Bat Masterson (standing), Charles Bassett, Wyatt Earp, M.C. Clark and Neal Brown (seated).

Earp spent his later years in Los Angeles and became friendly with the moviemakers. He and Tom Mix became pals and some say he helped out as a technical advisor for a few films. Many of the old-time cowboys and a few aging lawmen and outlaws hung out in the Gower Gulch saloons, reminiscing and waiting for casting calls.

Among the Earp brothers, many historians believe Virgil to have been the best lawman. Siding his brothers, Wyatt and Morgan, with Doc Holliday, Virgil was wounded on October 26, 1881, during the shooting at Tombstone's O.K. Corral. Two months later, during Christmas week, he was ambushed. A fusillade from five different shotguns left him bleeding in the dust of Allen Street. Although he survived, he was left crippled for life.

Some believe this Smith & Wesson .44 caliber American Model revolver, once the property of Tombstone Epitaph *editor, John Clum, is the one Wyatt Earp used at the O.K. Corral. The consensus among most historians, however, is that it was not. (Courtesy Autry Museum of Western Heritage)*

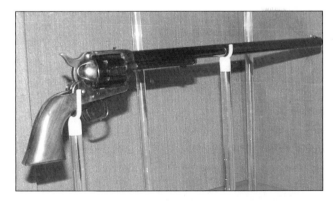

This SAA Colt .45, with its extra-long 16-inch barrel, came from the John S. DuMont collection. It has no known direct connection with Wyatt Earp, but shows the features of the Buntline Specials. (Courtesy The Autry Museum of Western Heritage)

The topstrap of the revolver's frame has been milled flat and routed so an adjustable rear sight could be installed. Note the hammer screw extending out past the side of the frame so it can be hinged to the top of the metal shoulder stock. (Courtesy the Autry Museum of Western Heritage)

The rear sight of the Buntline Special folds up to become a ladder rear sight, for use at extreme range. It's similar in function to those found on Winchester carbines. The shoulder stock is hinged at the top to the over-size head of the extended hammer screw. It hooks to a depression milled into the rear base of the backstrap and is drawn tight by a screw. (Courtesy The Autry Museum of Western Heritage)

This ivory-stocked Smith & Wesson New Model Number 3 was Virgil Earp's choice for enforcing the law. Many preferred the S&W revolvers for their faster extraction and reloading characteristics. (Courtesy National Cowboy and Western Heritage Museum)

Wells Fargo Chief Special Officer Fred Dodge added the sixgun issued to Wyatt Earp to his personal collection. (Courtesy The Autry Museum of Western Heritage)

Company-owned firearms were often provided for employees who had to maintain security. Wells Fargo issued this 5-1/2-inch barreled SAA .45 to Wyatt Earp. (Courtesy The Autry Museum of Western Heritage)

James was the eldest of the Earp brothers, but wounds sustained during his service in the Union Army during the Civil War kept him from becoming a lawman. Still, he was close to his brothers.

John Peters Ringold, better known as Johnny Ringo, was implicated in several killings, most notably the attempted murder of Virgil Earp. Several months after that act his body was found leaning against a tree, with a bullet through the brain. His boots had been removed, his feet wrapped, and his horse nowhere around. His death was ruled a suicide, but there was much speculation that Wyatt Earp had something to do with it. Earp was believed to have been in Gunnison, Colorado, at the time, but he is said to have confessed to the killing on his deathbed.

Actor Hugh O'Brian played Wyatt Earp in the television series, The Life and Legend of Wyatt Earp. The title is the same as that of the biography written by Stuart Lake. The show followed the book with extraordinary accuracy, but the accuracy of Lake's account of the man is in dispute. That, however, is probably more a reflection on Earp than on Lake who, in all likelihood, simply reported what he'd been told.

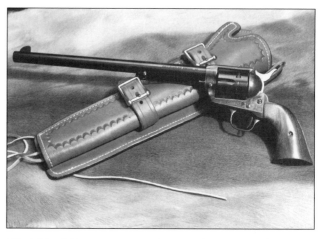

That Wyatt Earp ever owned or used a Buntline Special is very much in doubt, but its use on television created a great deal of public interest in that variation of the Single Action Army Colt during the late 1950s and early 1960s, so Colt began offering the revolver with a 12-inch barrel to the public.

Patrick Floyd Garrett

ALTHOUGH ONE MIGHT hardly know it, Pat Garrett did have a life before and after his association with Billy the Kid. However, his career was so lackluster that, had it not been for that association, it's unlikely that he would have been granted much more than a footnote in Western history. His life began auspiciously enough.

Born into a wealthy Alabama plantation family on June 5, 1850, his father, Col. John L. Garrett, moved the family to a cotton plantation in Louisiana in 1856. As did many among the Southern aristocracy, his parents lost everything as a result of the Civil War and died soon after it ended. Young Pat was reduced to working in the plantation store. In 1869 he moved west to Texas, where he found work as a cowboy in Lancaster.

Six years later, Garrett became a buffalo hunter, working the area around the Clear Fork of the Brazos River, in the vicinity of Ft. Griffin. It was during that period that he killed a man for the first time. Garrett insulted the man, who then attacked him with an axe. In self-defense, Garrett grabbed a .50 caliber buffalo rifle and shot him through the chest. Breathing his last, the man begged for forgiveness. Emotionally devastated, this was the end of his buffalo-hunting career.

Leaving Texas behind, Garrett drifted into New Mexico, where he blew his profits from the buffalo trade in a Tascosa gambling hall. His search for a job brought him to Ft. Sumner, where he found work with Pete Maxwell's cattle operation. That's when he first became acquainted with Billy the Kid.

Their early encounters seem to have been friendly. While there are stories of them being bosom buddies, there is no indication that they were more than casual acquaintances. For his part, Garrett began settling into the normal lifestyle of a maturing man. In 1879 he was married. Unfortunately, his young bride died during premature childbirth. Within a matter of months he was remarried, this time to his dead wife's sister. During that period he became a partner in a Ft. Sumner saloon and opened a restaurant.

In the summer of 1880, Garrett was persuaded to sign on as a deputy sheriff of Lincoln County, under Sheriff George Kimball. Then, in November, he ran against Kimball for the office and won. The primary demand of his constituency was apprehending Billy the Kid, who had reverted to his old ways of robbery and rustling after the murder of his boss, John Tunstall. Garrett rid the county of The Kid and his gang, but became the subject of controversy because of the local faction that regarded Billy as a heroic figure. When his term of office was done, he wasn't even nominated by his party for reelection.

Moving south, Garrett set up ranching again, along the Rio Hondo, but two years later, in 1884, he pinned on the badge of a Texas Ranger Captain, leading a force in pursuit of a gang of rustlers that were working the Texas-New Mexico border country. Six months later he left the Rangers, worked briefly for a detective agency, then as manager of the VV

spread, owned by an Englishman, Brandon Kirby. That job didn't last long either, so he returned to his own ranch on the Hondo.

Still drawn to law enforcement, in 1890 he ran unsuccessfully for the office of Sheriff of Chaves County. Angry and bitter when he lost, he pulled up stakes and moved on to Uvalde, Texas, to operate a horse ranch. Even though he was doing well in that venture, the badge beckoned once more and he returned to New Mexico to assume the office of Sheriff of Dona Ana County. Reelected twice, Garrett moved on in 1900, returning to Texas, where he ran a livery stable.

Theodore Roosevelt assumed the Presidency upon the death of William McKinley in 1901 and, soon after, appointed the aging killer of Billy the Kid to the post of Customs

Looking rather dapper in what appears to be a stylish (for its time) new suit, Pat Garrett was an impressive man. Lionized as the man who shot Billy the Kid, ending the career of one of the Old West's most vicious outlaws, his later career was rather lackluster. Were it not for the incident with The Kid, it's unlikely he would be remembered by history.

Collector in El Paso. Some claim that he did an excellent job in the Customs House, but made enemies for his refusal to lower duties on goods and livestock coming into the country from below the border. However, it would appear that his job performance must have been unsatisfactory; either that or some very powerful people were speaking against him in high places. Politically appointed bureaucrats rarely lose their positions, especially while their patrons remain in office. After five years, Pat Garrett failed to be reappointed and was again unemployed and returned to ranching. And, once again, he failed at that.

Pat Garrett's death was an inglorious end to a lackluster career. On February 29, 1908, while returning to his spread near Mesilla from a meeting in Las Cruces, where he was discussing the sale of his property, he was shot dead. One of his tenants, Wayne Brazel, admitted to killing Garrett, but claimed he'd acted in self-defense when the two argued over the legality of the sale. Carl Adamson, the prospective buyer who was riding in the dead man's buckboard, backed up Brazel's story of the event. Investigators noted that there were inconsistencies between the physical evidence and the stories they told, so Brazel was charged with murder. However, a jury found him not guilty. Pat Garrett, who had won fame in the act of but a moment, when he dropped the hammer on Billy the Kid, might never have achieved public notice were it not for that.

The sixgun Garrett used to end Billy's career is a .44-40 Colt SAA, with a 7-1/2-inch barrel, serial number 55083, that was shipped to B. Kitteridge and Co., of Cincinnati, Ohio, in April of 1880. It, and a Model 1873 Winchester, chambered alike, were surrendered by one of the Kid's fellow gang members,

Billie Wilson, when the outlaws were captured at Stinking Springs, in December of 1880. Garrett kept the nearly new guns for himself. He found them particularly to his liking because they used the same ammunition. Colt had begun making the SAA revolver for that cartridge in 1878, and having common chambering for both rifle and handgun was still very much a novelty at the time. While they remain mechanically sound, the guns were used extensively over the years that Garrett carried them. They have suffered minor surface pitting and the original finish is all but gone.

An interesting aside: Wilson was convicted of only minor offenses and escaped from custody soon after. He had apparently had enough of the owl-hoot life and went straight. After assuming the last name "Anderson," he later married, became a successful rancher in Terrell County, Texas, and was eventually elected sheriff there. For years he lived in fear that someone would recognize him. That happened more than 20 years after he'd assumed a respectable lifestyle. While in El Paso on official business, he ran into Garrett and was recognized. Instead of turning him in, Garrett quietly guided him through the petition process and helped arrange pardons for Wilson from both the Governor of New Mexico and President Roosevelt. The entire process was kept quiet and Sheriff "Anderson's" unsavory past never came out. Only after his death in 1911, at the hands of a drunk he was attempting to arrest, was the closely-guarded secret revealed.

Garrett's most successful years seem to have been during his time in Uvalde. Among the horses he raised was some excellent racing stock; including frequent winners at races from New Mexico to Louisiana. In 1891 some of his neighbors presented him with a cased

Chambered for the puny .32 Rimfire cartridge, Pat Garrett's Hopkins & Allen was carried often. Today's shooters would certainly question his choice of caliber, but such considerations are a modern conceit. Sometimes concealability takes a back seat to power. As well, there were no truly powerful pocket-size handguns available in his day.

and silver-plated .38 caliber Merwin & Hulbert Pocket Army revolver. Both the cover of the case and the left plaque of its ivory stocks bear its owner's name.

Another piece that was presented to him is a Model 1877 .41 caliber Colt Thunderer, with a 5-1/2-inch barrel. Obviously, he did have some friends and supporters in El Paso. Engraved and plated in silver and gold, with silver stocks, it is inscribed "Pat Garrett from his El Paso Friends" on the backstrap. "Customs Collector" is on the right stock and "Lincoln-Dona Ana-El Paso" on the left.

Garrett made a point of going armed at all times. When circumstances dictated that he do so unobtrusively, he sometimes carried a .32 RF Hopkins and Allen revolver. At other times it was with a Smith & Wesson Safety Hammerless .38 in his hip pocket.

While he used the 1873 Winchester he'd confiscated from Billie Wilson for nearly 30 years, it was essentially intended for man-hunting. When it came to hunting game for the table, he acquired a Model 1895 Winchester, chambered for the .30 U.S. cartridge, better known today as the .30-40 Krag.

Unlike many of his contemporaries, Garrett seems to have really enjoyed his guns and had a fondness for them. When he acquired one, it seems it became a permanent part of his personal collection.

Manuel Trazazas "Lone Wolf" Gonzaullas

FROM HIS NAME, alone, many suppose that "Lone Wolf" Gonzaullas was a Mexican-American. Actually, he was born in Cadiz, Spain, of naturalized American parents, in 1891. His father was originally from Spain, and his mother from Canada. One of the great Texas Rangers, he earned that nickname because in most of his investigations along the border and in the oil boomtowns of the 1920s and '30s, he worked alone. While he was an impressive figure of a man, with a reputation for expert marksmanship and no hesitation about resorting to gunplay when the occasion required, he also understood the value of scientific modes of investigation. For five years, from 1935 to 1940, he served as Superintendent of the Texas Department of Public Safety Bureau of Intelligence, developing a state-of-the-art crime library, rivaling that of the FBI. Fol-

lowing a distinguished career, he retired in 1951 to become a technical advisor for the entertainment industry and was instrumental in the founding of the Texas Ranger Hall of Fame, established in 1968.

Like many Rangers, Gonzaullas regarded his guns to be as much symbols of his authority as the badge that he wore. That shield was carved from a Mexican silver 5-peso coin. He made a point of carrying customized guns that were elaborately decorated so they would be noticed. Ordinary, law-abiding citizens tend to find such things impressive. Criminals tend to find them intimidating. Except for its Cutt's compensator, his Browning Auto-5 shotgun is pretty ordinary. It's made more useful, attractive and impressive by the addition of a beautifully hand-tooled leather cartridge carrier laced to the buttstock.

During most of the 20th century, Rangers carried either Government Model Colt .45s or Single Action Army .45s. At various times Gonzaullas used both. Factory-engraved, with "C" coverage, his 1911A1 was built in 1928. The face of the trigger is checkered and the trigger guard was cut off at the factory in order for the trigger finger of his big hand to find the trigger more quickly under stress. The ivory stocks have a Cuno Hel-

fricht-style carved ox-head with gold horns and a gold nose ring. Rubies have been set into the eyes. The SAAs sport 4-3/4-inch barrels, are gold-plated, with full coverage cattle-brand engraving. They, too, have carved ox-head ivory stocks. Opposite the ox heads are gold coins emblematic of the seal of the Lone Star State. While these decorations make the guns beautiful, what makes them most interesting are the mechanical

A big, tough, hard-nosed cop, Texas Ranger Captain "Lone Wolf" Gonzaullas was an expert at using fists and guns to enforce the law. He was also a thoughtful and intelligent lawman who pioneered scientific investigative techniques in the Lone Star State as Superintendent of the Department of Public Safety Bureau of Intelligence.

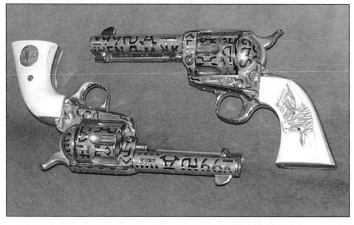

Elaborately engraved with a cattle brand motif, gold plated and stocked in carved and inlaid elephant ivory, "Lone Wolf" Gonzaullas' Single Action Army Colt revolvers were not merely decorative. The triggers are fixed to the rear of their trigger guards and the hammers widened and angled to permit them to more easily roll out from under the thumb for slip shooting a technique popular among lawmen in the early 20th century West for speed. It was very accurate at close range. (Courtesy The Autry Museum of Western Heritage)

features. Their triggers are welded to the back of the trigger guards. The hammers are slightly wider than normal and each is angled slightly to the inside in relation to the gun hand. This allows the hammer to slide easily from under the thumb as it is cocked and released for what is known as slip-shooting.

"Lone Wolf" Gonzaullas was reputed to have shot these handguns with unerring accuracy, even while holding them upside down. To his compatriots this was probably regarded as little more than an amusing stunt, but when word of it trickled down to the criminal element, it surely instilled fear. No doubt, it was meant to do so.

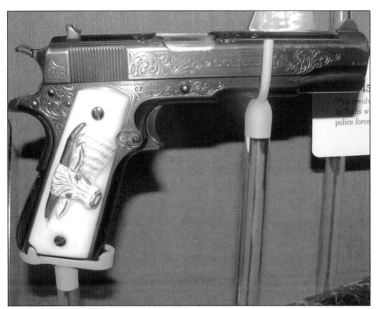

Texas Rangers were among the first lawmen to embrace the use of semi-automatic handguns for service. The near universal choice for that purpose was Colt's Government Model chambered for the .45 ACP cartridge. Many Rangers had both Government Model and SAA Colts and wore one type or the other depending upon the circumstances of a particular job to be done. "Lone Wolf" Gonzaullas' Government Model Colt .45 was scroll engraved at the factory. It was also made with the trigger guard removed to allow faster access for his large trigger finger. The elephant ivory stocks feature a carved ox head, with horns and nose ring of gold and ruby eyes. (Courtesy the Autry Museum of Western Heritage)

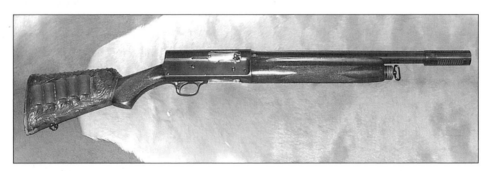

Browning's Auto-5 shotgun was the state-of-the-art semi-automatic shotgun in the 1930s, when "Lone Wolf" Gonzaullas was carrying his on stakeouts along the border. Outfitted with a Cutt's compensator to help control recoil and a beautifully hand-tooled, tightly laced leather cartridge carrier for a fast, convenient reload, this is no bird gun for a morning in the south Texas rice fields in pursuit of a goose dinner. It was set up to hunt smugglers bringing in contraband from across the border. (Courtesy The Autry Museum of Western Heritage)

Charles Goodnight

CHARLES GOODNIGHT WAS one of the Old West's toughest hombres and no stranger to gunplay. Born in Illinois in 1836, his father died when Charles was 5. Four years later, the family moved to the Brazos River country in Texas. The lad took to the Western life with gusto and was an accomplished bronco buster before he entered his teens. His expert horsemanship led to an interest in racing and by his mid-teens he was often jockeying winners across the finish line.

When he was in his early 20s, Goodnight and his stepbrother arranged a deal with a local rancher. In return for caring for his small herd of cattle, the pair could keep 25 percent of the newborn calves for themselves. Four years later they had 180 head. Then, in 1861, war brought with it a change in priorities. Having grown to manhood on the Texas frontier, Goodnight was an expert tracker and a skilled outdoorsman. He signed on with the Texas Rangers as a scout not to fight northern troops but to keep the Comanches from their depredations on the western frontier. In 1864, at the end of his enlistment, he returned to find his herd had been doing what came naturally and had grown to an estimated 5,000 head. As fortuitous as this was, Goodnight saw an even greater opportunity. By purchasing the entire herd of the neighbor from whom he'd gotten his seed stock and adding as many

mavericks as his men could gather, within a year he'd built the herd up to 8,000 head. The next step would be to take a portion of them to market.

At that time most herds were moved north to the Kansas railheads and, from there, were shipped to the Midwestern and Eastern markets. Goodnight proposed to seek out a new, potentially more lucrative market by taking his animals to Colorado and the mining camps and military forts then attracting a burgeoning population hungry for beef. However, the most direct route lay right through Comanche and Kiowa lands. Goodnight came up with a bold plan that would avoid the potential for armed confrontation, but it had a special set of dangers all its own.

Knowing that he and his crew were in for a long and difficult trek, he began making preparations. In the process, he came up with an idea that came to be a standard piece of equipment throughout the cattle industry in the West; he designed the first ever chuckwagon. By taking an ordinary wagon and adding boxes, cupboards and drawers, then equipping it with a carefully selected assortment of cooking pots, pans and utensils, it was transformed into an efficient kitchen on wheels.

While laying in provisions for the trip, Goodnight chanced to meet Oliver Loving, who was well known for his frontier experience and knowledge of cattle. To him he outlined his plan to take 2,000 head and strike out from the Brazos to the northwest, across the Llano Estacado to Ft. Sumner, on the Pecos River. Loving saw the wisdom in Goodnight's plan, but also understood the grave dangers, as well. Still, he thought the potential profits worth the risks and offered to lend his expertise to the enterprise. At that moment the two became partners.

With 18 hands to move the herd, they began the first leg of the trip, the 250-mile journey to the Concho River. The herd was rested briefly and well watered, then began the 92-mile stretch to the Pecos River with no water of any kind between. It was done in a 72-hour forced march that left about 300 animals dead or dying of thirst littering the landscape. A few miles from the Pecos the leaders smelled water and in short order the whole herd had stampeded. About 100 more animals were lost to drowning and from falling under the hooves of the others.

Even with such losses the trip was profitable. At Ft. Sumner the Army bought all the steers in the herd. Then, the cows and calves were taken due north, nearly to Denver. There, they were sold to a local cattleman, John Wesley Iliff, who would become owner of one of the biggest spreads in that part of the country. After paying off his crew, Goodnight headed home to Texas with a pack mule carrying his gear and $12,000 in gold.

The following year when they made the trek again, Loving died as the result of wounds incurred in a fight with Comanches. Goodnight made it through unscathed and continued herding cattle annually over the Goodnight-Loving Trail for several more years. In 1870 he decided to stay on in Colorado and purchased land near Pueblo. After three years he'd gone broke, partly because of a severe economic downturn. Texas beckoned once again; the moreso since he'd heard rumors of a hidden paradise in the Panhandle, that was ideal for raising cattle. Eventually he found it in Palo Duro Canyon and established the Old Home Ranch. The walls of the canyon formed a natural barrier to hold the cattle in and the floor of the canyon

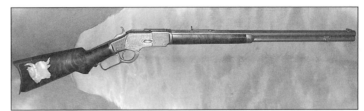

Charles Goodnight's Model 1873 rifle was a custom order from the Winchester factory. Its features mark it clearly as a richman's gun. Yet it wasn't just for show. The rifle's condition demonstrates that it saw considerable use. (Courtesy the Autry Museum of Western Heritage)

Charles Goodnight saw Texas grow from its infancy as a Republic to prominence as a great state in the 20th century. Texas-tough and Texas-rich, he was a shrewd businessman and a demanding taskmaster, but during his long life he contributed much to the state's growth and prosperity. He came to be known as "The father of the Texas Panhandle."

was lush with grass and water. When Goodnight persuaded the wealthy Irishman, John Adair, to invest in the enterprise, it became the JA Ranch.

Adair recouped his investment and reaped a handsome profit of more than half a million dollars, but he died in 1885 and Goodnight bought his widow out. He continued running the operation, earning millions of dollars in the process over the years, until he died in 1929 at age 93.

Charles Goodnight eschewed the use of strong drink, but smoked 50 cigars a day and chewed tobacco, as well. He was also notorious for his foul mouth and for being a skinflint. Although he drove a hard bargain, there were some things for which he was prepared to spend some of his vast wealth. One was fine breeding stock with which to improve his herds. Another was one of the finest Model 1873 Winchester rifles the factory ever made. Chambered for the .44-40 cartridge, the rifle is engraved, probably by one of the Ulrich brothers, judging by the style. It has a 24-inch octagonal barrel and its pistol-grip stock and the forend are made of presentation-grade

walnut. Prominent on the right side of the buttstock is a mother-of-pearl inlay of a shorthorn bull's head. Goodnight was among the first Texas ranchers to introduce the breed into the bloodlines of his herd. The rifle exhibits considerable wear and has a significant chip lost at the toe of the buttstock, so it appears obvious that it was more than just a decorative piece. The rifle clearly saw substantial use in its owner's hands.

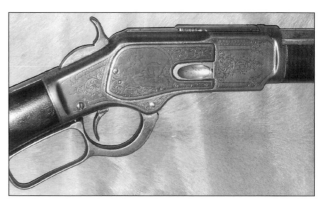

The engraving on Charles Goodnight's Model 1873 Winchester was probably done by one of the Ulrich brothers. (Courtesy the Autry Museum of Western Heritage)

John Wesley Hardin

A HEARTLESS, COLD-BLOODED murderer, whose killings were frequently motivated by racism and a vitriolic hatred of Yankees, John Wesley Hardin's propensity toward violence was evident as early as age 11, when he stabbed another boy during a fight over a girl. Wounded in the back and chest, the boy lived and Hardin's actions were ruled self-defense. But, that was just the beginning.

During a wrestling match he cut the face of an ex-slave named Mage with his ring. When Mage, carrying a stick with which to beat him, came after Hardin the next day, Hardin promptly grabbed his revolver and shot him dead. He was only 15 years old at the time and Texas, along with the rest of the South in these "Reconstruction" years, was under martial law. He took it on the lam to avoid capture by the army. Three black troopers who were assigned to apprehend him were gunned down from ambush. The killing had only just begun. Some say that, in all, he ended the life of 40 men, including one he murdered just for snoring. To be fair, that killing, it must be noted, was accidental. The sleeper in the room next to him was snoring so loudly that Hardin couldn't get any rest. He had yelled and banged on the wall to no avail in order to get the noisy sleeper to turn over and be quiet. At last, he resorted to shooting into the wall, thinking the noise would rouse him. Instead he put the man to sleep permanently. At least 16 deaths at Hardin's hand can be verified and many others were wounded before he was finally captured and sent to prison.

Wes Hardin's family had deep roots in the Texas soil, going back to the fight for independence from Mexico. His grandfather had been a Republic of Texas congressman and his father was a Methodist minister, teacher and lawyer. Born in Bonham, on May 26, 1853, it may be that his violent inclinations were formed, at least in part, by the passions stirred by the Civil War and resentment associated with the Federal occupation when it was lost. Clearly, there was a lot of hate in him and little, if any, sense of conscience. He was an unreconstructed Rebel who, though much too young to have served during official hostilities, continued to fight the war for years after Lee surrendered.

Before Hardin had reached his 17th birthday he had killed at least eight men. Governor Edmund J. Davis declared him a wanted man and ordered him "killed, jailed or hanged." During that time he had worked at several jobs, as a teacher, farmer and cowboy. When he learned the Governor didn't seem to have a sense of humor about his escapades, he decided to head for Louisiana, but was caught and arrested near the state line at Marshall, Texas. While being transported back for trial, he escaped, killing one of his guards in the process. Then, he hid out with some relatives near Smiley, Texas.

In the summer of 1871 he hired on for a trail drive to Abilene, Kansas. Along the way, he killed an Indian and six Mexican vaqueros. When he finally got to Abilene, he encountered Wild Bill Hickok. Some say that as long as Hardin minded his manners Hickok left him alone. Others maintain that Hardin got the drop on Hickok at one point and backed him down. Given the history of both men the latter scenario is probably a fairy tale. If Hardin had pulled iron on Hickok he probably would have dropped the hammer. If he didn't, Hickok almost certainly would have killed him.

The following year, at age 19, Hardin was back in Smiley and married his sweetheart, Jane Bowen. During the next two years he was involved in several more shooting scrapes and a blood feud in which some cousins of his were engaged. Two of his victims during that period were a couple of black state police officers sent to arrest him. He killed one and wounded the other with a bullet to the mouth.

Then, things were relatively quiet for a couple of years. During that time he was involved in just two killings. Matters came to a head, however, on his 21st birthday, in 1874. Hardin, one of his brothers, Joseph, and some of their friends were celebrating in a Comanche, Texas, saloon, when there was an altercation with a deputy sheriff by the name of Charles Webb. Webb ended up dead and Wes Hardin escaped, but his brother and two of his friends were caught and lynched by an angry mob. As far as the state of Texas was concerned, Hardin had crossed the line. This time he'd gunned down a white lawman. A bounty of $4,000 was placed on his head and the Texas

Wes Hardin had a history of violence before he'd reached his teens, was a killer by age 15, and a wanted man by the time he was just 17 years old. Here, he looks ready to attack the photographer taking his picture, who was very likely rather nervous about his customer's satisfaction.

Rangers were assigned to track him down. It was time to light a shuck and get out of Texas for good. With his wife and daughter he traveled to Florida by steamer under the assumed name, J.H. Swain Jr.

For the next three years Hardin stayed out of trouble. Living in and around Pensacola, and nearby Alabama, he made his way by buying and selling horses and cattle and as a timber merchant. During that time Jane presented him with a son and another daughter. John Wesley Hardin might never have been heard of again were it not for the fact that his wife couldn't bring herself to sever all ties with her family. Ranger Captain John Armstrong found out that her father, Neal Bowen, had regularly been receiving mail with a Pollard, Alabama, postmark. With that information it wasn't difficult to track Hardin down. He was arrested on a train at Pensacola Junction on July 23, 1877. When Armstrong and

another Ranger, Jack Duncan, confronted him, Hardin shouted, "Texas, by God," and tried to draw his gun. The hammer caught on his suspender strap and gave the Ranger the opportunity to clobber him over the head and take the fugitive into custody alive.

Back in Texas, Hardin was tried for deputy Webb's murder and on October 1, 1877, was convicted and sentenced to 25 years at hard labor in Huntsville State Prison. Considering his record, it's a wonder he wasn't sentenced to hang, but the charge was second-degree murder, not first, so the death sentence wasn't an option.

While it may be difficult to find much that's positive about Hardin, it must be acknowledged that he was a hard worker and reasonably intelligent. During his incarceration, while he wasn't making big rocks into little ones, he was applying himself to constructive purposes through the study of law; when he

Given to sudden, violent mood swings, John Wesley Hardin was quick to take offense at any perceived slight. Body counts vary somewhat according to the research one may believe, but the consensus seems to be that 40 men, give or take a few, met their demise at his hands. Most, it would seem, were murdered from ambush or during unexpected bursts of anger, for which they were not prepared. Few, if any, were given a fighting chance.

The elder John Selman, seated here with an unknown lad, possibly his grandson, put an end to Hardin's murderous career in El Paso's Acme Saloon one hot August night in 1895. Accused of murdering the murderer, a jury acquitted Selman, saying he acted in self-defense.

wasn't attempting to escape custody, that is. It's difficult to conceive, but Governor James Hogg was made to believe that Hardin had become a model prisoner so, in 1894, with nine years left of his sentence, Hardin was granted early parole for good behavior and released from prison on February 17 and a pardon was granted on March 16. His wife, Jane had died on November 6, 1892, so Hardin was a free man in all respects.

Moving to Gonzales, Hardin lived with his children for a while, passed the bar and established a law practice. From Gonzales he moved to Junction, where a young lady by the name of Callie Lewis lived. On the very day the two were married she must have seen something in him that either scared or disgusted her. Maybe both. Their wedding reception had barely started when she walked out on him, permanently severing their relationship. With nothing left to keep him in Junction, Hardin pulled up stakes and made his way to El Paso.

John Wesley Hardin might actually have been a competent lawyer, but he had little opportunity to display his skill at the bar, because few clients were willing to engage his services. With not much else to occupy his time, Hardin took to drinking and gambling.

Given his impulsiveness and short temper, this was unwise. Even worse was his affair with a beautiful and very married client, Mrs. Martin McRose. Her husband was wanted for a number of crimes and had taken refuge on the Mexican side of the border. Having been convinced that he could safely return to the U.S., McRose was gunned down by lawmen who were waiting as he crossed to the north side of the Rio Grande.

While Hardin was out of town on business for a couple of days, his girlfriend, the widow McRose, got herself drunk and, for some reason, fired her revolver on the city street. Arrested by John Selman Jr., a deputy constable for the city of El Paso, she was charged with being drunk and disorderly and discharging a firearm within the city limits. Considering the value of the dollar at that time, the fine of $50 that was imposed was pretty stiff. When Hardin returned to town and learned what the younger Selman had done, he was livid with anger. Encountering John Selman Sr. on the street, Hardin launched into an angry and threatening tirade. Considering that the elder Selman was himself a gunfighter of considerable note and the city's Chief Constable, that was a mistake; Hardin's most serious and final error.

The ejector rod housing on Wes Hardin's ivory-handled Colt .45 is missing. Could he have removed it to make it lighter and faster to handle, or was it merely lost at some time during its history? The left side of the barrel, at the muzzle end, is worn nearly flat, indicating long hours of practice drawing it from its holster. (Courtesy The Autry Museum of Western Heritage)

Having a second gun is faster than reloading. Wes Hardin's ivory-stocked .41 caliber Colt Thunderer was the back-up piece he carried the night he died. The gun retains little of its original finish, but it appears to have been maintained well. (Courtesy The Autry Museum of Western Heritage)

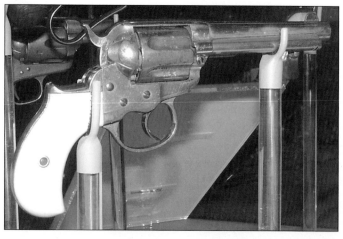

That night, less than an hour before midnight on August 19, 1895, Hardin was shooting dice with a local storekeeper named H.S. Brown in the Acme Saloon. The senior Selman walked through the door and moments later Hardin lay dead on the floor. The fatal shot passed through Hardin's left eye, but the coroner's report states that was an exit wound; that the entrance was from the back of his head. Selman disputed that claim, saying he'd called out to Hardin, who turned to face him and was shot when he reached for a gun. Hardin was carrying two revolvers at the time of his death, but neither was fired. The photo of Hardin's corpse shows three wounds. The other two include one to the right side of the chest and another in the upper right arm. All three appear to be entrance wounds, lending credence to Selman's account of the events. At trial Selman pled not guilty by reason of self-defense. Apparently his account was believed, because he was acquitted. Either that or the court decided against convicting Selman because it felt he'd performed a public service by causing Hardin to prematurely partake of the undertaker's services.

A .44 caliber Colt Model 1860 Army revolver is attributed to Hardin early in his career. Like most gunmen, however, he adopted the use of cartridge revolvers as soon as the opportunity presented itself. When he died, Hardin was carrying two such revolvers. One was an ivory-stocked 4-3/4-inch barreled, nickel-plated, .41 caliber Colt Thunderer, and the other a Colt SAA .45, also with a 4-3/4-inch barrel, but with the ejector rod housing missing. Also ivory-stocked, the sixgun is well worn and almost all the original finish is gone. It's uncertain whether the ejector rod housing has simply been lost over time or was deliberately removed. A clue is provided by the extreme wear to be found on the left side at the muzzle. It is so worn that the round contour is worn almost flat. This indicates that it was subjected to extraordinarily frequent fast draw practice. It's reasonable to suggest that the ejector rod housing was removed to lessen drag and lighten the revolver to make the draw a shade faster. That's just the sort of thing Hardin would have done.

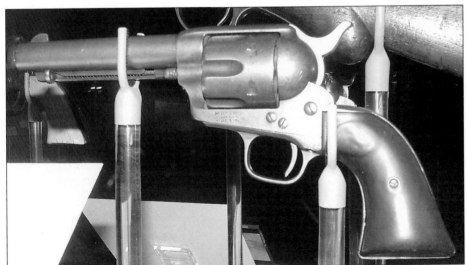

John Selman Sr. was worried and angry about Hardin's earlier threats against his son when he confronted Hardin in the Acme Saloon. When Hardin reached for his iron, Selman used this SAA .45 to put a permanent end to the killer's career. Nine months after that incident Selman was, himself, gunned down by fellow lawman George Scarborough in a dispute over money. (Courtesy the Autry Museum of Western Heritage)

James Butler "Wild Bill" Hickok

OF ALL THE lawmen of the "Old West," Wild Bill Hickok comes closest to the Hollywood image of the tough lawman and expert gunhandler. Known from his own time to this as "The Prince of Pistoleers," Hickok had a reputation for uncanny speed and unerring accuracy with his six-shooters. In many respects, he was justifiably regarded as a hero. Yet, like many of history's heroic figures, there were traces of clay on his pedestal and some seriously tragic aspects to his life, as well.

Hickok was born in Homer, Illinois (later renamed Troy Grove), on May 27, 1837. His parents, William Alonzo and Polly Butler Hickok, had moved there from Vermont the previous year. His father operated a general store and a small farm. Active in the abolitionist movement, his parents also ran a way station on the Underground Railroad, spiriting escaped slaves from the Southern states to safety in the North and in Canada. The Hickok children, of whom James Butler was the fourth of six, were often enlisted to assist in these clandestine activities.

To achieve such mastery of the handgun, that one may be regarded as a professional, requires diligent practice. Hickok was one of the few Old West gunfighters who seems to have truly appreciated fine firearms and enjoyed shooting for its own sake. He is known to have had a flintlock pistol of his own as a youngster and is said to have had another pistol of some sort by the age of 12, with which he became quite proficient. The latter was used extensively after he acquired it in a trade for some furs. He kept the family larder well filled with small game. We may only speculate as to what make or model it may have been, but when one considers that the year would have been about 1849, a pistol the size of an 1849 Colt Pocket Model would be about right for a child of that age. However, given the dates involved, one of the various Paterson designs could have been the means by which he honed his early marksmanship skills. With the available options at that time, those would appear to be the best candidates if, indeed, the gun was a revolver at all. There is no way to know for certain.

When he was 18 years old, Hickok got into a fight with another young man, a fellow teamster, named Charles Hudson. In the course of their fisticuffs both fell into a canal. Thinking,

This, perhaps the best-known portrait of Wild Bill Hickok, is somewhat revealing. Assuming that his revolvers and Bowie knife are placed as he usually wore them, we can determine whether he used a reverse draw or a cross-draw to bring his 1851 Colt Navy revolvers into action. Note that the butts of the revolvers are angled outward and that the knife is unsheathed. If he were to reach across with his left hand, as often as not his sleeve would catch on the point of the blade. He might even have stabbed himself in the arm. There can be little doubt that he practiced a reverse draw.

mistakenly, that he had killed Hudson, Hickok fled the jurisdiction. At Leavenworth, Kansas, he stopped running and settled in for a time. There, he joined "The Red Legs," General James H. Lane's Free-State Militia. In the 1850s Kansas was a hotbed of political and often physically violent controversy over the issue of slavery, but there is no record of Hickok's having any direct involvement in such conflicts. He held a variety of jobs, mostly as a teamster and as a farmhand for several years. For a brief period he was constable of the Johnson County township of Monticello. His first appointment as a lawman was most significant for its utter lack of excitement.

It seems odd that a man named James, not William, would be nicknamed "Wild Bill." There have been several explanations for that curious turn of events. The most plausible appears to be that at some point he was involved in a disagreement and in the resulting fracas, teamsters with whom he worked at the time likened him to a wild billy-goat. Whatever the circumstances may actually have been, the name stuck with him for the rest of his life.

Three pivotal events in Hickok's life seem to have affected the directions it took. The first occurred July 21, 1861, at Rock Creek Station, in Nebraska. The incident led to the shooting of a local bully, David McCanles. According to Hickok, he killed McCanles in a fair gunfight, then engaging and prevailing against his nine companions in combat, armed only with a six-gun and a Bowie knife.

The truth of the story appears to be somewhat less heroic. It seems that McCanles, his young son, William Monroe McCanles, and two adult companions, James Woods and James Gordon, came to Rock Creek to collect a debt. As McCanles and his boy entered the house, Hickok shot him from ambush with a plains-style rifle, then ran out of the house and shot and wounded Woods and Gordon with his 1851 Navy Colt. Hickok and several others then apparently pursued and finished the pair.

At trial, the accused were found "not guilty" of murder. The killings were ruled justifiable homicide in self-defense. There has been some speculation that McCanles may not have been armed and would not have brought his son if he'd been looking for trouble. That theory ignores the basic nature of the bully. It's quite probable that McCanles brought the boy to demonstrate that with bluff, bluster, threats and pure meanness he could intimidate others

Shown from left to right, Wild Bill Hickok, Texas Jack Omohundro and Buffalo Bill Cody performed together nightly in Ned Buntline's stage production of "Scouts of the Plains" during late 1873 until the spring of 1874, when Hickok finally acknowledged to himself that he had no talent as a performer.

Hickok's eyes were beginning to fail him by the time this photograph was taken. Some believe the probable cause was an advancing case of gonorrhea. If that was so, lacking the antibiotics that would be readily available a century later, had Jack McCall not killed him, "The Prince of Pistoleers" would probably have been reduced to complete blindness soon after.

into submission. If that was the case, it didn't work. The court's finding was probably more a reflection of a local dislike for McCanles than a vindication of Hickok and his accomplices' actions. In any event, the retelling of the story, with all its exaggerations, went a long way toward establishing "Wild Bill" Hickok's reputation as a tough man.

Springfield, Missouri, was the scene of the second pivotal event in Hickok's career. On July 21, 1865, he and David Tutt had a falling out over a woman. They agreed to meet in the town square to settle their differences with gunplay. Most accounts have it that Tutt fired first and Hickok took deliberate aim from 75 yards distant and shot him in the center of his chest, killing him instantly. It was a remarkable feat of marksmanship, especially considering the cap-and-ball arms involved. Hickok's reputation as a gunman was greatly magnified. This led to a succession of law enforcement appointments.

As the town marshal of Abilene, Kansas, the third pivotal event of Hickok's career occurred on October 5, 1871. It was then that he had a run-in with a gambler named Phil Coe over the latter's having fired a gun within the town limits. Coe claimed he'd merely shot at a stray dog, but suddenly turned his revolver on Hickok, who promptly shot him down. Alerted by the sound of gunfire, Mike Williams, one of Hickok's deputies and a close friend, came to the scene on the run to help. Some accounts say he stepped between Hickok and Coe. Others claim Hickok saw a man with his gun drawn, in his peripheral vision, and shot before realizing it was his friend. In either case, Williams was struck down by Hickok's hand and died soon after. Wild Bill Hickok was devastated by the incident and his part in it. Soon after he turned in his badge and went east to join his old friend Buffalo Bill Cody, who was working in a theater company.

It was at about the same time that it also became evident that Hickok's vision was rapidly failing. The cause of his affliction has been the subject of much debate. One of the most plausible explanations is advanced gonorrhea. He was well known to have had an eye for the ladies and numerous romantic encounters with women of easy virtue.

Buffalo Bill Cody, having all but forsaken life on the frontier for the lure of the stage, convinced Hickok that he should do the same. In the fall of 1873 he made his way to New York, where he appeared with Cody and Texas Jack Omohundro in the Ned Buntline production entitled *Scouts of the Plains*. Badly written and poorly produced, this utterly forgettable stage effort was made even worse by the complete lack of thespian talent of its star performers. Omohundro died soon after, of natural causes. Cody went on to establish his Wild West Show, which for decades was a great success. For his part, Hickok gave it up after seven months of fumbling lines, missing his mark and embarrassing himself nightly before audiences that came more for the opportunity to see these "heroes of the Wild West" in person, than to see good theater.

A complete failure as an entertainer and no longer capable, either emotionally or physically, of working as a peace officer, Hickok eked out a living as a gambler. This line of

Wild Bill Hickok was justifiably proud of his pair of ivory-stocked and engraved Model 1851 Colt Navy revolvers. The decoration was done in the style of Gustav Young, very likely by the master, himself. Much of the original finish has worn off from extensive use, but the metal and mechanical aspects remain in very good condition. Hickok took excellent care of them. (Courtesy The Autry Museum of Western Heritage)

work brought him to Deadwood, South Dakota, where on August 2, 1876, while playing poker, he was shot in the back of the head. His killer, Jack McCall, use a .22 caliber revolver. Ironically, all but one of the cartridges in McCall's gun turned out to be duds.

Numerous firearms have been associated with Wild Bill Hickok. Among them, a British-made Beaumont-Adams, a .44 Bulldog made by Hammond, that is said to have been on his person when he was killed, and the half-stocked plains rifle he is said to have used to shoot David McCanles. In addition, Hickok is reported to have, at various times, carried .44 caliber 1860 Army Colt revolvers and a Smith & Wesson Number 2 Old Army .32 rimfire.

The best documented Hickok guns are the pair of Colt's 1851 Navy revolvers given to him in 1869 by Massachusetts Senator Henry Wilson. Hickok had provided scout and guide services to Wilson during the politician's hunting trip.

Silver-plated and engraved in the style of Gustave Young, the revolvers are stocked in ivory, with an American Eagle carved on one side of each set. Wild Bill's name and the year they were presented are engraved on their backstraps, but his last name is misspelled, so the inscription reads, "J.B. Hickock 1869." Their finish shows extensive wear, attesting that they were carried and fired regularly. No doubt, Hickok took great pride in the ownership of such an elegant pair of revolvers.

John Henry Holliday

BETTER KNOWN AS Doc Holliday, this tubercular dentist came from a prominent Georgia family that managed to remain reasonably well off and politically influential, even after the end of the Civil War. His father, Henry B. Holliday, was by most accounts a kind and generous man who had served with distinction during the war with Mexico. When he returned home, he brought with him a young Mexican lad of whom he'd grown fond. It was his desire to offer the boy a chance at a more prosperous and productive life than the child could have hoped for in Mexico. Through that act of kindness he caused his own family irreparable harm. The child had tuberculosis, and Henry's wife, Alice Jane, contracted the disease. The couple's son, John Henry, was born in 1852. He caught the disease from his mother, but it wasn't until he was 20 years old and a recent graduate of a Baltimore college of dental surgery, just beginning his practice in Atlanta, that he was diagnosed. Holliday's physician offered little hope, recommending that he might live a few years longer if he were temperate in his habits and went to live somewhere like Colo-

rado. He did go west, but it took him a while to get all the way there. As to his habits, there was nothing temperate about them.

A good-looking young man, with a fine education and a promising career, suddenly given a death sentence by his doctor, Holliday's change in attitude toward life can be easily understood. He tried practicing his profession in Dallas, but few patients had much tolerance for a consumptive dentist coughing in their faces. He sank into depression and sought solace in the bottle, making a modest living by gambling. His occasional violent outbursts are thought by many to have very likely been his way of attempting suicide. Surely someone would put him out of his misery. It was not to be. Instead of dying in a year or two, Holliday survived for 15 years before succumbing to his illness at a sanatorium in Glenwood Springs, Colorado, on November 8, 1887. As he lay dying he seemed to be reflecting on the irony of his situation. For years he'd sought death at the hands of others. His last words were, "This is funny." With that, he gulped down a glass of whiskey and closed his eyes for the last time.

During the intervening years, Holliday wandered from one town to another, through Texas, Kansas, Colorado, New Mexico and Arizona. While in Dodge City, he happened upon a dry-gulcher one night, about to back-shoot Wyatt Earp with a rifle. Pulling his own iron, he intervened, winning the undying friendship of the marshal. However, it wasn't easy being Doc Holliday's friend. He was in one confrontation or another, involving gun-play or the Bowie knife, with such frequency that he seemed always to be moving on, one step ahead of the law or a lynch mob.

On the afternoon of October 26, 1881, Doc Holliday, in spite of Earp's attempt to dissuade him from joining in, became a willing partici-pant in what has become the best-known gun-fight in the history of the West, the one that came to be known as the gunfight at the O.K. Corral. During the fracas, Frank McLaury, as his dying act, shot Holliday in the hip, but it proved an inconsequential wound. A few

months later, on March 18, 1882, Morgan Earp was shot in the back and died within hours. Two days later Virgil Earp, who had been per-manently crippled in an ambush shooting just

Contemporary accounts indicate that Doc Holliday regarded a 10-gauge double-barreled shotgun, such as this one by West-ley Richards, to be indispensable in a gunfight. Usually he chose to use one with shortened barrels. This specimen's bar-rels retain their original length. (Courtesy The Autry Museum of Western Heritage)

Handsome, reasonably wealthy and well educated, Doc Holliday had a promising career in dental practice ahead of him until his physician informed him that he was dying of tuberculosis. He was transformed by the news into a depressed, sui-cidal and alcoholic wanderer.

after Christmas, accompanied Morgan's body and several family members to California, away from danger. Wyatt, his other brother, Warren, Doc, and a few others went out on a killing binge, hunting down those they felt were responsible for the harm that had come to the Earps. A lot of men died, but no charges against the Earps and their friends could be made to stick in court.

In most recent film depictions of these events, Holliday is depicted as carrying a Colt Lightning revolver, usually nickel-plated and sporting a short barrel. There doesn't seem to be any evidence to support this, but it is known that his preferred armament consisted of a sawed-off 10-gauge shotgun (which he used at the O.K. Corral) and a Colt SAA with a 7-1/2-inch barrel, that was also employed at that event.

Doc Holliday was, without question, a stone killer, an alcoholic and a whoremonger. He was known to cheat at cards. He probably wasn't especially good with a six-gun, which is evidenced by the number of adversaries he wounded, rather than killed. He was quick to take offense and bad tempered enough to be willing to shuck leather at any provocation. That made him a very dangerous man. On the other hand, he had one shining virtue, although it may have been grossly misplaced. He was loyal. Wyatt Earp was his friend, and he stood by him solidly. That may, perhaps, be the only good that remained in him.

DENTISTRY.

J. H. Holliday, Dentist, very respectfully offers his professional services to the citizens of Dodge City and surrounding country during the summer. Office at room No. 24, Dodge House. Where satisfaction is not given money will be refunded.

Advertising his professional services drew few patients to room number 24 of The Dodge House, where "Doc" Holliday set up his practice. The level of Doc Holliday's professional skill seems never to have been an issue. Between his contagiousness and his violent temper, most patients appear to have preferred having a toothache to risking death for the sake of its treatment.

Doc Holliday's wife, Katie Elder, identified this .45 caliber Colt SAA revolver as having been her husband's. Most sources that mention the matter at all seem to agree that this was the configuration he preferred for a personal handgun. It's unclear why Hollywood seems to have decided he liked short-barreled, nickel-plated Colt Lightning double action revolvers. (Courtesy The Autry Museum of Western Heritage)

Frank and Jesse James

THE PRELUDE, CONFLICT and aftermath of the Civil War shaped the public attitude regarding the James boys for nearly a century. These brothers were lionized by some as heroes in the best tradition of Robin Hood and condemned by others as thieves and murderers. With the hindsight of history, the latter definition clearly wins out. In the modern age the word terrorist would not be too strong a term to apply.

There is, for example, the tale that says that the James brothers robbed a bank, gave a significant portion of the take to a widow to pay her overdue mortgage. When the greedy banker, who had planned to foreclose on the property, had signed the paid contract over and started back to town, he was met along the road by Frank and Jesse and robbed of the money once again. No love was lost for carpetbaggers or bankers among Southern sympathizers, so many chose to believe this and other such imaginings, however unfounded they may have been in truth.

Born in 1843 and 1847, respectively, Frank and Jesse were the children of Robert and Zerelda James, who were married in Ken-

tucky in 1841, and moved to Missouri soon after. Robert was a Baptist preacher and a farmer, but, like many, he read in the newspapers of the vast riches to be found in the gold fields of California and yielded to temptation. Leaving his wife and four surviving children behind, he set off to make his fortune. What he got for his efforts was a severe case of pneumonia and, just three weeks after arriving in California, the pay dirt he'd hoped for turned out to be a grave.

Zerelda was remarried soon after Robert's death, to a farmer named Ben Simms. When he died in 1857, once again, she quickly remarried. This time it was to a local physician who was seven years her junior.

By the time Frank and Jesse were in their mid-teens, full-fledged warfare had already broken out along the Kansas-Missouri border. In the East the matter of states' rights engendered the greatest concern. In the West the hot-button issue was slavery, and whether Kansas would be admitted to the Union as a free or slave state. Throughout the decade of the 1850s, such copious amounts of blood were shed on both the abolitionist and pro-slavery side that the territory came to be known as "Bleeding Kansas."

When secession finally came, Frank James joined Quantrill's Raiders. In 1864, at age 17, Jesse followed his older brother's lead. William Clarke Quantrill had a long history of criminality before the war. With the hostilities now official, Quantrill offered his services to the Confederacy and was quickly accepted with a commission as a Captain in the C.S. Cavalry. This allowed him and his band of thugs to expand their predations under cover of supposedly legitimate military action. He quickly rose to the rank of Colonel. With time, the Confederate hierarchy came to realize that they'd nursed a viper at their figurative bosom and ordered the arrest of Quantrill and his "guerrillas."

By the fall of 1864, the James boys had split with Quantrill and joined, instead, the forces of Bloody Bill Anderson, a Quantrill disciple who, if anything, was even more vicious than his mentor. On the September 27 the two participated in one of the worst of a war full of atrocities on both sides. While they were sacking the town of Centralia, Missouri, a train

headed for Iowa, with 25 unarmed Union soldiers heading home from the war, stopped at the town's station. The men were removed from the train and murdered in cold blood.

When the war was over an amnesty was offered, but when Jesse attempted to turn himself in at Lexington, Missouri, the flag of truce under which he was riding seems to have been mistaken for a Confederate banner and one of the Union soldiers shot him in the chest. While Jesse recuperated, he, Frank and their cousin, Cole Younger, began planning a new career for which their "military" experience made them eminently qualified. One might also say they were quite innovative, as well, because they were the first in the history of the United States to engage in the daylight robbery of a bank during peacetime. They expanded their operation to train and stagecoach robbery and the armed theft of the box office receipts of public exhibitions.

Intimidation was a regular part of their modus operandi. In the course of their escapes, the James boys and their gang made a point of shooting indiscriminately, often wounding or killing innocent bystanders, including a 10-

In his youth, Frank James joined Quantrill's gang of anti-abolitionist cutthroats. He later switched his allegiance to Bloody Bill Anderson, an even more vicious criminal. Both gangs used the Confederate cause as a cover for their criminal enterprises.

Although he was tried for many crimes, Frank James ended up with a acquittals in all the cases brought against him. The politics of Reconstruction had more to do with the juries' findings than his guilt or innocence. Finally freed from custody in 1885, he never again ran afoul of the law.

year-old girl who was shot in the leg and an unarmed college student shot dead. One of the more significant aspects of their career seems to be that, while they had absolutely no hesitation shooting their victims or bystanders, only those victims who were within arms reach seem to have been in any mortal danger. They were such notoriously bad shots that it was the bystanders who had most to fear.

Throughout their predations, Jesse tried to sow doubt in the mind of the public by sending letters to newspapers declaring his innocence and offering an alibi for his whereabouts on the occasion of the particular crime in question. It was an interesting propaganda ploy and certainly added to the confusion and bolstered the position of his supporters. It's probable that in some instances others actually committed the crimes for which the brothers and their gang were accused. That, too, gave his protestations some credence. Nevertheless, there was still plenty of blame to be laid at their feet.

Lawmen, railroad detectives and agents from Pinkerton's frequently watched the home of Jesse and Frank's mother and stepfather. On the night of January 26, 1875, they had reason to believe that the brothers were in the house. Late that night a flare was thrown in through a window. As she tried to shove it into the fireplace it erupted into flames and in the ensuing fire, she lost most of her left arm. Her young son, Archie Samuel, Frank and Jesse's half-brother, died. Neither of the outlaws was present. The incident engendered more sympathy for them and an attempt to push an amnesty bill through the state legislature. It failed, but just barely.

Meanwhile, the crimes continued and rewards for Jesse, dead or alive, totaled more than $25,000. Brothers Charles and Robert Ford conspired to collect. They had joined the gang in time to participate in the last of the James gang's robberies, that of the Chicago-Alton Express train as it passed through

Jesse James posed for this studio photograph during the Civil War. Beneath the handsome and dashing appearance there lay a vicious young criminal who used the Colt's Model 1851 Navy revolvers tucked into his waistband for murder, robbery and intimidation, not to do legitimate battle for the cause of Southern freedom.

$25,000 REWARD
JESSE JAMES
DEAD OR ALIVE

$15,000 REWARD FOR FRANK JAMES

$5000 Reward for any Known Member of the James Band

SIGNED:

ST. LOUIS MIDLAND RAILROAD

Jesse, the younger of the James brothers, was the brains of the outfit and the more committed criminal. For that reason he got top billing on the wanted posters put out for their capture, dead or alive. The two were costing railroads, banks and merchants throughout the Midwest a lot of money, but their wanton and indiscriminate shootings were what made them most dangerous.

Glendale, Missouri, Aug. 7, 1881. Afterward, the Fords met with Missouri Governor Thomas Crittenden to discuss their plans to get Jesse.

On April 3, 1882, they were sitting with Jesse in the living room of his home in St. Joseph, planning their next robbery, when Jesse noticed a picture hanging askew on the wall. Standing, he removed his gunbelts and stepped to the wall. Standing on a chair, he reached up to adjust the picture when Bob grabbed one of the guns and shot him in the head. As Jesse turned and collapsed, dead, the brothers fled. Shortly after, Bob turned himself in and was promptly charged, tried and convicted of murder. However, the charges involved the earlier killing of a fellow bandit named Wood Hite, not Jesse James.

Governor Crittenden lived up to part of his bargain. Ford was pardoned immediately, but received only a fraction of the payment offered for Jesse's death. It has been suggested that the Governor and some of his cronies ended up splitting most of the reward money. Negative public feelings toward Bob Ford ran high and he was forced to leave Missouri. He ended up establishing a bar in what is now Creede, Colorado, and was shotgunned to death in a dispute over a missing ring a decade after killing Jesse James.

Frank James turned himself in six months after Jesse's death. Following multiple trials,

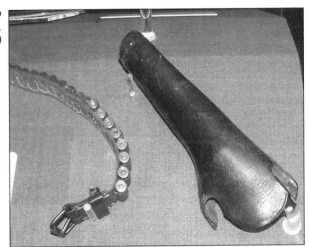

Frank James carried his Remington revolvers in what appear to be military holsters, with their flaps removed for quick retrieval. (Courtesy The Autry Museum of Western Heritage)

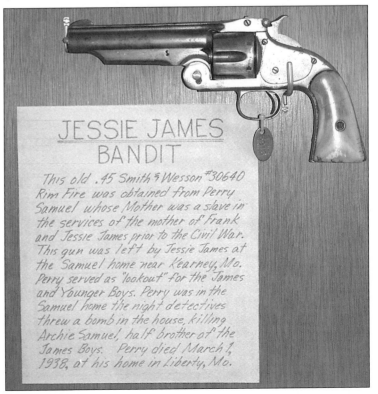

Claimed to be one of the revolvers Jesse kept at his mother's home, this cut down Smith & Wesson .45 Schofield is more likely just one of the many old used sixguns that were purchased for a few dollars around the neighborhood and sold to gullible tourists as "authentic" Jesse James artifacts. (Courtesy The J.M. Davis Museum)

JESSIE JAMES
BANDIT

This old .45 Smith & Wesson #30640 Rim Fire was obtained from Perry Samuel whose Mother was a slave in the services of the mother of Frank and Jessie James prior to the Civil War. This gun was left by Jessie James at the Samuel home near Kearney, Mo. Perry served as "lookout" for the James and Younger Boys. Perry was in the Samuel home the night detectives threw a bomb in the house, killing Archie Samuel, half brother of the James Boys. Perry died March 1, 1938, at his home in Liberty, Mo.

his pleas for leniency, coupled with local public opinion being overwhelmingly pro-Confederate, led to his final acquittal on all charges. In 1885 he walked free. From then until his death 30 years later, he worked at legitimate but mundane jobs. Never again did he run afoul of the law.

The behavior of their mother, Zerelda Samuel, following Jesse's death is instructive. She buried him in the front yard of her home and began selling tickets for 25 cents to those who wished to see the home and grave. She charged a quarter more for pebbles from the grave, which were sold as keepsakes. They were replenished regularly from a nearby creek. The guns, belts and holsters Jesse had removed just before he was killed were sold soon after for $15. Actually, not a bad price at the time for such well used revolvers. She is known to have regularly purchased quantities of used guns of all sorts and representing them as having belonged to Jesse when she resold them to the gullible. Perhaps she was merely pragmatic, but it's an unusual mother who will trade so freely upon the death of her child. It's easy to believe she was simply greedy.

Frank James is known to have preferred the .45 caliber Remington Model 1875 revolvers. He carried a brace of them in cut-down military holsters. In his later years he appeared for a time in a Wild West Show where he carried as a prop a .32-20 Bisley with a 5-1/2-inch barrel.

Jesse used Colt's Model 1851 Navy revolvers through the Civil War and beyond, but once metallic cartridge revolvers became available he quickly switched. The guns he was using when he died included a Colt SAA .45 and a Schofield .45. In all likelihood they were both loaded with the shorter Schofield cartridge, which would fit both guns, in order to avoid the problems inherent in mixing ammunition. Since both brothers were such poor marksmen, it probably didn't matter much to either of them what they used. Their choices were likely made on the basis of convenience and availability.

This is one of the pair of Model 1875 Remington revolvers carried by Frank James. (Courtesy The Autry Museum of Western Heritage)

Bill Jordan

A MAN OF enormous stature, both physically and in personal character, Bill Jordan was courtly with the ladies, good humored and generous with his friends, patient and friendly toward his fans and a criminal's worst nightmare. The speed of his draw was legendary and the level of his marksmanship was amazing. Born William H. Jordan, on February 12, 1911, in Cheyneyville, Louisiana, he grew to be a self-effacing southern lad of 6 feet, 7 inches in height. With his wide shoulders and enormous hands, he was an imposing figure. Were it not for his ready smile, others besides the criminal element might have thought him fearsome. After attending Louisiana State University, Jordan joined the Border Patrol. It was the early 1930s and the organization had just been formed.

Aside from his Patrol duties, Bill Jordan was a member of the Marine Corps Reserve. As such, he was called to active duty during World War II. Serving with distinction in the Pacific Theater, he fought in the battles for Eniwitok, Iwo Jima and Okinawa where he led a team that specialized in removing enemy holdouts from the caves in which they hid. Returning to the Border Patrol after the war, Jordan continued to serve until his retirement in 1965. He then became an NRA Field Representative, serving in that capacity for 10 years.

During the years following WWII, Jordan's skill with a sixgun gained him national attention, and makers of arms and accessories often sought his advice. Don Hume began making a holster of Jordan's design that became standard issue for uniform wear with most law enforcement agencies nationwide. He also designed revolver stocks that improved control during rapid fire and aided point shooting. Carl Holstrum, President of Smith & Wesson during much of the 1950s, came to Jordan for his input as to the features to be offered for the ideal lawman's revolver. The result was the K-frame Model 19, which is chambered for the .357 Magnum cartridge. It was significantly lighter and faster to handle than any previous revolver in that chambering and became one of the best selling of all law enforcement handguns and a favorite among shooting sportsmen, as well. He, in company with several other lawmen and gunwriters, was also instrumental in the creation of the .41 Remington Magnum cartridge.

Although it's somewhat dated by current standards, Jordan's book, *No Second Place Winner,* remains a valuable learning tool and has become a classic. Following his retirement from the Border Patrol, and after leaving his position at the NRA, Jordan began writing magazine articles. Most had to do with hunting, while some were humorous tales of his days in harness with the Border Patrol.

Bill Jordan was a lawman's lawman, a man of unflinching integrity and a true southern gentleman. In recognition of his many contributions to his profession, his country and the shooting sports, he was the fourth man selected as a recipient of The Outstanding American Handgunner Award. He died Oct. 4, 1997.

His ready smile and the merry twinkle in Bill Jordan's eye are indicative of his usual demeanor when he was among friends and fans. His behavior among criminals and enemy soldiers was anything but friendly.

With its bobbed hammer and oversize stocks of his own design, Bill Jordan had this rebarreled Smith & Wesson Model 10 set up for double-action speed shooting to use in the exhibitions of his amazing speed and accuracy. (Courtesy The Autry Museum of Western Heritage)

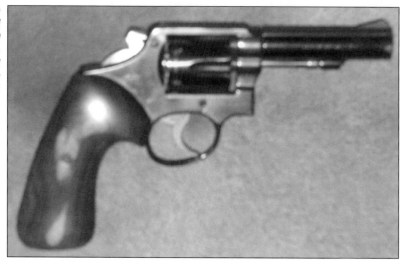

Elmer Keith

RANCHER, HUNTER, PACK-GUIDE, prolific writer and arms and ammunition experimenter, Elmer Keith was all of these, and so much more. Yet, although he held a commission as a Lemhi County, Idaho, deputy sheriff for many years, he was never a professional peace officer. Nor is there any public record that he ever actively participated in a gunfight, although there were a few narrowly avoided. No one who ever knew him could doubt, however, that he had the skill at arms and the mindset required to acquit himself well, had he ever been involved in such an incident. Actually, that's the most probable reason that he never had to fight. During those few confrontations that might have been reduced to gunplay, the opposition considered the risk of survival too low to be worth taking the chance. He is included here, because throughout most of the 20th century Elmer Keith's influence in all aspects of the development of the art and science of shooting was arguably greater than that of any other individual.

Elmer Keith was born to Forrest Everett and Linnie Neal Keith on March 8, 1899, in Hardin, Missouri. In 1905, his parents moved the family to Helena, Montana, but returned to Missouri soon after. Then, a few years later, they moved back to Montana permanently. They lived in Helena again, for a time, but in 1911 moved to Missoula. On the family's first night there they rented accommodations in a rooming house. At 2:30 in the morning an arsonist torched the building and the young Elmer was horribly burned. It took almost a year for him to recover sufficiently to resume most of his normal activities, but he was left badly scarred for life.

The worst of his injuries was a severely deformed left hand. The burns had left it doubled back, claw shaped, pressed against the wrist. Burn care and orthopedic surgical techniques were limited in the best of situations in the early 20th century. Western Montana was far removed from any such expertise. Folks made do as best they could. Keith was determined to return his hand to its normal position and recover as much use of it as he could. When local doctors refused to operate, he and his parents took the matter upon themselves. First the youngster was anesthetized with as much Old Grand-Dad bourbon whiskey as was necessary. Then, his father turned the hand around, in the process tearing still-healing skin and muscle, until it was straight. His mother bandaged it carefully and it was splinted to a smooth board. During that "operation" and the next few days that followed, the pain was excruciating for the boy and the jug of Old Grand-Dad continued in service. Within a few weeks, however, the hand began to heal. Interesting from a medical standpoint, part of his homemade therapy was to wear a buckskin glove, into which his mother dripped tallow. The glove protected the hand, while the tallow softened and lubricated the newly-growing skin. While his mother was simply using her own good sense in the matter, that technique is not far removed from accepted protocol in today's medical establishment.

No one at the time would have understood the term "physical therapy," as it is used today. In Keith's case, it consisted of nothing more than hard work; some of it everyday ranch chores and some at the National Biscuit Co. plant, where he shoveled coal, hauled it in a wheelbarrow, filled shipping boxes with the company's products, and stacked those as high as he could manage. In time, his left hand regained excellent function.

Beginning with an old muzzleloader and quickly graduating to a .22 rifle, Keith started shooting when his age was still counted in the single digits. By the time he'd reached his early teen years, he was a certified NRA Expert high-power rifleman and a competent shotgunner. As a handgunner, he cut his teeth on a Colt Model 1851 Navy revolver. The .36 caliber sixgun was used often to provide small game for the Keith family table. However, his life-long love of hand-

gunning began with a Single Action Army Colt, with a 7-1/2-inch barrel, blued, with case hardened colored frame, stocked with checkered wood and chambered for the .32-20 cartridge. He earned the money to purchase it by winning the $50 prize he and his brother shared for successfully riding a notorious bucking mule during the final appearance of the Buffalo Bill Wild West Show in Helena.

While the Colt .32-20 proved to be very accurate, and provided an excellent learning tool on which to hone his long-range shooting skills, the youngster quickly determined that it was severely underpowered for use on larger animals. While his experiments with big-bore handguns and bullets with flatter, wider noses and cases loaded with heavy powder charges led, ultimately, to a broad acceptance by the shooting public of handguns for hunting medium and large game, that was not his initial intent. Foremost in his mind seems to have been maximizing the effectiveness of the handgun as a daily work tool.

Romantics, particularly those weaned on a steady diet of Hollywood-inspired folklore, imagine the cowboy's handgun as intended for defense against outlaws and renegades. To be sure, it was generally considered an essential part of any cowboy's outfit, but its primary purpose was for use on aggressive horses and

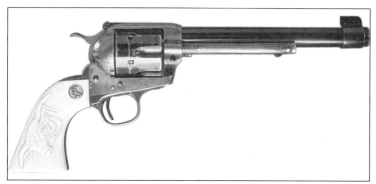

It was with this revolver that Elmer Keith developed the heavy .44 Special loads that would lead to the introduction of the .44 Magnum cartridge. Much customized, it features a King action job with a wide Bisley hammer. The topstrap of the frame has been milled almost flat and routed to accept installation of an S&W adjustable rear sight. The high front sight, mounted on a barrel band, aids precision accuracy at long range.

Known as the Keith Number 5, this modified Colt SAA revolver has a Bisley-style hammer and a wide trigger. The topstrap of the frame is built up and milled flat for added strength and has an adjustable rear sight. The oversize cylinder pin is much easier to grasp for removal than the standard type.

cattle or to dispatch severely injured or diseased livestock. The occasional small game animal taken for the cook pot or varmint shot for protection of livestock was far more frequent a use of the pistol than was the settling of interpersonal disputes. This was especially so by the time the 20th century had entered its second decade.

There was little in the way of literature on the subject to provide Keith with guidance as he developed his theories and applied his experiments. Some of the loads he developed proved to be downright dangerous, as attested to by the guns he ended up destroying in the process. One must bear in mind, however, that the metallurgical and design strengths of some of the handguns with which he worked in the years prior to World War II were wanting.

His experiments with the .38 Special cartridge were influential in the development by Phil Sharpe and Douglas Wesson of the .357 Magnum cartridge. His work with the .44 Special was directly responsible for the advent of the .44 Magnum cartridge. Likewise, he championed the concept of the .41 Magnum cartridge, primarily as a replacement for the .38 Special, which was regarded by many as woefully inadequate for law enforcement and sport shooting.

While he seems best remembered for his work with handguns, for which he was elected the first recipient of the Outstanding American Handgunner Award in 1973, Keith's work with rifles intended for big game was also noteworthy. He is, for example, directly responsible for the development of the .338 Winchester Magnum cartridge, which derived from his early experiments with the .333 and .334 OKH wildcat cartridges.

Elmer Keith owned dozens of firearms in his lifetime. Many would today be considered

Here is a quartet of .44 Magnum Smith & Wesson Model 29 revolvers, with various levels of decoration. All are wearing carved ivory stocks. The one at the top originally had a 6-1/2-inch barrel, but Keith had it cut to a more comfortably handling 4-1/2 inches. Today, most owners of engraved guns refuse to shoot them, but that's what they were made for. In most instances, not shooting a gun because it's engraved would be like not kissing a girl because she's pretty.

prized collector's items if unaltered, but his were working guns. They were intended for shooting and any alteration that improved their performance was, in his mind, worth doing. To be sure, a firearm with documented provenance associating it with Keith is a collector's item in its own right. However, for others to alter similar guns would, in most instances reduce their value substantially. Major arms manufacturers later adopted in whole or in part many of the improvements he made to his own guns. A good example is the Single Action Army Colt that combined the SAA and Bisley gripframes to form what he called the Number 5 revolver. It also has a wider trigger and a Bisley hammer spur. In 1986 Sturm, Ruger and Co. introduced its Bisley Model, which has nearly identical features.

Much of Keith's work in development of bullet design and potent powder charges for the .44 Special cartridge was done with a SAA Colt with a 7-1/2-inch barrel. The topstrap of its frame has been modified to resemble those of the early flat-top target revolvers made by Colt. An adjustable rear sight, made by Smith & Wesson, and a pinned front sight, set into a barrel band, provide for precise aiming. A Colt Bisley hammer spur replaced the original, to permit the sights to remain visible with the hammer down. He made no secret of his preference for .44 and .45 caliber single-action Colts for use on large game. When the Ruger Blackhawk and Super Blackhawk were introduced, he was very much impressed with their greater intrinsic strength and the much-improved reliability of their wire and coil springs. The original Colts use flat springs.

Elmer Keith understood the metallurgical limitations of Smith & Wesson's pre-war N-frame revolvers. With the massive amount of steel in their cylinders, the .357 Magnum cartridge worked wonderfully with them, but heavy loads for .44 and .45 caliber cartridges strained their capacity. The better steels and improved lockwork of the post-war era were another matter entirely. By the mid-1950s both S&W and Ruger began chambering revolvers for the .44 Magnum cartridge. The new, longer case was used to prevent the substantially hotter ammunition from being chambered in, and severely damaging, older .44 Special revolvers.

The experimental ammunition used in the development of the .44 Magnum cartridge proved very accurate and even more powerful than Keith had anticipated. However, as provided to the public, Remington's earliest available ammunition offering was disappointing. The lead SWC bullets used were too soft and the powder charges too hot, causing severe leading and poor accuracy. Such power quickly stressed the revolver's lockwork. In short order he developed a handload that optimized .44 Magnum cartridge performance while remaining within the strength parameters of the revolvers that used it.

Together with Border Patrolman Bill Jordan, Keith met with representatives of Smith & Wesson, Remington, Winchester, Ruger, and others during the 1964 NRA Convention in Washington, D.C. There, they lobbied for the introduction of .41 Magnum revolvers and ammunition, primarily for the use of lawmen. A few months later, both guns and ammunition were available. S&W provided Keith with the first of them-a consecutively numbered pair. They came with the 3/8-inch-wide triggers and the hammers shortened 1/4 of an inch from standard, just as Keith preferred them. In his later years, Elmer Keith was seldom out of reach of one or more of his .44 or .41 Magnum S&W revolvers.

Over and above Keith's myriad contributions to the shooting sports, his experiences and accomplishments provide examples of integrity, self-reliance, fairness and honesty; all qualities to be emulated.

Three of Keith's favorite SAA Colts are illustrated here. He was especially fond of carved ivory stocks on his sixguns. The Number 5 revolver, at the bottom, has a gripframe combining the Bisley at the top and the standard SAA at the bottom. The parts are welded together and the design makes the revolver's recoil easier to control with heavy loads, so follow-up shots can be fired more quickly.

Elmer Keith is striking a pose with two of his pet Smith & Wesson .44 Magnum revolvers.

In this photo, taken sometime in the 1950s, Keith is seated on the steps of the back porch of his Salmon, Idaho home. He's displaying his customized Colt .44 Special in its hand tooled, carved leather Lawrence #120 rig.

William Barclay Masterson

A CANADIAN BY birth, and best known to history by the name, "Bat" Masterson, the name given our subject was actually William Bartholomew. He was born Nov. 26, 1853, in Rouville County, in the Province of Quebec. His parents, Thomas and Catherine Masterson, were farmers who appear to have either had something of a wanderlust or just been seeking warmer climes and richer soil. By the time their second of seven children was 14 years old, the family had moved from Quebec to New York, then to Illinois, and finally settled in Kansas.

It's unclear for what reason, but at some point in his late teens William changed his middle name to Barclay. There is also some question as to the reason his nickname became "Bat." By all accounts he was a feisty young man, quick to do battle. That may have been the origins of his nickname, but most historians seem to think "Bat" is a reference to the cane he used both to assist his limp and as a weapon he sometimes used to subdue his foes.

His first significant job away from the family farm found the 18-year-old Bat and his elder brother Edward contracted to the Atchison, Topeka and Santa Fe Railroad grading its track line near Dodge City, Kansas. The pay was good, but the labor was grueling. With his earnings, he outfitted himself to take up the somewhat less physically demanding and far more lucrative occupation of the buffalo hunter. This brought him to his first notable confrontation, the Battle of Adobe Walls.

The plains tribes had begun to feel the severe pressure brought upon them by the buffalo hunters. The business was not only a major source of revenue for those who provided hides, meat and bones for the commercial market, it was also a part of the government's strategy for pacifying the Indians who depended upon the buffalo for their livelihood. Commercial hunting evolved into wholesale slaughter which, combined with disease and the deleterious effects of severe weather and drought, brought the American bison to the edge of extinction. A Comanche war party, under Quannah Parker, attacked a party of hunters encamped at Adobe Walls, inflicting severe damage. The attackers were ultimately driven off. The long-range accuracy of the buffalo rifles made the fight too costly for the raiders. Masterson fought well in that confrontation and a brief, three-month stint as a scout for General Nelson A. Miles followed.

Masterson's first recorded gunfight involved a jealous rival for the affections of a dancehall girl named Molly Brennan. Sergeant King, a soldier from Ft. Elliott, burst into the saloon where she worked, shooting as he came. One of his rounds struck Masterson in the pelvis. That injury is what caused him to require the use of a cane. In the exchange of gunfire, Molly was hit and killed. It's not clear whose shot struck her. Some say it was King's and that the bullet passed through her and struck Masterson. Others allege that she was hit with a stray round from Masterson's gun. It is nearly 130 years too late to sort things right.

It took some time for his injury to heal, but Masterson returned to Dodge in 1877, where he hired on as a deputy sheriff. That November he ran for the top position in the office and won. His record on the job was good enough that by 1879 he'd earned a deputy U.S. Marshal's commission, as well. Those dual responsibilities notwithstanding, a call from his former employer, the AT&SF Railroad, brought him to Trinidad, Colorado, where a dispute over the right-of-way over Raton pass into New Mexico with the rival Denver & Rio Grande Railway had deteriorated into a shooting war. Masterson and his "troops" won out but his constituents back home in Dodge City don't seem to have appreciated the cavalier manner in which he left them to take up the railroad's cause. He lost his bid for reelection.

For the next half dozen years, Bat Masterson wandered the West as a gambler and some-time lawman or hired gun. By the mid-1880s he'd become more interested in sports than gunslinging. He married a lady named Emma Walters in 1891. Settling for a time in Denver, he promoted prizefights and horse racing. By then he was also doing some writing for the newspapers. This slowly evolved into a new career, and by 1902 he'd moved to New York City.

Fashionably attired in an impeccably tailored suit, Bat Masterson usually dressed in high fashion. He might easily have been mistaken for a well-to-do Eastern businessman, rather than one of the toughest lawmen of the Old West.

President Theodore Roosevelt, very much a fan of Western lore, was an admirer of Masterson. Probably motivated by potential political advantage, it being seen as a law and order move, he gave the erstwhile gunfighter an appointment as deputy U.S. Marshal for The Southern District of New York. When Taft became president, he rescinded that com-

An ill-fitting set of Bakelite stocks has replaced the plastic staghorn on the revolver used by Barry in his role as Bat Masterson. The revolver was renickeled and its barrel shortened to 4 inches. The ejector rod housing was retained by cutting it back to match. (Courtesy The Cody Firearms Museum)

Most of his contemporaries in the West tended to wear their hair long. Not Bat Masterson. His tonsorial styling may have given trailherders and railroadmen the impression that he was just another fastidious dude they could run roughshod over. Anyone who thought that was in for a big surprise. Perhaps, Masterson intended it that way.

mission. Masterson didn't seem to mind. It was interfering with his sports interests, anyway. Beginning in 1907, he began writing as a featured sports columnist for the *Morning Telegraph* newspaper; a job he held until he died, ironically, with his boots on. On October 25, 1921, he slumped over at his typewriter, dead of a heart attack.

Colt's records show that Bat Masterson preferred the 4-3/4-inch barrel length on his favorite handgun, the SAA Colt. Over the course of his years in the West, he ordered several directly from the factory, including at least one on Dodge City's Long Branch Saloon stationery. In one letter he'd been very specific as to the features he wanted with it, including nickel plating, that the trigger be "easy" and the front sight higher and thicker than standard. When last heard of, that revolver was in a private collection, but there are many others that are purported to be "genuine" Bat Masterson guns. Most are the product of a bit of chicanery on his part. While living and working in New York, he was often approached by people interested in buying "the" gun he carried during his days as a

In his later years Bat Masterson became a respected sportswriter for The New York Morning Telegraph newspaper. He continued to dress well, but his gunfighting days were done and there was no indication he ever missed them.

Western gunfighter. Ever the entrepreneur, Masterson purchased numerous old sixguns from the local pawn shops for a few dollars and sold them to willing collectors for more than twice the going rate for a similar revolver purchased new. It was a sweet racket.

His interest in making a fast buck, combined with his notoriety as a gunman, led Masterson to do something no other Western gunfighter had ever officially done. He endorsed a specific product. In this instance it was Savage's little .32 caliber semi-automatic pistol. In an advertising brochure he averred that all the old-time gunfighters would have preferred having one of these pistols, because it would deliver "10 shots quick!" Never mind that in most instances it would require several more rounds to put a man down than would be needed with a .45, he was being paid for his opinion, so he would deliver what the customer wanted. Of its kind, it really was a pretty good pistol, to be sure. However, few people thought in terms of terminal ballistic efficiency in those days. If made today such an endorsement would have utterly destroyed any credibility he might have had.

From 1958 until 1961 actor Gene Barry portrayed Bat Masterson in the NBC television show of that name; complete with "cane and derby hat," as the opening theme song described. That was about as far as the historical accuracy of the show went.

Ed McGivern

AGAIN, WE INCLUDE an individual never known to have drawn down on another human, but whose expertise and reputation precluded any such necessity. During the decades immediately prior to and following World War II, Ed McGivern was probably the world's most famous handgunner. At the dawn of the 21st century, his name lives on among the more ardent enthusiasts of the sixgun, but it has long since faded from most public memory.

Where his contemporary, Elmer Keith, was renowned for long-range precision with the revolver and an enormous body of private research into practical and theoretical ballistic performance, McGivern was famous for his close-range speed and accuracy and the ability and willingness to teach such skills to others. Records he set stood unbroken by all challengers for more than half a century. There are those, however, who would point out that there are significant differences between the handling qualities of the revolvers McGivern used and those used by his modern challengers. No slight is intended toward the latter, but it would be interesting to compare performances with identical equipment.

Speaking of equipment, the effectiveness of that with which McGivern's expertise was measured has been called into question. It still exists, and when calibrated and tested, it

was found to be equal to the accuracy of our modern devices.

Ed McGivern was a university graduate, whose areas of study were concentrated in the sciences, including: mathematics, electronics, anatomy, physiology, psychology and physics. The results of his studies were compiled in his book, *Fast and Fancy Revolver Shooting.*

Semi-automatic pistols are all but ignored in McGivern's work, which will surprise many modern shooters, especially when they learn the reason. McGivern was so fast on the trigger that he could actually fire all the ammunition in a revolver faster than can be done with a semi-automatic. Observers at his exhibitions often reported that they believed he had fired his revolver only once, but were amazed to see five holes in the target and as many empty cartridge cases ejected from the cylinder. It should be pointed out here that it remained common practice at that time, as a matter of safety, to carry even double-action revolvers with an empty chamber under the hammer.

A sign painter by trade, McGivern was by no means well off financially. His shooting and related experiments were expensive, but in many ways McGivern was an artist, and artists often have patrons to support their work. Walter Groff, a Philadelphia businessman, was fascinated by McGivern's skills and accomplishments. Groff became McGivern's patron and made certain that he never lacked for ammunition or any firearm with which he might wish to experiment. Because his shooting activities left him no time for handloading, McGivern worked exclusively with factory ammunition. Groff had cases of it shipped directly to him from the ammo makers.

When the Master Sixgunner died in 1957, the 16 handguns that were a part of his legacy were willed to Groff. When Groff, himself, died, his will specified that 14 of the McGivern handguns were to be donated to the NRA. The remaining two were passed to Groff's long-time friend and fellow shooting enthusiast, Henry Stewart, of Wynnewood, Pennsylvania. Of those, one is a very scarce Colt SAA .357 Magnum. It has a factory-altered front sight. A small, L-shaped cut

was made in its rear face and a dimple with a small dot of white paint to fill it replaced the original bead front sight, which has been lost. McGivern was known to favor bead or dot front sights. This one was regulated to strike point of aim at 25 yards using a dead-on hold.

For the most part, McGivern used double-action Smith & Wesson revolvers along with a few Colts of comparable size and caliber. Of considerable interest is that none of their actions were modified in any way. All were factory stock, just as any other shooter might purchase. Tests the NRA conducted in the 1970s demonstrated that the accuracy they were capable of providing was also typical of others of their type. McGivern had no advantages whatsoever in terms of the equipment at his disposal. His remarkable performance with them was purely a matter of talent.

A portly, rather ordinary looking man, Ed McGivern's commonplace physiognomy belied the speed and accuracy with which he could use a revolver. Unlike most highly skilled shooters, who simply practice until a technique works for them, McGivern first applied the scientific method to solving a shooting challenge. That made what and how to practice more meaningful, so in the end he mastered a technique more thoroughly than most pistoleros.

McGivern's book, Fast and Fancy Revolver Shooting, *is one of the early classics of firearms literature. He was often the subject of magazine articles such as the cover story in the October 1974 issue of* American Rifleman. *The target shown was shot from 25 yards over sandbags, using Winchester's 145-grain .38 Special loads.*

President Theodore Roosevelt

THE 26TH PRESIDENT of the United States was an avid hunter, general outdoorsman, conservationist, soldier and statesman. As fond as he was of guns and shooting, he was an incredibly poor marksman because of his poor eyesight. Nevertheless, as with all else in his life, he persevered.

Roosevelt was born October 27, 1858, into a well-to-do and politically influential family. He was a sickly child and doctors were concerned that he would live a short and miserable life, but as he came of an age to understand his circumstances, he chose to begin a regimen of vigorous exercise in the belief that it would improve his health. He was correct. Although he was doomed to wear spectacles throughout his life, he grew stronger, more vigorous and athletic as he grew to manhood.

His formal education included attending the finest primary and secondary schools and graduating from Harvard University, but his natural curiosity inspired studies far beyond the bounds of ivy-covered walls. Roosevelt was particularly interested in the natural sciences, which made him unusually well acquainted with wildlife and conservation issues. Fascinated by stories of the Wild West and the adventures to be had there, the realities of which were continuing to unfold during his youth, he arranged to participate in a big game hunt in the Dakota Territory in 1883. Roosevelt's host, a transplanted Scot named Gregor Lang, and his guide, Joe Ferris, had expected a typical dude, rich, spoiled and expecting to be waited upon hand and foot. What they got was a talkative young man who was insatiably curious, possessed boundless energy and was more than willing to do for himself whenever possible. While his poor vision handicapped his hunting, the 25-year-old Easterner remained enthusiastic and managed to bag a few trophies. His most important acquisition was a growing love and respect for the land; so much so that he determined to set up ranching, himself. That enterprise lost a lot of money, but he stuck with it for 16 years, mostly as an absentee owner. But his appreciation of the West, its people, land, flora and fauna continued throughout his life and was a major motivation in his move to establish the National Park Service. He was also the founding member of the Boone and Crockett Club, dedicated to promoting the conservation of wildlife, its habitat and establish and maintain ethical hunting standards.

In 1903, during Roosevelt's term as President, Congress established The National Board for the Promotion of Rifle Practice to promote marksmanship training for civilians in order to provide for future military needs. It has evolved over the years to become the Civilian Marksmanship Program, which offers surplus firearms and ammunition to qualified individuals for competition and training.

The serious social aspect of firearms use was not lost upon Theodore Roosevelt. During his ranching days he pursued and captured a couple of thieves and brought them to justice at the point of his engraved Model 1876 Winchester. His Colt Single Action Army .44-40, lavishly embellished by Nimschke, saw extensive use. Leading his Rough Riders in Cuba, he used his government-issue Model 1889 double-action revolver, chambered for the .38 Colt cartridge.

Companion to Theodore Roosevelt's Model 1876 Winchester is the .44-40 Colt Single Action Army revolver he frequently carried. It, too, is engraved and stocked in carved ivory. On the right side the stocks bear a stylized rendition of its owner's initials. (Courtesy The Autry Museum of Western Heritage)

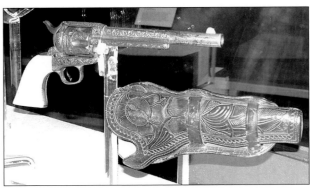

Roosevelt's SAA Colt revolver was carried in a finely crafted drop-loop holster with a floral carving pattern. The sixgun has seen a great deal of use at its owner's hands, as demonstrated by the amount of wear to its nickel finish. The holster wear and flaking of the nickel notwithstanding, the revolver was well maintained and demonstrates no evidence of abuse. (Courtesy The Autry Museum of Western Heritage)

In stark contrast with the pampered lifestyle and tailored suits one might expect of a child of privilege, Theodore Roosevelt was as self-reliant as his skills would allow. Seated here with a Bowie knife tucked into his belt and his engraved Model 1876 Winchester in his hands, he's dressed in a buckskin shirt and trousers he made himself.

With it, he shot at least one Spaniard. In 1896, while serving as New York City Police Commissioner, Roosevelt arranged for the first standard issue handgun for that agency, the .32 Colt New Police revolver. Serial #1 of the initial factory order was presented to him. Even during his presidency he felt it prudent to go armed. He was descending the steps from the second floor of the White House one day, enroute to a political affair, when he stopped suddenly, patted his chest, turned and went back to his room, exclaiming as he did so that he'd forgotten his gun. It would be interesting to know how many other presidents were not willing to rely solely upon the Secret Service for their personal protection. He seems also to have had some disdain for gun control laws. On one occasion he was in Massachusetts to deliver a speech at Harvard. While leaving his room to go to the event, he tucked a revolver into the breast pocket of his jacket. With him was the university president, who commented that carrying a concealed weapon was illegal there. Roosevelt was unimpressed and went armed, anyway.

During his days in the Dakota Territory, one of Roosevelt's favorite rifles was a Sharp's .45-90. His shotgun was a 10-gauge double barrel by Chicago maker, Thomas. Roosevelt appreciated the many advancements in firearms design and cartridge development that were occurring during his lifetime. After his political career, he went on an extended safari in Africa during which he collected hundreds of animal specimens for museum exhibits. His primary armament for that trek included a pair of Model 1895 Winchesters, chambered for the .405 Win. cartridge and a sporterized Model 1903 Springfield .30-06. Another rather interesting rifle owned by Roosevelt is the Model 1894 Winchester chambered for the .30-30 cartridge that he fitted with a Maxim silencer to dispatch the woodchucks in his garden without disturbing the peace of his neighbors at his family estate, Sagamore Hill.

Theodore Roosevelt died in his sleep, in 1919, at the age of 60. Many regard him as the nation's greatest president. Among firearms enthusiasts there are few dissenters.

Winchester's Model 1876 was a popular rifle in the West during the time Roosevelt was there. Few, however, were decorated so elaborately. (Courtesy The Autry Museum of Western Heritage)

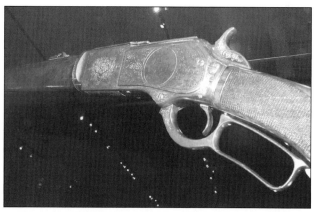

Profusely engraved by L.D. Nimschke, Roosevelt's rifle also features a highly figured walnut stock with pistol grip and checkering. Although he used it extensively, it retains most of its original finish, indicating that he cared for it with the attention such a fine rifle deserves. (Courtesy The Autry Museum of Western Heritage)

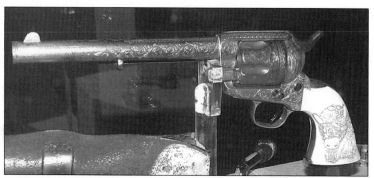

The ivory stock panel on the left side of President Roosevelt's Nimschke-engraved Colt .44-40 bears the hand carved likeness of a buffalo's head. (Courtesy The Autry Museum of Western Heritage)

Skeeter Skelton

LONG, LEAN AND ramrod straight, Charles A. "Skeeter" Skelton looked every inch the Texas lawman he was. He was born in the west Texas panhandle town of Hereford, in Deaf Smith County, on May 1, 1928. There wasn't much cash around during the Depression years of his childhood, but it's unlikely that Skeeter Skelton ever thought of himself or his family as poor. Like most country folks, his parents and grandparents knew how to make do with what they had and with whatever nature's bounty provided. The way he told it in the "Me and Joe" stories that were for years a great favorite with the readers of *Shooting Times Magazine,* nature provided very well and he made the most of it for the dinner table.

World War II was over before Skelton had grown to an age to serve, but Skelton joined the Marine Corps shortly after hostilities ceased. After his military hitch he tried college for a time, but quit to become a patrolman with the Amarillo, Texas, Police Department. Service with the U.S. Border Patrol came next. With that elite outfit he helped guard our southern borders against smugglers and illegal aliens in Arizona.

It may have been a measure of homesickness that brought him back, or, perhaps, a desire to give back to the community in which he was raised. Whatever the reason, Skelton returned to Deaf Smith County to serve, first as a deputy, and then as its Sheriff. During his time in elective office he gained a reputation as a tough, but fair, lawman and a skilled and intelligent investigator. That led him to federal service, first as a narcotics agent for the U.S. Customs Service, then as a Special Agent in Charge for the U.S. Drug Enforcement Administration. He retired from service in 1974.

As distinguished as his career behind the badge was, the public best remembers Skeeter Skelton as a writer. He began that phase of his career with an article published in *Guns Magazine* in the late 1950s. The subject was methods for carrying a concealed handgun. Readers were impressed with the sound advice he offered regarding many aspects of guns and shooting, and the modesty and good humor with which he told his stories demonstrated that he didn't take himself too seriously. By the early 1960s Skelton had a following among devotees of the shooting sports, handgunners in particular. A life-long shooter and hunter, Skelton knew what worked and why. Firearms manufacturers and ammunition and accessory makers began actively seeking his input. In 1966 he began writing exclusively for *Shooting Times Magazine* and served as its Handgun Editor for 21 years, authoring more than 400 articles and four books; two softbound and two hardcover.

Skelton was as popular among his peers in the firearms industry as with his readers. That was demonstrated in 1978 when he was presented the prestigious Outstanding American Handgunner Award. He was its sixth recipient.

Skeeter Skelton owned dozens of firearms over the course of his lifetime. His first serious handgun was a Single Action Army Colt Bisley Model that had started life chambered for the .41 Long Colt cartridge. Ammunition was scarce for that round and not particularly given to premium accuracy, so a .38-40 cylinder was exchanged for the original. Since bores were nominally the same, the switch made the sixgun a good learning tool for a youngster just getting seriously into the shooting game. He always had a fondness for SAA Colts, but recognized the greater strength inherent in the Ruger single-gle action revolvers. It was the latter that he used most often for heavy handloads. Of all the guns he carried as a lawman, his favorite was the .357 Magnum Smith & Wesson Model 27, with a 5-inch barrel. The late Deacon Deason originally made the stocks he designed for it. They feature a thinner panel than the factory type. Similar in some respects to the old Roper design, the stocks have a slight swell at the center and become thinner near the bottom of the panel, then flare out slightly to give the edge of the hand a measure of extra support. These are particularly useful for fast double-action shooting. Precisely the same design is available today from Colorado craftsman Ted Adamovich, of Blu Magnum Grips. After a long illness, Skeeter Skelton succumbed to liver disease on January 17, 1988, at Sun Towers Hospital in El Paso, Texas.

During the course of his many years behind the badge Skeeter Skelton used many different handguns in the line of duty. His favorite was this Model 27 Smith & Wesson. Chambered for the .357 Magnum cartridge, it has a 5-inch barrel, which he regarded as an ideal compromise between the handiness of the 4-inch version and the improved accuracy of the 6-inch version. It is fitted with the stocks made to his specifications by Deacon Deason. (Courtesy The Autry Museum of Western Heritage)

Skeeter Skelton was one of the great Texas lawmen of the 20th century and looked the part. He wore with honor the badges of the several agencies he served during his career. His interest in guns and shooting beyond the requirements of his official duties led to a thorough knowledge of the subject, which he shared generously with others through his writing. His recommendations were practical, and provided with an element of humor that delighted his readers.

Myra Maybelle Shirley, a.k.a. Belle Starr

THE TRANSFORMATION FROM the rather plain name with which Myra Maybelle Shirley was born, to the more romantic sounding one by which she is best known, is reflected in the way she has been portrayed by Hollywood. Attractive, even beautiful women have played that role. Had the films been striving for accuracy, at least in terms of physical resemblance, they would have done better choosing plain, if not ugly actresses.

Most accounts say she was born in Carthage, Missouri, but the truth is she was born in Washington County, Arkansas, on February 5, 1848. Her parents had migrated from Virginia and settled there in the 1830s. While she was still an infant, John Shirley and his wife Eliza left Arkansas and settled in Carthage. There, the family prospered and young Myra was provided with every educational advantage a proper young lady of the mid-Victorian era. At The Carthage Academy for Young Ladies she learned the social graces, studied music, mathematics and classical languages.

The brutality of war was brought home to the Shirley family when, in 1863, Myra's brother, Edward, was killed by federal troops and the hotel her father owned was burned to the ground. John Shirley packed his family and all the belongings they could manage into a wagon and set off for Texas, where they settled near Dallas, in the town of Scyene. Once again the family did well, but in late adolescence Myra's hormones seem to have begun overcoming the manners and morels she'd been taught. Her family heartily disapproved of Cole Younger, the young tough, a former member of Quantrell's Raiders, who had come sniffing around. They saw little to approve of when John Reed, a young man of lazy habits and criminal proclivities that she'd known back home in Carthage, came calling. Only the shame associated with out-of-wedlock pregnancy overcame parental objections and the couple was married. But there has always been an element of doubt about the actual paternity of the daughter she bore, whom they named Rosie Lee, but called Pearl.

The young family moved to southern California to avoid Reed being prosecuted for killing a man. There, he took up the lucrative business of robbing stagecoaches. A second child, this time a son was born in 1871. But things were getting hot for them once more and just ahead of a posse, the Reed family made a run for it and headed back to Scyene. The business Myra ran there, a livery stable, seemed on the surface to be legitimate. Actually it provided a front for the "laundering" of stolen horses that Reed was rustling in the Indian Territory and moving south to convert to cash.

The law finally caught up with Reed, who was killed by a deputy sheriff in a shootout near Paris, Texas, in 1874. Subsequently, the young widow sold her business, dumped her children with her family and started a new career as a faro dealer in Dallas. This was the beginning of a long downhill slide.

She moved to Kansas in 1877 and set up housekeeping with Cole Younger's cousin Bruce. That relationship lasted about three years. She then married Sam Starr, one of the sons of outlaw Cherokee Tom Starr, and joined in the family business, rustling cattle and horses. They took up residence in the Cherokee

REWARD
$10,000
IN GOLD COIN
Will be paid by the U. S. Government for the apprehension
DEAD OR ALIVE
of
SAM and BELLE STARR

Wanted for Robbery, Murder, Treason and other acts against the peace and dignity of the U. S.

THOMAS CRAIL
Major, 8th Missouri Cavalry, Commanding

Belle Starr had little respect for the property of others, though she was not known to be the killer her husband, Sam Starr, was. A thief and rustler, with distinctly anti-Yankee attitudes, Union authorities were willing to spend a lot of money to stop her predations.

Mounted as a proper Victorian lady should be, using a side-saddle on her mare, Venus, Belle Starr affected the manner of a well-bred woman. However, in her personal life she was anything but discriminating in her breeding habits. The revolver holstered on her right hip appears to be a Smith & Wesson American Model, a variation of the large-frame Number 3 series.

Nation, near Eufaula. Finally, at least in name, she was the Belle Starr of legend. In spite of the $5,000 reward posted for the capture of the pair, Judge Isaac Parker seems not to have been particularly impressed by their criminality. They were captured in 1882, but released in less than six months. The light of their romance seems to have gone out during their separation, however, because she soon began bestowing her feminine favors on a much younger man, named Blue Duck. When he went off to prison in 1886, John Middleton began warming her bed. That didn't last very long, either. Within a few months, he was shot to death. There has always been some suspicion that Sam Starr may have had something to do with the disappearance of his rivals from his bride's life, but nothing was ever proved. Not that it mattered much, because he was killed in a shootout just before Christmas, 1886.

Jim July was next to share her bed. A cousin of Sam Starr's, she insisted he adopt the family name. Presumably because she liked the one she had and didn't want to change it. He might have made a better choice in bedmates. By now it should have been evident to anyone who might have cared that establishing a romantic relationship with her was not conducive to a long and happy life. He died resisting arrest. Two other lovers, Jack Spaniard and Jim French, also met an early demise. The only one who survived into old age was Cole Younger, but he spent 25 years of his life in a Minnesota prison.

Belle Starr met her end returning from an overnight trip with Jim July. He pressed on to Fort Smith and on her way home she was blown from the saddle of her mare, Venus, by a shotgun blast in the back. The date was February 3, 1889, just two days shy of her

Holding what appears to be a cocked Model 1877 Colt Lightning revolver in her right hand, one may wonder what she has in mind for the photographer. A Single Action Army Colt revolver rests in a cross-draw holster on her left hip.

Standing by her man, Belle Starr posed for this studio portrait with her paramour of the time, the Cherokee criminal, Blue Duck, whose wrists are shackled. The photo was taken in Ft. Smith, Arkansas, as he awaited trial.

41st birthday. Ever since, dime novels and motion pictures have labeled Belle Starr the "Bandit Queen." There are many ways one may describe her, but a queen of anything is hardly one of them.

Belle Starr did go armed much of the time. There is no record, however, that she ever shot anyone or participated in a shoot-out. Notwithstanding, the "lady" did pack iron. The photo taken of her mounted side-saddle on her mare, Venus, has her promi-nently displaying what appears to be a Smith & Wesson American revolver in the holster on her right hip. A studio portrait of her shows what appears to be a double-action Colt Model 1877 held straight down but cocked, and a bone- or ivory-handled SAA holstered cross-draw on her left hip. A well-worn .45, with a 4-3/4-inch barrel, alleged to have been hers, is on display in The Autry Museum of Western Heritage. It

appears she was content to carry whatever was available at any given time.

This very ordinary Colt .45 has been attributed to Belle Starr, indicating that she very likely changed guns when-ever it was convenient, just as she did lovers and hus-bands. (Courtesy The Autry Museum of Western Heritage)

Bill Tilghman

HAD HE BEEN born 50 years later, Bill Tilghman might have had a very different career. His good looks could have made him a western movie hero. It seems more than strange that one such as William Matthew Tilghman Jr., whose career as a lawman spanned nearly five decades, was all but ignored by the sensationalist press of his own time and later by an entertainment industry willing to capitalize on the names of many lesser men. Some of his exploits were precisely of the sort Hollywood often fictionalized about others. Sam Elliot's recent TV movie, *You Know My Name,* was a rare glimpse at the remarkable career of one of the great western lawmen.

"A real live nephew of (his) Uncle Sam," as the songwriter, George M. Cohan would have put it, Tilghman was born in Ft. Dodge, Iowa, July 4, 1854. When he was a toddler, his family moved to Kansas, where he was raised on a farm near Atchison. As a young man, he, like many others who would become lawmen, honed his marksmanship skills as a buffalo hunter. There followed a stint as an army scout, headquartered at Ft. Dodge, Kansas. In 1877 he began his career behind the badge as a deputy sheriff in Ford County, Kansas.

It seems that there must have remained something of a wild streak in the still youthful Tilghman, because the year after he became a deputy, he was arrested twice for stealing. Whatever the circumstances that lead to that behavior, he quickly mended his ways; perhaps because shortly after those incidents he married and soon began raising a family. Never again was he known to tread on the wrong side of the law. With growing maturity came respectability and the confidence of the community. In 1884 he was appointed Dodge City Marshal.

In 1889, the 35-year-old lawman pulled up stakes and moved. The Oklahoma District Land Rush opened portions of Indian Territory to legal white settlement. The promise of fertile land and the expected economic growth apparently attracted Tilghman. He filed a claim in Guthrie, but soon found a badge once more pinned to his shirt; this time as the Perry City Marshal. Three years after arriving in Oklahoma, Tilghman won appointment as a deputy U.S. Marshal.

The Indian Territory, which became the State of Oklahoma, had, early in the 19th century, been established by the federal government as a homeland for native tribes displaced by the encroachment of white settlement in the East. Prior to the Civil War, it had also become a favorite destination for escaped black slaves and outlaws fleeing justice. Because the territory was, at first, reserved exclusively for native settlement, only federal peace officers, the U.S. Marshals, were authorized to enter those lands to arrest and extradite criminals wanted elsewhere in the United States. Available lawmen were so few that the lawless element could expect that only the most brazen among them would attract interest. Unless his crimes had been especially vile, the outlaw who didn't draw attention to himself within the borders of I.T. could often go about unmolested. There were, however, some really bad hombres who needed catching.

At that time, U.S. Marshal Evett Nix administered the Marshal's Service offices headquartered in Ft. Smith, Arkansas, where Judge Isaac Parker, "The Hanging Judge," presided over court proceedings. Nix hired Heck Thomas, Chris Madsen and Bill Tilghman to go after the worst of the outlaws. The trio, who came to be known as "The Three Guardsmen," usually operated independently, but kept in close contact, so that each would know the location of the other and be able to coordinate their efforts whenever the need should arise.

While there were many desperados of particular interest to the law, none was more sought after than Bill Doolin, the leader of a gang known as the "Oklahombres." A different brand of outlaw than most, Doolin had a shrewd and calculating mind and became a robber for the sake of the money, not because he was a sociopath. That didn't make him any less dangerous. Doolin planned his crimes carefully to minimize risk and maxi-

mize profits. Family concerns and ill health were weighing on him and he was seriously considering retirement when Tilghman took up his trail.

Disguised as a minister, Tilghman caught up with the ailing desperado at the resort in Eureka Springs, Arkansas, where Doolin had gone "to take the cure," soaking in the natural hot springs from which the town derives its name. When the lawman got the drop on him, the outlaw's every instinct was to pull his own iron and fight, but after a few seconds' thought, he must have decided that it wasn't a good day to die. Soon after he'd been brought in, Doolin escaped from jail and made his way to New Mexico. When he returned for his wife and child several months later, he was found, and this time made a fight of it. The posse killed him.

Tilghman continued in public service throughout his life, with such posts as that of U.S. Marshal, Oklahoma State senator and as Chief of Police of Oklahoma City. In 1915 he wrote, produced and directed a motion picture entitled, *Passing of the Oklahoma Outlaws,* a six-part serial that, unlike many movies, did not portray a glamorized image of the outlaws.

In one capacity or another, Tilghman remained a lawman into old age. When he was 70, he accepted the post of Marshal in the oil boom-town of Crawford, Oklahoma. There, in a rare unguarded moment, Wiley Lynn, a pro-

More than a century has passed since Bill Tilghman's "Sunday-go-to-meeting" sixgun was made. Fitted with a 4-3/4-inch barrel and mother-of-pearl stocks, it was nickel-plated and engraved by Cuno Helfricht. This beautiful specimen of the classic .45 caliber Colt Single Action Army revolver remains in mint condition and may never have been fired. (Courtesy The Autry Museum of Western Heritage)

Taken during his buffalo hunting days, this photo shows Bill Tilghman appearing somewhat disheveled, quite unlike the well-groomed lawman he would become.

hibition officer of questionable character, gunned him down.

Over the course of his long career, many firearms must have passed through Bill Tilghman's hands. Based upon contemporary observations and personal quotes attributed to him, Colt's Single Action Army revolver seems to have been the handgun he most preferred. A 5-1/2-inch .38-40 he owned was among several guns he traded to a gentleman named Merle A. Gill. Well used, but in good condition, just how much of that use occurred in Tilghman's hands could be difficult to determine, particularly in view of the fact that he was known to have favored .45 caliber revolvers.

One .45 Tilghman owned appears to have seen little use. Nickel-plated, with two-piece mother-of-pearl handles and engraved by Cuno Helfricht, this beautiful SAA Colt six-gun is in such pristine condition that it may never have been fired. Made in 1893, if any use whatever was put to it, it was probably as a "Sunday-go-to-meeting" gun, worn only for special occasions.

In his middle years, Tilghman, who was much feared by the lawless element, came to be loved and respected with equal fervor by

With marriage, a family and the responsibilities associated with his office, Bill Tilghman took on the appearance of a serious professional.

By the time Tilghman had reached middle age, he was one of the nation's best-known and most respected lawmen. His career in public service was the stuff of legend. He was the living embodiment of the Western lawman so often idealized in motion pictures. Oklahomans came to know him simply as "Uncle Billy."

Known in his day as "The Hanging Judge," Isaac Parker's actual record indicates that he was as fair and impartial a jurist as a defendant or his attorney could wish. Tilghman, in his capacity as a Deputy U.S. Marshal, served Parker's court and was known as one of "The Three Guardsmen."

the citizenry whom he served and protected. Known far and wide for his kindly nature, he was affectionately dubbed "Uncle Billy." During his tenure as Chief of Police in Oklahoma City, a grateful citizenry presented him with a gold-plated, engraved and ivory-stocked 2nd Model .44 Special Hand Ejector, made by Smith & Wesson.

A tough lawman, a loyal public servant and a devoted family man, Bill Tilghman stands tall among the best-known figures of the Old West. He remains a shining example of what it truly means to be a "Peace Officer."

All that is known of this well-used 5-1/2-inch Colt, chambered for the .38-40 cartridge, is that Bill Tilghman once owned it and traded it to a collector named Merle A. Gill. The circumstances under which Tilghman may have acquired or used it are unknown, but it's similar to one he got from John Wesley Hardin. (Courtesy the J.M. Davis Muesum)

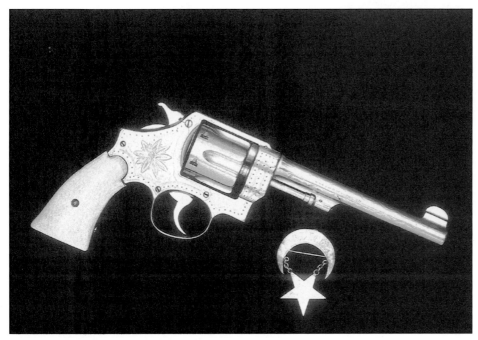

Shown here with Tilghman's badge, is a Smith & Wesson 2nd Model .44 Hand Ejector revolver that was presented to him by "The grateful citizens of Oklahoma City." Lightly engraved, the revolver is gold-plated and has ivory stocks. (Courtesy National Cowboy and Western Heritage Museum)

Tom Threepersons

TOM THREEPERSONS WAS "an enigma wrapped in a riddle," to borrow a phrase. Part of the problem is that there were two men with nearly identical names and they were contemporaries. One was a Canadian member of the Blood nation and the other was born in the United States, ostensibly a Cherokee. Tom Three Persons, the Canadian, was a champion rodeo cowboy whose immortality was assured when he rode the outlaw bucking horse, Cyclone, at the Calgary Stampede in 1912. Prior to September 7, 1912, 127 cowboys had attempted and failed to ride that big, black bronc. Three Persons not only rode him for time, he rode him to a standstill!

Stories that claim the Cherokee Tom Threepersons was at one time a member of the Royal Canadian Mounted Police are rooted in an unfortunate personal failing of Three Persons. As much as the Canadian liked horses, he also liked whiskey. During his all too frequent periods of incarceration for public intoxication at Ft. McLeod, Alberta the mounties availed themselves of his talents and had him break the rough stock brought in for remounts.

The American lawman, Tom Threepersons was, according to his death certificate, born July 22, 1889, in Vinita, Oklahoma, in the northeastern part of the state, right in the heart of the Cherokee Nation. However, the name Threepersons doesn't appear in the tribal records as a Cherokee surname. That's not necessarily definitive. As much intermarriage as there was among whites, Indians and Negroes in that area, the lines of ethnic heritage were often quite blurred.

Absolutely no record of Tom Threepersons appears prior to February 1916, when he was mentioned in a newspaper account of a local rodeo in Douglas, Arizona. A few weeks later Pancho Villa and his band of cutthroats, known as Los Dorados, "The Golden Ones," invaded Columbus, New Mexico. In short order, General John J. "Black Jack" Pershing was on the border forming up his troops for the punitive expedition into Mexico. It appears that Threepersons was directly involved, but it's unclear what exactly his role was. He may have signed on as a civilian scout, or as a stock wrangler. By February of the following year the troops had returned, and by May Threepersons was doing his patriotic wartime duty working at the U.S. Army Remount Depot at Fort Bliss. He continued working there until some time in 1920.

It was during his years at Ft. Bliss that Threepersons is believed to have sustained a serious head injury, the result of a kick by one of the animals. A silver plate was installed to correct the damage to his skull. It was to cause him problems for years to come.

Tom Threepersons left the Remount Service to become a police officer for the city of El Paso. Always a hotbed of smuggling activity, the recently passed Volstead Act, which ushered in the era of "The Noble Experiment," prohibition, turned the town downright volatile. The local distilleries, breweries and bars moved south of the border and their products swiftly began heading northward in the hands of contrabandistas, the Mexican smugglers. Patrolling a beat on the south end of town, Threepersons and his partner, Juan Escontrias, found themselves right in the thick of the action. Gunfights were frequent. In the

aftermath of one, Threepersons ended up hospitalized with a bullet in his chest.

During the summer of 1922 Threepersons made the first of several job changes in his law enforcement career, hiring on as a Federal Prohibition Agent. It's likely he did so for the increase in salary, but by the end of the year he had turned in his badge. Elements within that agency were corrupt and Threepersons valued his outstanding reputation for integrity. Early in 1923 he was working in Mexico for the Cudahay Packing Company, which was experiencing serious problems with rustlers. It was a risky business, indeed. American pistoleros were not well tolerated by either the Federales or the banditos and he soon moved on.

Usually identified as a Cherokee, Tom Threepersons was likely of mixed ethnicity. This photo, probably taken in the mid-1920s, shows him posing with his short-barreled .30-30 Winchester carbine. The belt and holster look remarkably like John Wayne's trademark rig.

Badge
Colt .45 caliber revolver with holster
This revolver was used by Tom Threepersons throughout his career in Texas with a variety of law enforcement agencies (the San Antonio police force among them).

Tom Threepersons' Colt Single Action Army .45 is nickel-plated, has a 4-3/4-inch barrel and carved mother-of-pearl stocks. The rifle-type front sight was installed to improve accuracy.

Back in El Paso by the summer of 1923, Threepersons was in harness behind a badge, once again. This time it was with the U.S. Customs Service and, once again, he was battling contrabandistas bringing illegal booze across the Rio Grande. He must have been costing the smugglers a lot of money, because by 1925 they had placed a $10,000 bounty on his head. They wanted him dead and several attempts to collect that "reward" were made. The pressure involved with near nightly stakeouts and constantly having to watch his back to avoid assassination probably prompted his resignation from the Customs Service in November 1925. Before the month was out, he was wearing the badge of El Paso County's Sheriff's Department, but his tenure there was brief. He resigned in August 1926, following an argument regarding the disposal of some contraband.

For the rest of that year and into the spring of 1927, Tom Threepersons worked at a local ranch, maintaining windmills. In mid-April, he was once more a member of the El Paso Police Department, but now a detective, rather than a beat-cop. That lasted only until 1929. During his nine-year career as a lawman, he'd been shot twice and struck by an attempted assassin's automobile. The old head injury was beginning to plague him with severe headaches. It was time to quit.

Threepersons sold some of his guns and he and his wife, Lorene, moved to Silver City, New Mexico, where they spent most of the rest of their lives. He worked for several ranches and as a hunting guide. In 1933 he went to New York for surgery, to correct the problems he'd been having with his head. A partial paralysis had developed and surgery was the only solution. It seemed to do the trick. In 1962 the couple moved for the last time, settling into retirement near his old stomping grounds at Safford, Arizona. His wife passed away in 1968 and he quickly remarried. Then, on March 29, 1969, he suffered a heart attack and died a few days later, on April 2.

Contrary to some reports, Tom Threepersons was never a U.S. Marshal, nor was he ever a Texas Ranger, although he certainly knew and worked with many members of both agencies. Although his time behind the badge was relatively brief, it was served honorably and under extraordinarily tough and dangerous circumstances. His skill with firearms was widely acknowledged on both sides of the law. The tools he used in his trade were well chosen. There were two Model 1894 Winchesters, both chambered for the .30-30 cartridge. One was a standard carbine and the other, a Trapper's Model with a short barrel, for close work. A First Model .44 Hand Ejector, the so-called triple-lock, was his double-action service revolver. The best known of his guns is a Colt SAA, nickel-plated, with a 4-3/4-inch barrel and steerhead carved mother-of-pearl stocks. The latter is unique in one respect, in that the front sight is a replacement. The sight was intended to be for a rifle and sits slightly higher than a normal SAA sight and is much more narrow at the top, making deliberate, aimed shots more precise.

As fine a lawman as he was, Tom Threepersons might now be little more than a

The holster style that bears the Threepersons name exposes the gripframe, hammer and trigger of a revolver and cants the muzzle slightly to the rear. It makes retrieval in an emergency quite swift.

footnote in Texas history, if it were not for the holster design that bears his name. At the time he was serving the law, automobiles were rapidly replacing hay-burning horsepower for patrol work. In town, beat cops relied on shanks mare. Until then, most holsters were little more than leather sheaths intended to protect a handgun and prevent it from being lost. Most covered the gun almost completely, leaving just the grip-frame in the open. Often, the gun was entirely covered by a flap, as with military holsters. The object was to make certain it was there when it was needed, not to facilitate speed of the draw.

In an automobile, conventional holsters made access to one's weapon difficult. On patrol, ambush was a frequent threat. When attacked, an officer needed to be able to respond in an instant. To that end Tom Threepersons designed a holster that left the hammer exposed and easily reached by the thumb, with the leather angling down and across the partially exposed cylinder to the forward edge of the uncovered trigger guard. It was worn high on the belt and a slight butt-forward angle helped speed the draw.

Threepersons took his idea to saddle and holster maker Tio Sam Meyers, who made it a reality. Others found it desirable and, beginning in 1922, it appeared in Meyers' catalog. Years later the firm was sold and became El Paso Saddlery. It remains one of the most popular items they make.

Part Two

THE REEL GUNFIGHTERS

Rex Allen

THE LAST OF the singing cowboys, Rex Allen was one of the few "B" Western stars that really was a cowboy. Born December 31, 1922, in a sleepy eastern Arizona town called Wilcox, and raised on a nearby ranch, Allen grew up working with horses and cattle. Guns were normal tools of everyday life.

It's difficult enough making a living cattle ranching. Doing so in such arid country and growing up during the Depression made it that much harder for Allen. True to his Western roots, he first tried earning a living on the rodeo circuit. Music had been a big part of his life at home, in church and in school, so he apparently decided that using his pleasant baritone and mail-order Sears, Roebuck guitar seemed a better way to make money.

Allen's musical talent got him some regular radio time on Phoenix station KOY, which led to some recordings. By the mid-1940s, he'd made the big time, in terms of country and western music, by signing on with Chicago radio station WLS on their show *National Barn Dance*. That got him national attention and a radio show of his own on the CBS network. Republic Studios noticed. Here was a handsome young man who could ride, shoot and, best of all, sing! Rex Allen was a natural for the musical "B" Western genre. He signed a contract with Republic in 1949 and headed for Hollywood.

Had all this happened 10 years earlier, Rex Allen might have had a long career on screen, but the timing was bad. In the early 1950s, television was the new phenomenon. Millions of new viewers were staying home, instead of going to the movies, to watch their favorite shows. Kids who had flocked to the Saturday matinees could watch Hoppy, Gene, Roy and the Lone Ranger from the comfort of their living rooms, because all four of them, as well as several others, had forsaken the big screen for the small one. It was the end of an era, but in the brief period between 1950 and 1954 Allen made the most of it. Beginning with *Arizona Cowboy*, Allen starred in 35 films, all but the first of which featured his horse, Koko. Arguably the most handsome of Western movie horses, Koko was a Morgan, with a dark brown sorrel coat and contrasting white mane, tail and blaze on his face. He was billed, "The Miracle Horse of the Movies."

Rex Allen's own forays into television involved some commercials, a short-lived country and western variety show and the series *Frontier Doctor*, which ran for just one season, from September 1958 to June 1959. There were occasional non-Western films, but he turned to an entirely different area of the entertainment industry to make his living once the Westerns dried up. His resonant baritone, combined with superb diction and his southwest accent, combined to provide an appealing sound that was a natural for narrating Walt Disney's nature films. He estimated having done about 150 such features over the course of 30 years with that studio.

During his first days at Republic, Rex Allen was shown around the lot and introduced to many of the executives and performers there. One of those among the many he met was John Wayne, who welcomed him warmly. Before Allen left his office, Wayne reached into a drawer and removed a Colt Bisley .44-40 revolver. Handing it to the newcomer he said, "Here Kid, I want you to have this, it's always been lucky for me. I used it when we shot *Red River*. Maybe it'll be lucky for you."

"One of those among the many he met was John Wayne..."

Just because the gun doesn't show up in the film doesn't mean the story isn't true. It might very well have been used in some scenes, but ended up on the cutting room floor during the editing process. In any event, the gun has been re-blued and now wears a nicely figured set of oversize sambar staghorn stocks.

Almost as soon as Allen arrived in Hollywood, he began outfitting himself with the accouterments associated with a "B" Western movie star. Along with the fancy shirts, distinctive hat and colorful neckerchiefs, he had to have a saddle adorned with silver, with matching bridle, chest strap and martingale for Koko, and a pair of engraved sixshooters with distinctive stocks and a gunbelt and holsters as elaborately decorated as his horse's tack. When his career on screen was over, and the folks in his hometown established a small museum in his honor, it was all placed on exhibit there. Unfortunately, thieves broke in one night and stole it all. The saddle and tack were recovered, but the guns and rig have never been found.

Expensive as those sixguns and leather were, Allen used them for just a few of his

Rex Allen's almost boyishly handsome features, winning smile and pleasant singing voice made him a natural for the singing Western movies. Unfortunately for him, it was a fading fashion. Within just a few years such films were a thing of the past.

films. They were very heavy and restricted movement, so that jumping on and off horses, running, and engaging in choreographed fights was very difficult. He was perfectly happy to begin wearing just one revolver. That was a nickel-plated SAA with a 5-1/2 inch barrel and no front sight. It was passed on to his son, Rex Jr., who is also a singer, for use on stage.

Although it was clear to everyone directly involved that Rex Allen was hired on at Republic to replace Roy Rogers, who was leaving to do television, Allen didn't want to appear to be anyone's substitute. For that reason he did a number of things a bit differently, so folks wouldn't be as inclined to make direct comparisons. One of those was to wear his six-gun(s) butt forward on screen. He'd been doing it for about two years before finding out that "Wild Bill" Elliott had done the same long before he came along.

Although he came to the movies too late to develop the legendary popularity of some of his better known predecessors, Rex Allen was among the top five Western movie performers during his relatively few years doing oaters. Abbreviated though his on-screen career may have been, between his musical talent and the narrations he did for movie shorts and commercials, his was a very real but quiet suc-cess. He died December 17, 1999, two weeks before his 77th birthday.

A big, chocolate brown sorrel, with a white mane and tale, many consider Koko to have been the best looking of all the B movie mounts.

Allen and his horse, Koko, made a great team. The same trainer that worked with Roy Rogers' horse, Trigger, schooled Koko.

Appearing in a cameo role, Roy Rogers figuratively handed over the reins to Allen in one of the new-comer's early films.

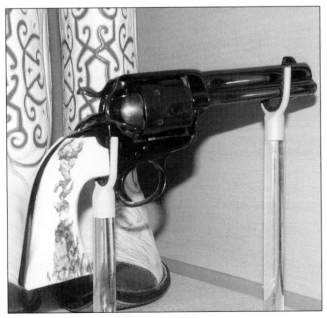

Its roots in the John Wayne film, Red River, may be questionable, nevertheless, The Duke gave this .44-40 Bisley to Rex Allen when he first reported for work at Republic Studios. Allen later had it reblued and a set of Sambar stag stocks installed.

Rex Allen looks like he's all business in this promotional still. The sixgun in his hand is one of a pair that was stolen several years later. They were never recovered.

Gene Autry

BORN SEPTEMBER 29, 1907, in Tioga, Texas, Gene Autry's father, a tenant farmer, moved the family to nearby Ravia, Oklahoma, when he was a youngster. Working with horses and cattle were a part of everyday life when he was growing up, and music was a part of family and community life. He began singing at the tender age of 5, as a member of his grandfather's church choir. At age 12 he bought a mail-order guitar from the Sears and Roebuck catalog and taught himself to play. By the time he'd reached his early 20s, he was an accomplished musician.

Hollywood legend has it that Gene Autry's show business career began when Will Rogers heard him playing his guitar and singing to while away the time between tending to his duties as a railroad telegrapher at the Frisco Line station in Chelsea, Oklahoma. The humorist expressed admiration for his talents and advised him to seek a professional career. With encouragement from such a figure, Autry made his way to New York City, to seek his fortune.

Whether or not Will Rogers actually played a part in the story (he probably did), Autry's trip east was a complete failure. Nevertheless, he persevered. Upon returning to Oklahoma he found a slot at Tulsa radio station KVOO. Although he received no pay for those perfor-

mances, he came to the attention of people in places where he would come to be paid very well. During that time, he had great success with his recordings of the songs *That Silver Haired Daddy of Mine* and *The Yellow Rose of Texas*. In 1933 he was signed by WLS, in Chicago, as a regular on the weekly nationwide broadcast of *National Barn Dance*.

Talking pictures were still new and Western movie producers had started adding musical interludes in their adventure films in order to draw a wider audience. Autry's pleasant voice, and the Oklahoma twang of his accent, made him a natural for such a venue. In 1934 a bit part in the Ken Maynard film, *In Old Santa Fe*, by Mascot Pictures, was arranged for him and his radio sidekick, Smiley Burnett. Their performances were a hit. Meanwhile, Maynard, who was one of the top players of the time, was in trouble. Studio heads were growing tired of his abusive, drunken behavior on the set and off. He'd been scheduled to do a serial entitled *The Phantom Empire*, but the studio gave it to newcomer, Autry, instead.

The 1935 film was a flop with the critics, but a box office success. His first starring role brought Autry to the attention of both Monogram Pictures and Republic Studios. Republic beat Monogram to signing him. There he made 58 films between 1935 and 1947, when he switched to Columbia Pictures.

Although his early performances as an actor were somewhat rigid, and never really became fluid, he seemed completely at ease during the musical portions of his films and eventually began to appear more confident during the dramatic parts. The action was certainly up to the standards of the 6- to 12-year-old Saturday Matinee moviegoers who were the mainstay of his audience. In the meanwhile, they and their parents listened faithfully to the broadcasts of Gene Autry's *Melody Ranch* radio show and purchased recordings of his songs by the tens of millions.

When the United States entered World War II, he was the top Western movie box office draw and his radio show, broadcast nationwide by the CBS network, was among the most-listened to in the country. Today, in the early years of the 21st century, relatively few people have experienced radio as a general entertainment medium. Modern fare is mostly limited to news in one format or another, talk shows and recorded music. During the decades of the 1930s, 1940s and 1950s, variety shows, dramas, situation comedies, soap operas and other formats were broadcast nationally. For those who have difficulty with the concept, it has often been suggested that they think of it as "television without the pictures." The stars of those shows were very well paid and Gene Autry was among them. However, with his country at war, he felt an obligation to serve, so early in 1942 he volunteered and was sworn into the U.S. Army during a broadcast of his radio show. The starting salary at his new job was just $21 per month.

Initially, the Army Special Services Unit put him to work doing camp shows to entertain the troops, recruiting and soliciting money in War Bond drives. As long as he remained in the U.S. he was able to continue doing the radio shows, because it was usually possible to do so from remote locations, but there was no time for making movies. How-

Always mindful that he had an image to uphold, Gene Autry wore fancy Western-style clothing whenever he was in public. Even his tuxedos were tailored with a Western cut. Although he rarely carried engraved revolvers in his films, highly embellished sixguns are often seen in studio stills, such as this.

ever, Autry wanted to serve in what he believed to be a more meaningful capacity, so he took flying lessons on his own time, and, when he'd earned his pilot's license, had himself transferred to the Air Transport Command. His new assignment had him ferrying troops and supplies to combat zones in such far flung places as Burma, China, India and North Africa.

During Gene Autry's absence from Hollywood, his position as top Western movie draw was taken over by Roy Rogers and never quite recovered. Still, he remained hugely popular and went right back to work making movies for Republic as soon as the war was over. A contract dispute that was eventually settled in the courts allowed him to leave Republic in 1947. He then made a deal with Columbia Pictures that was one of the most lucrative of his motion picture career. It called for him to make four movies per year and to take a 50 percent profit split. He went on to do 31 films there, for a lifetime total of 89 features, one serial and several bit player and guest roles. In 1950 his production company, Flying A Pictures, began doing *The Gene Autry Show* television series. It went on to produce five additional Western series for TV, including: *The Range Rider, Death Valley Days, Annie Oakley, The Adventures of Champion* and *Buffalo Bill Jr.*

An astute businessman and a wise investor, Autry put his show business earnings to work for him in other venues, some of which included real estate, hotels, and, eventually, the California Angels baseball team. The last of these was the fulfillment in some measure

of a childhood dream. At one time he'd wanted to play professional ball and won a slot with a team, but declined their offer because the pay was $50 a month less than he was making as a railroad telegrapher.

Autry became a very wealthy man, but he retained the simple personal values of his upbringing. He appreciated his fans and earned a fierce loyalty among his employees and friends. He was a Western man, born and bred, who understood the struggle and hardship, the heroism and occasional folly involved in the real history of the American West and he wanted the story to be told factually. To that end he established The Autry Museum of Western Heritage, located in Los Angeles' Griffith Park, which opened in 1988. Rated as one of the best museums of its kind, it houses many documents and historical artifacts and one of the world's finest collections of firearms, many of which were once the property of pioneers, gunfighters and entertainers. Included are some of his favorite guns.

In his films Autry carries a single SAA Colt, usually a nickel-plated one with either a 5-1/2- or 4-3/4-inch barrel. It's usually engraved and wears either ivory or mother-of-pearl stocks that are often carved. It's curious that his gun belt, which bears hand-tooled floral carving, is usually one made for two holsters, yet only the right one is installed. There's plenty of gunplay in those pictures, but not a great deal of it at his hands. Autry wears his rig with the casual assurance of one whose skill is such that he can afford to ignore it until it's needed. Of course, when he does reach for his six-shooter, Autry usually shoots

The sixguns on Champion's bridle are actually aluminum forgings, but in several of his films Autry's audience is made to believe they are real. Real revolvers were actually tried in some of Gene Autry's early films, but they proved too heavy and uncomfortable for the horse.

the gun from his opponent's hand or the draws so quickly that the bad guy halts his actions in mid draw.

The revolver Autry used for personal appearances during rodeos and fairs was a nickel-plated and engraved SAA converted to fire only .22 Short blanks. It appeared for sale at auction in 2001. The performer had it modified in order to make it quieter, out of concern for the hearing of the youngsters in his audience.

Those he chose for other personal appearances and photographic sessions were particularly ornate. Among them is a 4-3/4-inch SAA bearing ivory stocks with a floral motif, elaborately engraved, plated in yellow gold and inlaid with tiny flowers of red, white and blue gold. Another, with floral-carved ivory stocks,

nickeled, with a 4-3/4-inch barrel, has full coverage American scroll engraving. On the under side of the barrel, its owner's signature appears in a raised gold inlay. Bordering on the ostentatious is a matched pair of gold-plated revolvers, with full-coverage engraving that's reminiscent of the style of Cuno Helfricht. Each of its ivory stocks bears a simplistic eagle carving with ruby eye.

Gene Autry felt that his fans had certain expectations of him and he tried to live up to them. When he appeared in public it was almost always in elaborate western costume, with the same sort of flamboyant shirts and colorful boots he wore in the movies. The six-guns he used were clearly intended to complement the image he intended to project.

Richard Boone

(Paladin)

EVEN WITHOUT THE severe pockmark scars left by adolescent acne, Richard Boone would have been an unlikely candidate for roles as a leading man. To be sure, during most of his career he was a character actor, not a leading man. While not what might be called ugly, one would be hard pressed to think him handsome. Yet, there was a certain dignity about him that audiences found appealing enough that he was quite believable in such parts.

Boone's career on television is an eclectic mix. He played a doctor in his first series, called *Medic*. He appeared regularly in several anthologies. *The Richard Boone Show* was a repertory theater for television that he hosted. As the title character in *Hec Ramsey*, he played an aging gunfighter, turned deputy sheriff cum scientific investigator. Set at the turn of the 20th century, it put a unique face on the usual Western fare.

In Western movies, Richard Boone was most often cast as the heavy. Among his most memorable roles were those in *Hombre*, with Paul Newman, and *Big Jake*, with John Wayne. The bad men he played in those films simply reeked of evil. Audiences could almost smell the brimstone when he was on camera. Still, it is the courtly, mercenary gunfighter, Paladin, in *Have Gun - Will Travel*, for whom he is best remembered by Western buffs.

Richard Boone came by his name honestly; he was born with it in Los Angeles, on June 18, 1917. Moreover, the historical association with his surname is genuine, as well. He was a nephew, seven generations removed, of *the* Daniel Boone, of legendary frontier fame.

Dressed entirely in black when on the job, the hero, or perhaps anti-hero, Paladin, carried what he called in the opening of the first episode, a custom-made "Hamilton" revolver. In a remarkable example of the ignorance of Hollywood writers when it comes to firearms, the weight of pull of its trigger was stated to have been a mere 1 ounce. Any experienced shooter will know that 2 *pounds* is considered a hair trigger. With a trigger pull of an ounce, the weight of the main spring on the cocked hammer would be sufficient to fire the revolver, so that bit of fluff is plainly ridiculous. In reality, the revolver is a perfectly ordinary 1st Generation Colt Single Action Army with a 7-1/2-inch barrel. It was carried low-slung in a Hollywood-style black leather fast-draw rig, distinctive only for the silver chess knight affixed to the holster.

During the late 1950s and early 1960s, when the TV series was created and presented for its first run, Westerns on television spawned fast-draw as a major competitive sport. As compelling as most of the Paladin episodes were, there was one thing about the main character quite evident to every adherent to the sport. The lyric of the theme song with which each episode opened and closed referred to him as "a fast gun for hire." He was, in reality, remarkably slow on the draw.

Boone's character didn't rely solely on that long-barreled Colt. Just in case he lost his primary armament, which he often did, Paladin kept a double-barreled Remington derringer hidden behind the front skirting of his gunbelt. The .41 rimfire cartridge for which that little hideout gun was chambered was originally loaded by the ammunition factories with 13 grains of black powder to propel a conical bullet weighing 130 grains. Its muzzle velocity of 425 feet per second is about the same as that of a good air rifle. To be sure, at or near contact distance it would be possible to do serious harm with it; maybe even cause a fatal wound. If there was much distance for it to cover, the bullet might very well simply bounce off the individual struck with it-especially if he were wearing a heavy coat. The adversaries Paladin faced with it reacted more as though they'd been put down by a blast of buckshot.

Unauthentic as the gunplay of the series was, there were intellectual qualities to the screenplays and sufficient action to make it very popular with audiences. As for Richard Boone, there's little to suggest he was personally interested in the shooting sports. Nevertheless, he owned at least one gun, which he obtained from his father-in-law. It is a 9mm Belgian Browning Hi-Power that remains in mint condition and is regarded as one of the finest pistols of its kind. If nothing else, Boone had good taste in personal protection.

Dressed all in black as the character Paladin for the CBS television series Have Gun - Will Travel, *Richard Boone holds the revolver supposedly custom-made for the protagonist. The costuming suggests an almost* film- noir *anti-hero.*

During the period of the television series' first run, this was probably the nation's best-known business card.

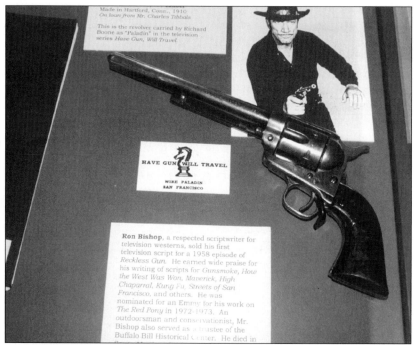

Paladin's revolver is, in reality, a perfectly ordinary 1st Generation Colt .45 caliber Single Action Army Model with a 7-1/2-inch barrel. (Courtesy Cody Firearms Museum)

In spite of long familiarity with the firearms of the Old West, Richard Boone chose a more modern firearm for use in the real world. This, his 9mm Browning High-Power pistol, was purchased around 1970 and sold by his widow several years after he passed away.

In his youth and in the years following his presidency, Theodore Roosevelt was a seeker of grand adventure; first in the American West, then in Africa and Central America. Although poor vision prevented him from becoming the marksman he wished to be, he was a connoisseur of fine firearms and could afford the best. To accompany him on his hunts in the Dakota Territory he chose this handsome example of the Model 1876 Winchester. L.D. Nimschke engraved the rifle and Winchester's craftsmen fitted it with a pistol grip stock; an unusual feature for this model. The wood of both the buttstock and forend is finely checkered and of exhibition-grade quality. *(Courtesy The Autry Museum of Western Heritage)*

One of several of Gene Autry's personal parade saddles, this one features hand-carved black leather. The saddle, tapaderos, breast collar, and bridle are profusely decorated with hand-tooled silver and gold. Master craftsman, Ed Bohlin, created this masterpiece. *(Courtesy The Autry Museum of Western Heritage)*

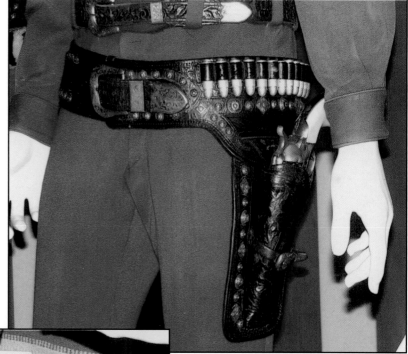

Hand-carved black leather, silver spots, buckle and billet tip make Clayton Moore's Lone Ranger rig a handsome one. His sixguns, unfortunately are all show and no go. The pair was put together from a couple of well-used relics found in a pawn shop. Their long barrels were cut, without replacing the front sights. The guns were then nickel-plated and cheap plastic stocks of simulated ivory were fitted. Since they were never seen in close-ups, audiences never saw how badly they were put together. (Courtesy The Autry Museum of Western Heritage)

The gunbelt and holsters shown here are nearly identical to Roy Rogers' first set. The sixguns, however, are not real. This rig was used when Rogers made personal appearances in places where having real guns might present legal problems. (Courtesy The Autry Museum of Western Heritage)

The Great Western Arms company presented these revolvers to John Wayne in 1955. He carried them in his final film, The Shootist. They rest here on red velvet in their fitted case. The ivory stocks have taken on a golden hue with age. (Courtesy The National Cowboy Hall of Fame and Western Heritage Center)

Colorful banners such as this announced the coming of Buffalo Bill's Wild West Show and Congress of Rough Riders of the World. The Rough Riders portion of the title referred to representatives of the great equestrian societies, such as the American cowboy, the plains Indians, Russian Cossacks, Argentine gauchos and others. (Courtesy the Buffalo Bill Museum)

Many old cartridge boxes are brightly colored and can make an attractive display for collectors. This one, a box of .38-40 shot cartridges, was meant for the use of trick shooters firing at aerial targets, usually fragile glass balls similar to those that are still used for Christmas tree ornaments. (Author's collection)

The shot cartridges in this box are topped with a fragile, thin wooden shell that from a distance makes them appear to be conventional ammunition with a copper-coated lead projectile. (Author's collection)

Even with several feature films and two television series to his credit, native Oklahoman Dale Robertson never quite achieved the level of Western stardom he sought. In his first TV series, Tales of Wells Fargo, he played an investigator for the company. His gimmick was being right handed, but wearing his gun and shooting it with the left. The second series, The Iron Horse, had him as a gambler who wins a nearly bankrupt, half-built railroad in the Old West. This lovely brace of fully engraved, nickel-plated Single Action Army Colt .45s with carved ivory stocks, belonged to Robertson. They were done with a 19th century railroad theme to commemorate that series. (Courtesy The National Cowboy Hall of Fame and Western Heritage Center)

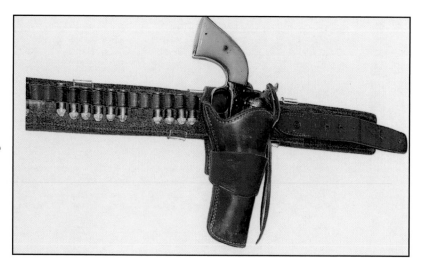

John Wayne's well-worn, ivory-stocked, old Colt .45 resides in a gunbelt and holster made by Arvo Ojala. The rig is based upon one originally created for The Duke by Bob Brown, who made gunleather for many of the Western movie players. (Courtesy The National Cowboy Hall of Fame and Western Heritage Center)

Virgil Earp is said to have owned this ivory-stocked Smith & Wesson New Model Number 3 revolver. Although not as fast to bring into play as the more popular SAA Colt, these were very accurate revolvers and, with the break-top opening and automatic extraction, could be loaded, fired, then reloaded much more quickly than the Colts. (Courtesy The National Cowboy Hall of Fame and Western Heritage Center)

This cartridge box dates to the late 19th century, when the likes of Annie Oakley and Doc Carver were performing their trick shooting acts. It contains .32-20 shot cartridges, an ammunition type used mostly by exhibition shooters. Those who wanted a round that wouldn't shoot far, but could be used to dispatch small varmints, like rats or starlings, also used this ammo. (Author's collection)

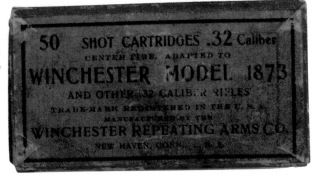

A slightly longer than standard case for these .32-20 rounds assisted in reliable feeding through a rifle's action. A cardboard wad was used to hold the shot charge in place, as was common practice with conventional shotgun shells. (Author's collection)

Ken Maynard's parade outfit included this richly embellished Mexican-style saddle, decorated in silver and gold, a black hat and a white one, to match the outfit of the day, a set of silver spurs and, of course, the finely tooled gunbelt and holsters with their matched pair of silver and gold handled Colts. *(Courtesy The Autry Museum of Western History)*

During the 20 years James Arness played the role of Matt Dillon in the television series, Gunsmoke, he carried, at one time or another, one of two Colt Single Action Army .45s. With time, both suffered considerable wear to their finish and the prop department had them reblued. Both were fitted with replacement stocks of nicely figured genuine Sambar staghorn and had 7-1/2'inch barrels. Colt made this one in 1901. *(Courtesy The Cody Firearms Museum)*

Script writers came up with a fanciful description of the Paladin sixgun, as used by Richard Boone in his long-running series, Have Gun-Will Travel. However, it's not, as they characterized it, a "...custom made Hamilton, with a 1-ounce trigger pull," but a factory standard early 1st Generation Colt Single Action Army .45. *(Courtesy The Cody Firearms Museum)*

Its finish worn to gray metal, this Colt .45 SAA revolver is just the sort that Hollywood studios and firearms rental firms began selling off in the 1960s and 1970s, because they had evolved from being merely "old guns" to desirable collectibles. Colt made this one in 1877. Dan Blocker, who played the character, Hoss, in the long-running television series Bonanza, *carried this one (Courtesy The Cody Firearms Museum)*

A notorious crusader against the private ownership of handguns, Canadian-born actor Lorne Greene had the role of family patriarch, Ben Cartwright on TV's Bonanza. *Contradicting his personal beliefs, Green's character carried this nickel-plated, walnut stocked Colt .45. The long shank of the holster for the beautifully hand-tooled rig in which he carried it is typical of the low-slung fast-draw styling of the period. (Courtesy The Cody Firearms Museum)*

During the last quarter of the 19th century Smith & Wesson's New Model Number 3 revolvers were regarded as among the most accurate handguns available. Annie Oakley and her husband, Frank Butler, concurred. This pearl-handled example, chambered for the .38-44 target cartridge, was used in their act. (Courtesy The Cody Firearms Museum)

In battle, as well as for hunting, Buffalo Bill preferred the range and power of a rifle, but for close-up personal defense he preferred a small, concealable, pistol tucked into a pocket, rather than a holstered revolver. He purchased this pair, made by Henry Deringer, the premium maker of such pistols of the era, in 1865. (Courtesy The Cody Firearms Museum)

Gene Autry's Flying A Productions filmed the Annie Oakley *television series for CBS in the early 1950s. Gail Davis played the title character. Because her tiny hands were too small to manipulate the Colt SAA revolvers, usually used in Western productions she was equipped with a pair of Colt's Police Positive revolvers, of which this is one. Nickel-plated with staghorn stocks, the revolver was fitted with a dummy ejector rod housing on the right side of the barrel in order to make it appear less modern and more like the traditional Western sixshooter. (Courtesy The Cody Firearms Museum)*

These Colt SAA .45 caliber revolvers were a gift to Roy Rogers from his friend, Medal of Honor winner Audie Murphy. (Courtesy The Roy Rogers and Dale Evans Museum)

Gary Cooper owned this vintage 1894 SAA Colt .45. This is likely the revolver he used when he won the Academy Award for Best Actor in the classic, High Noon. *While the gutta percha (hard rubber) stocks are well worn, the revolver's finish is nearly perfect. That's because it was professionally restored in the early 1950s and treated gently after that. Judging by the quality of the work and the case hardened colors of the frame; it was probably done at the Colt factory. (Courtesy The Cody Firearms Museum)*

As is usual with gold-plated revolvers that are subjected to much use, the finish on these revolvers is worn. Still, they are very rare and desirable collectibles because they have smooth bores to facilitate their use with shot cartridges. Originally owned by the Miller Brothers 101 Ranch Wild West Show, Roy Rogers used them for his own shooting demonstrations at fairs and rodeos. The yellowed stocks are simulated ivory. (Courtesy The Roy Rogers and Dale Evans Museum)

Gene Barry used this Colt SAA revolver when he played the title role in the television series, Bat Masterson. *At that time it was fitted with plastic simulated staghorn stocks, but they've been replaced with the ill-fitting Bakelite plaques seen here. The revolver was subjected to a most unprofessional polishing job and had its barrel bobbed to 4 inches, with the ejector rod housing being relocated, as well. It was then badly nickel-plated. This is another instance of a sixgun looking fine on screen, but only because it was never subjected to a close-up. (Courtesy The Cody Firearms Museum)*

It has been alleged that this LeMatt revolver was used in the Johnny Ringo *television series, which starred Don Durant. However, some modifications made to that gun are not present on this one and the star has stated that there was only one used during the production of the show. There is, therefore some doubt as to this one's provenance. (Courtesy The Cody Firearms Museum)*

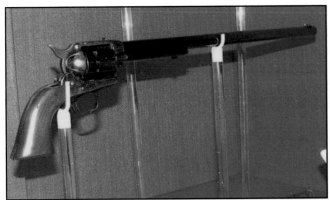

Colt began offering the Single Action Army revolver with barrel lengths longer than 7-1/2 inches in 1876. The price to the consumer was $1 for each additional inch. Thus, at $8.50 extra this one, with its 16-inch barrel, cost the average working man the equivalent of a week's wages for the extra barrel length. It would have been an expensive undertaking for Ned Buntline to give five of them to the lawmen of Dodge City, even if they had 12-inch barrels. There is no independent indication that Wyatt Earp had such a revolver. (Courtesy The Autry Museum of Western Heritage)

Roy Rogers' third sixgun rig featured gold trim around the top edge of the belt. The revolvers were fitted with carved mother-of-pearl stocks instead of the staghorn seen on his earlier guns. Nudie's Rodeo Tailors, of North Hollywood made the belt and holsters.

Pearl stocks, a dummy ejector rod housing and gun leather featuring fine floral carving and a traditional-style drop-loop holster lent a needed Western flavor to Dale Evans otherwise modern looking double-action revolver. (Courtesy The Roy Rogers and Dale Evans Museum)

Monte Hale posed for this publicity still wearing a pair of long-barreled, ivory-handled SAA Colt cartridge revolvers, but is carrying a muzzleloading Springfield musket and powderhorn instead of a more appropriate lever-action rifle. He was a singer, not a historian, so one may forgive his error. The photographer probably didn't know any better and the prop man obviously didn't care.

Roy Rogers remains slim and trim in this publicity still, as he handles two of the most famous sixguns of the Hollywood cowboy era.

Here is one of the finest examples of an engraved 19th century Colt Single Action Army revolver extant. The embellishment was factory done by the meistergraver, Cuno Helfricht. It is nickel-plated and wears a lovely set of mother-of-pearl stocks, a particularly fragile material, that is still perfect. This handsome sixgun belonged to famed lawman, Bill Tilghman. (Courtesy The Autry Museum of Western Heritage)

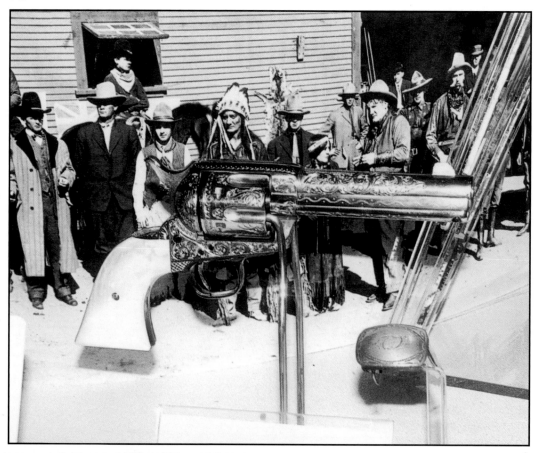

This .38 Special Colt Bisley Model revolver is one Ed Bohlin embellished for himself. Bohlin was a Swedish immigrant who came to America to be a cowboy and went on to make elaborately decorated boots, saddles, gunbelts and holsters, usually accented with silver or gold, for movie cowboys, rodeo stars and wealthy horsemen. He was also an engraver of excellent talent. The sixgun is replete with silver inlays and the stocks are silver, with gold inlays. The silver cartridge block contains 50 rounds of nickel-plated Remington-UMC ammunition. There's even a silver cleaning rod, with a gold-inlaid carved silver handle. The man did a superb job for his customers, but he knew how to treat himself well, too. (Courtesy The Autry Museum of Western Heritage)

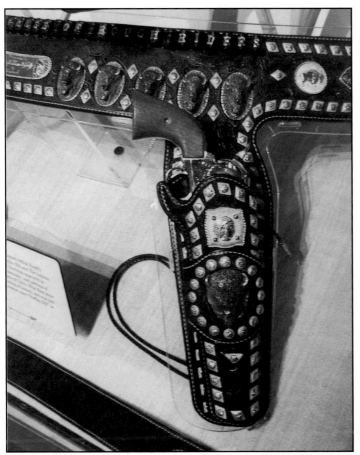

Paul Newman wore this lovely rig during his portrayal of William F. Cody in the film, Buffalo Bill and the Indians, *or* Sitting Bull's History Lesson. *Although it was not a great movie, some of the props and wardrobe were first class. The revolver, by the way, is not real. It's a dummy, simply used to keep the holster's shape. (Courtesy The Autry Museum of Western History)*

This ivory-stocked and fully engraved revolver, with its Bisley-style hammer, has been attributed to Judge Roy Bean, the cantankerous antithesis to honorable jurisprudence, who ran Langtry, Texas with an iron hand. Its provenance is weak, however, and it probably never was his. (Courtesy The Autry Museum of Western Heritage)

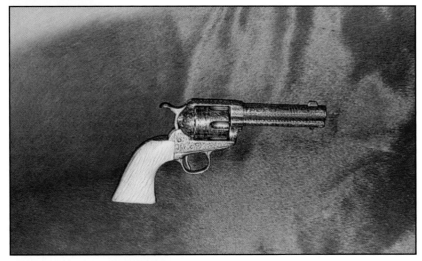

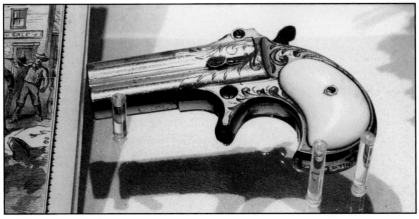

In his later years, Buffalo Bill gave up carrying his cap-and-ball pistols by Henry Deringer in favor of this modestly engraved, nickel-plated and ivory-stocked .41 Rimfire Remington Derringer. (Courtesy The Autry Museum of Western Heritage)

The "Dead Man's Hand," black aces, black 8s and a Jack of Diamonds got that name when Wild Bill Hickok was killed while holding it. Jack McCall shot Hickok in the head from behind. The revolver is one of a pair of Gustave Young-engraved Model 1851 Navy Colts that were presented to Hickok by Massachusetts Senator, Henry Wilson. (Courtesy The Autry Museum of Western Heritage)

Pat Garrett's .38 S&W caliber, ivory-stocked, Merwin & Hulbert Pocket Army revolver was a gift from some of the citizens of Uvalde, New Mexico. For a time, Garrett raised horses on a ranch near there. Properly placed, the revolver's unusual folding hammer prevents it from catching on clothing when the gun is drawn. (Courtesy The Autry Museum of Western Heritage)

Better, though not by much, than the proverbial "sharp stick in the eye," Pat Garrett's little Hopkins & Allen .32 Rimfire revolver shows significant wear, indicating that he often carried it. There is, however, no evidence that he ever used it in a fight. Still, having it and knowing it was there might have been a comfort on occasion. (Courtesy The Autry Museum of Western Heritage)

At personal appearances Buck Jones carried this revolver in his Ed Bohlin rig. The numerous superbly engraved silver inlays on the sixgun, the ivory stocks with still more silver inlays and the quality of the workmanship suggests that it, too, may have been embellished at the hands of Ed Bohlin.

Engraved in the American scroll style, Tom Mix's Remington Model 8 rifle is stocked with magnificently figured walnut. It is certainly one of the most decorated specimens of its kind. (Courtesy The Autry Museum of Western Heritage)

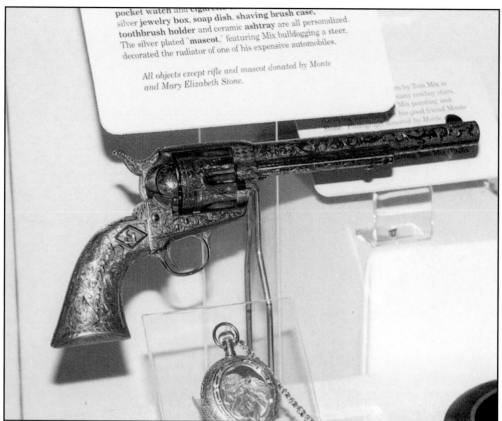

pocket watch and cigare...
silver **jewelry box**, **soap dish**, **shaving brush case**,
toothbrush holder and ceramic **ashtray** are all personalized.
The silver plated "**mascot**," featuring Mix bulldogging a steer,
decorated the radiator of one of his expensive automobiles.

*All objects except rifle and mascot donated by Monte
and Mary Elizabeth Stone.*

Tom Mix was well known for his generosity to others, but he didn't spare himself in the process, as this revolver demonstrates. Some might think it ostentatious, but those who appreciate fine firearms recognize it for the work of art that it is. Probably created at the hands of Ed Bohlin, the tight scrollwork strongly suggests European influence. (Courtesy The Autry Museum of Western Heritage)

Monte Hale arrived at Republic Studios too late to become a major "B" Western star because the age of the singing cowboy was coming to a slow end with the advent of television. Nevertheless, he went along with the program and for personal appearances wore fancy duds and leather and had a handsomely embellished sixshooter created for him. Its hammer and cylinder are gold-plated. The stocks are silver, inlaid with gold and the rest of the revolver is nickel-plated. (Courtesy The Autry Museum of Western Heritage)

Monte

Texan Monte Hale's winni...
won him a contract with Repul...
1946 through 1950, he starred...
as a singing cowboy.   At the en...
occasionally appeared on televis...
most notably forming part of the...
with James Dean and Elizabeth...

Prince of the Pl...

William Boyd

(Hopalong Cassidy)

IN MUCH THE same manner as Clayton Moore's personification of The Lone Ranger, Hopalong Cassidy became William Boyd's alter ego. After the first few films in which he portrayed that role, Boyd was usually costumed in black, from the high crowned Montana-style peak of his wide-brimmed Stetson, complete with stampede string to keep it in place, to his high-heeled boots. In some of the later films a lighter colored outfit of similar cut was worn, but the black outfit had almost become a uniform, and Hoppy wasn't really Hoppy, except in black. The only standard symbols of virtue that the character maintained was his snow-white horse, Topper, matched by his own head of thick, prematurely white hair.

The original literary character of Hopalong Cassidy, as created by Clarence E. Mulford, early in the 20th century, more closely resembled that of Festus Haggin, as played by Ken Curtis, in the later episodes of the television series, *Gunsmoke*. Hollywood has never lacked for literary license. In this instance it was a real stretch from the heavy drinking, cussing, bad tempered and generally nasty, yet somehow admirable character of the books to the thoughtful, clean-cut, highly moral pillar of the community that was portrayed on screen. Moreover, there was no indication in the movies as to the origins of the character's peculiar nickname. The books make it clear that it derives from Hoppy's severe limp; the result of an old gunshot wound. When it came down to the finale, both the literary and the cinematic versions were, however, gunslingers of the first order.

Boyd was born in Hendrysburg, Ohio, on June 5, 1898, and his family moved to Oklahoma when he was still a youngster. Both his parents died when he was in his teens, making it necessary for him to quit school in order to earn a living. Working at a succession of jobs requiring more brawn than brains, he moved slowly westward, finally making his way to Hollywood in 1919. There, he managed to find a few bit parts in the silent movies. Finding that he liked playing make-believe for money, he moved quickly to featured, then leading roles. Ten years later he was a major motion picture star commanding a six-figure annual income. Then, in 1931, a case of mistaken identity brought his Hollywood dream world crashing down around him. Another actor of the same name, whose venue was the stage, rather than films, became embroiled in a scandal involving an arrest during a wild party, featuring illegal alcoholic beverages (this was the era of prohibition), gambling and rumors of a sex orgy. A photo of the innocent Boyd accompanied a newspaper account of the event. Protestations that he'd had nothing to do with the incident were to no avail. An egg cannot be unbroken and Boyd's stardom was shattered by the scandal. During the two years that followed he found work in only four films produced by minor studios. At the same time, he sought solace in the bottle, which affected his work and further damaged his reputation.

In 1933, Harry "Pop" Sherman negotiated the film rights to the Hopalong Cassidy stories and character. He is said to have envisioned one of the most popular character actors of the period, James Gleason, in the leading role. Gleason's roles were often those of a prizefighter's manager, hard-boiled newspaper editor and tough big-city police detective. His parts were usually played with a sense of wry humor. A wiry little man, he would have been perfect in the role Mumford's books described. Sherman's plans for Boyd had the down-and-nearly-out actor playing the role of Cassidy's antagonist or that of his sidekick. Boyd had another idea. He managed to talk Sherman into giving him the leading role. Before acquiescing, Sherman elicited a promise from Boyd to give up drinking; it was a promise kept in the best traditions of the "Code of the West."

The Hopalong Cassidy series was originally to have been limited to six or seven films, but went on to 41 released by Paramount and another 25 from United Artists, for a total of 66. While a half-hearted attempt to remain true to Mumford's version of the character was made in the first film of the series, entitled simply,

In full Hopalong Cassidy costume, William Boyd poses with his engraved, ivory-handled Colt revolvers drawn. The gunbelt he wears has some unusual features. Contrasting white lacing and cartridge loops with the otherwise black leather draws the eye's attention. The holsters are mounted a bit farther forward on the belt than most and, rather than a solid piece, the shank that connects them is split. It appears this would give the rig much more flexibility than more traditional Hollywood Buscadero rigs; an important consideration if the wearer has to frequently mount horses or run.

Hop-a-Long Cassidy, succeeding episodes of the long-running saga had the hero portrayed as an intelligent, thoughtful and literate man, slow to anger and of kindly, good-humored disposition. When confronted by criminality, however, our hero becomes an indomitable force, striking terror into the hearts of evildoers. The usual "B" movie formula of the period was used in the films. It featured a trio of players in the protagonist roles, one for comic relief, another to get into trouble and the hero to set it all straight. As a bonus, the "A" studios from which the Cassidy oaters came provided a higher standard than usual for sets and locations. Thus the series had a more polished look that appealed to a broader audience.

When, in his later films, Boyd/Cassidy changed from his trademark black costume into the light, it's interesting to note that there was something of a transformation of his character's persona, as well. In that outfit the double rig is replaced with a rather plain, drop-loop single gunbelt and holster, although one of the ivory-handled nickel-plated Colts is retained. The character becomes more like a *film-noir* private detective. One could have changed the set to a city environment, trading the horse, Topper, for a sports car, the clothes to a baggy double-breasted suit and exchanging the Peacemaker for a snubnose Detective Special and the script could have been followed with little additional change. Sherman halted the series in 1944 because costs of production were becoming too great. The profit margin was no longer enough for it to remain worthwhile. By this time, however, the role had become so much a part of Boyd's life that

he felt compelled to continue. Two years later Boyd purchased the rights to the films and the Hopalong Cassidy character. A program promoting Cassidy merchandise developed and radio shows were followed by the newly popular medium of television. Boyd leased the

After Boyd stopped doing the Hopalong Cassidy films, Hayden teamed with Hoppy's earlier sidekick, Jimmy Ellison to reprise their roles together, but this time as the co-heroes.

Boyd is said not to have liked being around children before assuming the role of Hopalong Cassidy, but having experienced the starry-eyed admiration of his young fans he came to enjoy them and feel a responsibility to set a good example.

rights to his feature films to NBC, and then produced 52 original half-hour shows. His final film appearance was in the parade sequence of the Academy Award winning feature, *The Greatest Show on Earth*, which was made by his first Hollywood mentor, Cecil B. DeMille. In failing health, Boyd retired as a millionaire soon after that film. His fans remember him as he had been, rather than in illness. He died of Parkinson's disease in 1972.

The character of Hopalong Cassidy, as portrayed by Boyd, demonstrated more than mere marksmanship with the sixguns on his hip. In one film he also demonstrated a measure of knowledge of forensic ballistics by matching the bullet removed from a shooting victim to that of the revolver belonging to the chief heavy. The Hopalong Cassidy revolvers were a pair of engraved, nickel-plated .45 caliber Colt Single Action Army models, and have factory medallions inlaid into their ivory stocks. Judging by the manner of their inlays and the other features of the revolvers, they were probably made at about the time Boyd assumed the role of Cassidy. They are otherwise unremarkable, save for the 5-1/2-inch length of the barrels. The Hopalong Cassidy gunbelt, on the other hand, is distinctive. It's a beautifully crafted drop-loop rig, floral carved, with numerous small silver conchos and white-laced border trim on the outer edges and white leather cartridge loops.

"B" Westerns often used a standard formula in which the hero would have two sidekicks, an older man for comic relief and a good and loyal younger one who often got into trouble and had to be helped out. George "Gabby" Hayes as the character "Windy," and Jimmy Ellison as Johnny Nelson sided Hoppy in the 1930s.

In the 1940s, Hoppy's sidekicks were comedian Andy Clyde in the role of "California" Carlson and Russell Hayden as "Lucky" Jenkins. Later, Rand Brooks took over Hayden's role.

Russell Hayden started out with the name Pate Lucid, which might have been all right for a heavy, but wouldn't quite do for a hero.

By the time it found its way to the Autry Museum, Hayden's belt and holster were showing severe wear. His Colt .45 had also seen extensive use. (Courtesy The Autry Museum of Western Heritage)

The Hopalong Cassidy films and television shows earned a great deal of money for William Boyd but, as was the case with many "B" Western stars, the big money was in product endorsements and merchandising "official" equipment, such as cap guns, clothing, bikes, watches, bedding and a host of other products that appealed to their young fans. (Courtesy The Autry Museum of Western Heritage)

Johnny Mack Brown

BEFORE HIS NAME ever appeared on a screen credit or theater marquee Johnny Mack Brown was famous. Playing halfback for the University of Alabama, his nickname became "the Dothan Antelope." His collegiate football career brought him national attention when he caught a 65-yard pass and scored the winning touchdown against the Georgia Tech team during the 1926 Rose Bowl. A year later, in a real nail-biter, Brown intercepted a pass, then ran it back for a touchdown in the final seconds of the Rose Bowl against the Washington Huskies, snatching a 20-19 victory that got him elected to the 1927 All-American team. Decades later he would be inducted into the All-American Hall of Fame, The College Football Hall of Fame and The Rose Bowl Hall of Fame.

Brown was offered and accepted a slot as an assistant coach with the University of Alabama football team when he graduated, but while he and his team had been in California he'd taken the time to do a screen test. Shortly after starting his coaching job, a call came from Hollywood and he headed for the West Coast. With his good looks and athletic phy-

sique it wasn't long before the small parts with which he started led to bigger roles, then stardom. The films were mostly dramas and romances, not many Westerns, and they were all silent. When movies began to talk, studio heads at MGM, where he was one of the rising young stars, listened. They didn't like what they heard. A native son of the Deep South, Brown was born September 1, 1904, in Dothan, Alabama, and his slow Southern drawl simply didn't fit in with the sophisticated and urbane parts in which he'd most often been cast. MGM let his contract lapse. That, however, didn't stop him. Brown shopped himself around to the other studios and managed to keep working.

Although his voice and speech mannerisms weren't right for urban settings, it was soon obvious to studio executives that those characteristics, combined with his natural athleticism, made him perfect for Westerns. Ironically, Brown's excellent education and the courtly manners of his upbringing made him a welcome member of Hollywood's High Society-a rare circumstance among "B" Western stars. That he was regarded as one of the best polo players in the film community, a sport particularly popular with that crowd in the 1930s, certainly helped, but Johnny Mack Brown was well-liked for himself. His skill with horse and mallet might have gained him entry in some circumstances, but it was his winning personality that kept him there.

Between 1935 and 1937 Johnny Mack Brown was moving about from one studio to another, making Westerns at MGM, Universal, Republic, Paramount and Supreme. The frequent exposure brought with it a large measure of audience recognition and popularity. In a time when singing cowboys were the coming craze, Brown sang not a note. He relied upon action, with fisticuffs and sixgun to satisfy the audience. By the end of the decade, Brown had settled down at Universal Studios. There, he was frequently paired with

Bob Baker or Tex Ritter in the action sequences, and sidekicked by Fuzzy Knight.

By 1943, Monogram Studios was feeling the financial loss that resulted after its most popular cowboy hero, Buck Jones, perished in the Coconut Grove fire the year before. They needed a replacement, but grooming a new face would take too much time and money. An established star would bring in the box office receipts much more quickly and in greater amounts, at a fraction of the cost of the publicity program that would be required trying to sell a newcomer to the fans. Johnny Mack Brown proved the perfect solution to their woes. He hired on and rode for the Monogram brand for the next decade.

During his years with Monogram, Brown was most often paired with Raymond Hatton as his sidekick. The two did 47 films together. Hatton

In the mid-1930s, Johnny Mack Brown found his new niche in the film industry, as a "B" Western star. The gun leather he's wearing in this publicity still is about as fancy as his ever got. It's modestly decorated with silver spots, a plain silver buckle and fish-scale stamping. This is one of the few instances in which he wore a two-gun rig. The revolvers are stocked with faux staghorn.

was a classically trained character actor, whose flair for humor was nurtured during the silent years in the Mack Sennett comedies. Rather than the broad, nearly slapstick, humor practiced by most of the sidekicks of the genre, his was a more droll wit that appealed to a more sophisticated audience. Yet, the measure of his talent was illustrated by the fact that even the youngsters who spent their Saturday Matinee dimes to see a Johnny Mack Brown feature could get the jokes. He differed in one other respect from most sidekicks. Instead of carrying a worn, plain and very conventional Colt Single Action Army revolver, his sixgun was usually an ivory-handled Bisley with a 7-1/2-inch barrel, chambered for the .32-20 cartridge. He often wore it butt forward on his left side.

Johnny Mack Brown went into semi-retirement when his contract with Monogram ended in 1952. From then on he made occasional guest appearances on television and appeared on the big screen once in a while as late as 1966. During his 25 active years and 15 years of part time work on screen, he appeared in nearly 170 films. Heart disease killed him at 70, on November 14, 1974.

An avid outdoor sportsman, Brown fished and hunted often with his son Lachlan, and Charles Starrett was their frequent companion afield. In private life he preferred shooting shotguns, but he was a master sixgun handler on screen and off. Few in Hollywood, or anywhere else for that matter, were his equal at twirling, flipping and spinning a single-action revolver. In keeping with his rough and tumble screen persona, Johnny Mack Brown's gun leather was usually simple and workmanlike. Once in a while he'd wear something modestly decorated, but by no means elaborate. The only manner in which he bowed to the usual "B" Western hero mold was that of his horse and its silver-mounted tack. He rode a palomino named Rebel, the name of which had to be changed from its original, Reno, because a frequent leading lady in his films was Reno Blaire, also known as Reno Browne. It simply wouldn't do to allow any confusion between the names of horse and lady.

The revolvers Johnny Mack Brown used were sometimes blued, sometimes nickel-plated. On rare occasions they were engraved, but almost always stocked with

Audiences seldom saw Brown with a nickel-plated and engraved revolver, like the pearl-handled sixgun he's handling here.

plastic faux staghorn, mother-of-pearl or an ivory or ivory-like material. It seemed he was willing to use whatever the prop department had to offer at any given time. Not even barrel length seemed to matter. He usually used revolvers with 4-3/4-inch barrels, but if the prop man gave him one with a 5-1/2-inch barrel, he'd use it. One of his own guns has pearl stocks and a 7-1/2-inch barrel. The only constant seems to have been that whichever sixgun he had in his holster, he used it well.

In a publicity still from one of his last movies, Montana Desperado *(1951), Johnny Mack Brown is protecting Virginia Herrick from the bad guys. His revolver is a plain blued Colt Single Action Army revolver with imitation staghorn stocks. His gunbelt and holster are plain and unadorned.*

Gary Cooper

ALTHOUGH HE WAS born in Helena, Montana and raised in its environs, Gary Cooper was by no means a cowboy in his youth. His parents had emigrated from England and his father was a lawyer, who later served on the state Supreme Court. The family owned a small ranch, but his mother, regarded the ranch hands to be a rowdy and unsuitable influence on her sons and packed Francis (the name Gary was actually given at birth on May 7, 1901) and elder brother Arthur off to an English public (what Americans would call, "private") school for a "proper" education. With the outbreak of World War I, the boys returned to Montana. Frank, who was too young to serve, continued his schooling and helped out on the ranch, while Arthur joined the Army. Frank found work on the ranch anything but romantic. Shoveling manure at 5 a.m. in 40 degrees below freezing weather held no appeal whatever.

Later, while at Grinnel College, in Iowa, Frank found he had a talent for drawing cartoons and caricatures. He envisioned a sterling career as a political cartoonist. In 1920 he returned to the ranch to recuperate after fracturing a hip in an automobile accident. As a measure of physical therapy his doctor recommended he ride horses. With practice, he got pretty good at it.

When an elderly cousin, who was living in Los Angeles, passed away in 1924, Cooper's parents pulled up stakes and moved there to handle the estate. Following soon after, he applied for work in his chosen field with the local newspapers, but they weren't hiring green political cartoonists, so he took what work he could find. Among the jobs he held were those of a photographer's assistant and a dry goods salesman. Then, one day, he happened to bump into a couple of old friends from Montana, who told him all about their jobs as extras and stunt riders in the movies. He quoted one as telling him, "in rodeo you're paid to stay on a horse. In films it's for falling off." The $10 a day they were paid, plus a box lunch, sounded pretty good to him, so he joined them.

During the next couple of years Cooper worked a lot. He also became ambitious. He began thinking in terms of a Hollywood career beyond mere stunt work. He approached Nan Collins, a casting director and actor's agent and she agreed to represent him. She observed, however, that there were already two actors named Frank Cooper working in Hollywood. The industry could hardly support a third. A name change was in order. She was from Indiana and suggested the name of her hometown, Gary, as his new first name. Cooper agreed, but later quipped, "It's a good thing she didn't come from Poughkeepsie."

Several of Cooper's earliest films were Westerns, including one of his first starring roles, the title character in the third motion picture version of Owen Wister's *The Virginian*. Over the course of his 3-1/2 decades on screen, Gary Cooper appeared in more than two dozen Westerns, several of them great classics. Among those may be included such cinematic gems as the aforementioned *The Virginian*, as well as *The Plainsman, High Noon, Vera Cruz* and *They Came to Cordura.*

Gary Cooper took his Westerns pretty seriously. Like many of his contemporaries, he preferred using his own guns whenever it was practical to do so. One such is a Colt Single Action Army revolver with a 4-3/4-inch barrel of 1894 vintage. Chambered for the .45 Colt cartridge, it is known to have been used in several of his films, including *Vera Cruz* and believed to be the one he carried in his best known role, that of the Hadleyville town Marshal, Will Kane, in *High Noon*. Cooper's six-gun was professionally refinished, probably some time between 1950 and 1955, probably at the Colt factory.

Gary Cooper's movie career spanned more than 35 years. In that time he played a wide variety of roles in comedies, mysteries, contemporary dramas and historical screenplays, but he was never far from his roots in Westerns.

Gary Cooper's personal Colt .45 six-shooter was used in several of his films, including, it's believed, his most famous role, Marshal Will Kane, in High Noon. *(Courtesy The Cody Firearms Museum)*

In this publicity still from the 1950 Western, Dallas, *Cooper is seen as he is best remembered, as the tall, quiet Westerner, slow to anger, but dangerous when pushed to his limits.*

Gail Davis
(Annie Oakley)

FROM THE LATE 1940s through the mid-1950s, Gail Davis, perky, petite and pretty, in a tomboyish sort of way, was the secret love of most of the pre-adolescent boys in the United States. Even though girls were "yucky" to most boys that age, here was one that could ride and shoot with the best of the cowboy heroes. Interestingly enough, she really could, too. She could sit a horse as well as any of them and regularly appeared with her boss, Gene Autry, doing a sharpshooting act in rodeos. With her blue eyes, winning smile and honey-blonde hair, usually done up in pigtails, she was the very picture of the all-American girl. Truth to tell, a lot of the older brothers, fathers and uncles of those little kids found much about her to admire as well. Little wonder, during high school and college she won a total of eight beauty contests.

Born Betty Jeanne Grayson on October 5, 1925, Davis grew up in Little Rock, Arkansas. Her father, a physician, started in private practice, but became a state health officer. A graduate of Little Rock High, she studied drama at Harcum Junior College in Bryn Mawr, Pennsylvania, and went on to the University of Texas at Austin. Like many budding

young performers starting out during World War II, she entertained the troops at camp shows when her studies permitted. She met Gene Autry, who was serving in the Army Air Corps, during one of them.

After graduation, Davis moved to Hollywood to start a professional career. An agent found her working at the Plaza Hotel and got her a tryout at MGM where, in 1946, she appeared on film for the first time with Van Johnson and Janet Leigh in a lighthearted film entitled *Romance of Rosy Ridge*. Soon after, RKO bought her contract, but when Howard Hughes purchased the studio a short time later, hers, along with many others, was abruptly canceled. Undaunted, she began looking for roles as a freelance actress. She had no trouble finding them.

Republic Studios put Davis to work regularly. There, she was cast in films starring Roy Rogers, Monte Hale and Rocky Lane. Because she was freelancing, she was also able to work at Monogram, where Johnny Mack Brown and Jimmy Wakely used her talents. Over at Columbia Studios she was featured with Charles Starrett and, in 1949, did *Cow Town*, the first of her 14 feature films with Gene

Autry. Between 1948 and 1953 she did 25 "B" Westerns. When Autry began doing his television series in 1950, Gail Davis came along and appeared in 15 episodes. At the same time she was popping up in episodes of *The Cisco Kid* and *The Lone Ranger*. When his Flying A Productions began branching out to other series, like *The Range Rider* and *Death Valley Days*, Autry found a place for her in them, as well.

In 1953 Autry decided the time was right for a Western heroine for little girls to look up to. His initial plan was to use an unknown in the role, but when she heard that he was looking for someone to star in *The Annie Oakley Show*, Davis dressed the part as she thought it should be costumed and walked into his office determined that the role would be hers. It didn't take much convincing. For the next five years, in the minds of her fans, Annie Oakley

lived in Diablo, Arizona, rode a horse named Target, was sweet on the town deputy, Lofty Craig (who towered over her), and was constantly getting her little brother, Tagg, out of hot water.

After her series folded, Gail Davis continued working with Gene Autry for a while on the personal appearance circuit and did occasional guest spots on television shows. One of her most entertaining outings had her back in the sharpshooting business, challenging Mayberry's sheriff, Andy Taylor, in a skeet match.

Gail Davis began to fade from public view in the early 1960s. With her 40s fast approaching it was time to quit playing the girl-next-door sort of roles she always had. She continued to do occasional fan conventions for most of the rest of her life, but her regular job from then on was that of a per-

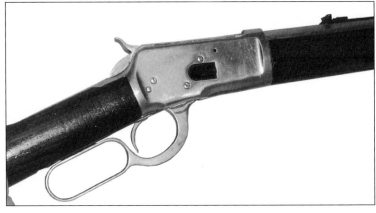

Take the pigtails out and brush her hair, then put a fancy ball gown on her, but leave her impeccable makeup in place and one can easily imagine Gail Davis as the beauty queen she was during her school years.

Gail Davis used this .32-20 Model 1892 Winchester for the rifle scenes in her Annie Oakley *series. It was blued when it came from the factory, but nickel-plated at some later time. Since then the plating has flaked off, leaving a bare, polished surface. (Courtesy The Autry Museum of Western Heritage)*

former's agent. Davis was 71 years of age when she passed away on March 15, 1997.

While it's doubtful she could have competed with the real Annie Oakley, Gail Davis was an excellent markswoman. Of course the guns she used as Annie Oakley in her TV series used blanks exclusively. With the aid of the special effects crew, she could hit anything the script called for. The rifle she used was a Model 1892 Winchester, chambered for the .32-20 cartridge. At one time it had been nickel-plated, but it now has bright and shiny bare metal. The usual movie sixgun, a Single Action Army Colt, is large enough to have looked overwhelming in her tiny hands, so the prop department equipped her with a pair of nickel-plated Colt Police Positive revolvers. They were given a more traditionally western look by the addition of nicely figured staghorn stocks and by attaching to each a dummy ejector rod housing on the right side of the barrel. When Annie Oakley, in the person of Gail Davis, used them, there was no question of her competence.

Nicely figured sambar stag stocks and a dummy ejector rod housing that's been contoured to the frame and screwed to the right side of the barrel make Gail Davis' Colt Police Positive revolvers look more "western." The Single Action Army Colts they are intended to resemble were much too large to appear comfortable in her tiny hands. (Courtesy The Cody Firearms Museum)

The Annie Oakley series characters included her love interest, Lofty Craig, and little brother, Tagg. Brad Johnson and Jimmy Hawkins played them, respectively.

Originally, Gene Autry intended Gail Davis, as Annie Oakley, to be a Western heroine for little girls to look up to. Usually their brothers and some older male relatives found her appealing as well.

Gordon "Wild Bill" Elliott (Red Ryder)

BORN OCTOBER 16, 1903, and raised on a ranch in the vicinity of the northwestern Missouri town of Pattonsburg, Gordon Nance, who would one day become Western movie star "Wild Bill" Elliott, was a natural for cowboy roles. He grew up riding horses and working cattle and, by his mid-teens, was an accomplished rodeo contestant. The acting bug seems to have bitten early. As was the case with many of his generation, William S. Hart was his boyhood hero and young Gordon wanted to be like him. However, he had the intelligence and maturity to prepare himself for a career in films rather than simply run off to Hollywood as a starry-eyed hopeful. First, he attended Rockhurst College (now a university) in Kansas City. Then, he trained at the Pasadena Playhouse, one of the best theatrical houses in the nation. It was at about this time that he changed his surname to Elliott.

There were a few Westerns among his early films, but those roles were minor and he was cast as a heavy. Beginning with the 1925 silent film, *The Plastic Age*, which starred Clara Bow and Gilbert Roland, the majority of his films were dramas with a modern setting. While taking whatever movie roles became available, he continued working in live theater, perfecting his craft, until at least 1932. By then he was becoming well known to the casting directors and was getting work in all manner of films, including comedies, dramas, musicals, historical epochs and mysteries. He even did a Tarzan film, *Tarzan's Revenge*, which starred Glenn Morris in the lead. Still, he'd made about 60 pictures before landing a featured role in a Western, the 1936 film, *Trailin' West*. Several more followed in quick succession and in 1938 Columbia signed him to star in the 15-chapter serial, *The Great Adventures of Wild Bill Hickok*. That's how he came to pick up the handle "Wild Bill." After doing that role, the name just stuck; so much so that after a few more films he was billed from then on either as Bill Elliott or Wild Bill Elliott. By the end of the 1940s, all vestiges of the name he was given at birth were gone, when he changed his name legally to William Elliott. That's also when, for the first time, he wore his sixguns butt-forward for a reverse draw. Whether he was emulating Hickok or Gary Cooper, who'd played the role in *The Plainsman* in 1936, is unknown.

The Hickok role was the turning point for Elliott's career. It was followed almost immediately with *In Early Arizona* and a succession of other feature oaters and another serial, *Overland With Kit Carson*. Elliott had found his niche. As a "B" Western star the money was good, he got top billing in his films and, for an actor of his caliber and a horseman of his skill, the work was relatively easy. As one of the few leading players in that genre with a strong acting background, he raised the bar of expectation in his young audiences and made it possible for their parents to better appreciate the greater level of maturity in the performance, as well.

In 1943 Elliott moved from Columbia to Republic Studios. There the budgets for his films were greater and the talent cast in his films was of a much-improved quality. In his first films with "The Little Studio in The Valley," he was billed as Wild Bill Elliott. George "Gabby" Hayes, himself a classically trained actor, who played sidekick to most of the "B" Western stars of the period, provided the comic relief for the stories. The lovely and elegant Anne Jeffreys, whose early background was in opera, was selected as his leading lady, playing a variety of roles, each with equal aplomb. It was at this stage of his career that Elliott permanently turned his revolvers butt forward for a reverse draw. Wearing them in that manner became his trademark. That's also when he began using his classic apology to the bad guys in his films. After winging them with a surgically placed shot from the hip or clobbering one with a vicious one-two pair of punches, he'd deliver a variation of the line, "I'm sorry I had to do that. As a rule, I'm a peace-loving man."

Long and lean, with a strong jaw line, Wild Bill Elliott's physical resemblance to the cartoon character, Red Ryder, the role he played in 16 films and for which he is probably best remembered, is interesting. A reluctant hero, the character is an ordinary cowboy working on a ranch owned by his aunt, known simply as "The Duchess." When trouble befalls, Red Ryder must rise to the occasion. In the series he was paired with a young Indian boy, Little Beaver, who was played by Bobby Blake, now better known as Robert Blake of the TV series, *Baretta*.

Wild Bill Elliott came by his nickname by playing Wild Bill Hickok in a 1938 Columbia Pictures serial. The name fit and it stuck. Eventually he changed his first name, legally, from Gordon to William. Elliott is shown here with one of his best screen partners, his horse, Thunder.

Except for the actual color of his hair, Wild Bill Elliott closely resembled the cartoon character, Red Ryder, which was the subject of his longest-running film series, 16 pictures made between 1944 and 1946.

Elliott succeeded Don "Red" Barry as Red Ryder and passed the role on to Allan "Rocky" Lane, when he began doing "A" films in 1946. He remained under contract to Republic until 1951, when he was signed by Monogram (later Allied Artists). There he did a few more Westerns, but in 1954 began doing mysteries. He retired in 1957 to raise horses on his Nevada ranch. He died there on November 6, 1965.

Shown here with his horse, Cyclone, Donald Barry was the first of Republic's Western stars to take on the role of Red Ryder. In much the same manner as Elliott became known as "Wild Bill" for the Hickok role he played, Barry was ever-after nicknamed "Red."

Elliott's pair of Single Action Army .45s wore 5-1/2-inch barrels and wore a better grade of plastic stag stocks than usual, but are otherwise remarkable only for the manner in which they were worn; with their butts forward. This necessitated a reverse draw. This is the revolver the actor carried on his left side. The rig was crafted by master leathersmith Bob Brown, who created many of the "B" Western gunbelts and holsters. (Courtesy The Autry Museum of Western Heritage)

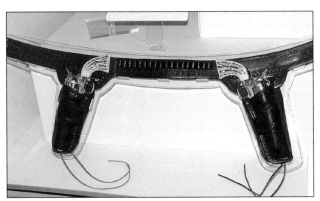

"Red" Barry carried these 4-3/4-inch barreled SAA Colts when he portrayed the Red Ryder character. As with so many cinema sixguns, these were badly polished, then nickel-plated and fitted with plastic stag stocks. Since they were never shown in close-ups, it didn't matter as long as they fired their blank cartridges on cue.

Billed as "America's Fightin'est Cowboy", Allen "Rocky" Lane followed Wild Bill Elliott in the role of Red Ryder. Although he could handle the shoot-'em-up scenes with the best of them, his films featured some of the best fight scenes Republic Studios, famous for the choreography of such episodes, ever did. Later in his career, Lane became the voice of the talking horse in the TV series, Mr. Ed.

James Garner
(Maverick)

WITH WRY GOOD humor, James Garner has for nearly five decades made a career of playing the reluctant hero and off-beat philosopher, Bret Maverick. Even with other successful television series and some very popular movies to his credit, Garner has never completely shed himself of this, his most popular role. Filmed by Warner Bros. for the ABC television network, the series first aired in 1957. Quoting his "Dear old Pappy," Maverick's reluctance to involve himself in any form of violent confrontation, particularly any that involved gunplay, was exemplified by the philosophical observation that: "He who fights and runs away, can run away another day." Yet, in spite of all his best efforts, as often as not, the Maverick character is, inevitably, forced to resort to the sixgun on his hip.

Maverick, an itinerant gambler, knows full well the value of being armed to the teeth! In an episode of the short-lived return of the series in the 1980s, there is a scene in which a poker tournament is about to take place. The town lawman goes to great pains to see to it that none of the participants is packing heat. Maverick is asked to hand over the revolver on his hip. Then, the one in his hat, up his sleeves, in pockets, etc., until about 15 guns

have been deposited on the seemingly endless pile of hardware of which he's been divested. Finally, the lawman is satisfied, but Maverick breathes a sigh of relief when it's revealed to the audience that he still has one more stashed on his person. While he may have no desire to engage in violence, he appreciates the dangers of not being prepared should the need arise.

There is little difference in the characters played by Garner in such movies as *Support Your Local Sheriff, Support Your Local Gunfighter* and *Skin Game.* Nor in the television detective drama, *The Rockford Files.* For all the tongue-in-cheek humor of the aforementioned productions, Garner demonstrates the breadth of his talent as a performer and a very real understanding of the mechanics of gun handling in his portrayal of the controversial Wyatt Earp in *Hour of the Gun.*

During its initial run, and later, in syndication, Maverick was one of the most popular Western series on television in a period when there was a glut of similar shows to be seen on every channel, at virtually any hour of the evening. The self-effacing charm with which the role was played and the more realistic attitude that shooting people and the risk of being shot are things to be avoided, seems to have been appreciated by the hierarchy at Colt. Without being didactic about the subject, what was being demonstrated was responsible gun ownership and use. That was viewed as a good thing.

To be sure, the proliferation of productions in the Western genre had a very positive influence upon sales of Colt's Single Action Army revolvers, too. A little positive publicity gained by honoring the popular star of a successful series could only help boost the bottom line a little more. Thus, Colt's president, Fred A Roff Jr., was pleased to present James Garner with an SAA revolver. Made with a 4-3/4-inch barrel, blued, with case hardened colors, the .45 caliber sixgun was fitted with a nicely figured set of two-piece walnut stocks. On the left side, a five-pointed silver star is inlaid

with the stock screw at its center. On the right side is inlaid an engraved oval plate that is blind to the stock screw. The center of the oval inlay is blank, with room enough for further inscription, if desired, but nothing more was ever added to it.

After the presentation, Garner carried the revolver during filming of succeeding episodes of the series and it seems to have seen extensive use. It remains in about 90 percent condition, but exhibits some blue wear near the muzzle of the barrel, around the sharp edges of the face of the cylinder and its flutes and a ring around the locking notches that indicate some possible timing problems in need of correction. The case hardened colors are beginning to fade. Still, it remains a handsome piece and was a fitting tribute to one of the most enduring of television characters.

Insofar as possible, Maverick, as portrayed by James Garner, relied upon his wit, charm and poker skills to deal with his adversaries. Just in case that didn't work, he carried a sixgun to back his play.

If he failed at solving problems amicably, or at least nonviolently, Garner's character, Maverick, could resort to gunplay. Although he made every effort to give the impression that his abilities were minimal, audiences were confident that he could handle a six-shooter with the best of them.

Although there is some evidence that its lockwork requires some attention, the Colt Single Action Army revolver that the factory presented to James Garner retains about 90 percent of its original finish. The left side stock panel is inlaid with a five-pointed silver star.

A large oval, suitable for engraving a name or motto, was inlaid into the right stock panel of the James Garner Colt. Nothing was ever done about it and it remains blank.

The backstrap of Garner's SAA Colt was factory-inscribed with his name, that of the character he was playing at the time and that of Colt's president, Fred A. Roff.

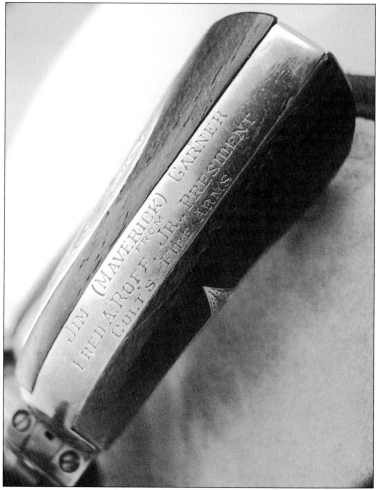

Monte Hale

MONTE HALE HAD no intention of becoming an actor. It happened practically by accident. What he really wanted to do was sing and play music and that ended up barely happening at all. It all began during World War II when he was appearing with a traveling USO camp show, entertaining troops. Several well known actors and musicians were involved in a War Bonds sales drive and talked him into joining the group to accompany veteran minstrel and sidekick, Lee White, for the few weeks left of the tour. He proved to be a good musician, had a nice singing voice and the group seemed to like him very much, because they wrote a letter to Herbert Yates, the president of Republic Studios, telling him about the talented young man with whom they'd just been working. Yates, always on the lookout for fresh new faces, offered to give Hale a try. A friend gave him enough money to make the trip and hold him over for a spell. The year was 1944 and, all of a sudden, he was under contract to do movies. After playing a few small parts to get his feet wet, Hale was headlining in his own series of "B" Westerns.

A genuine westerner, Monte Hale was born in Ada, Oklahoma, and raised on a ranch near San Angelo, Texas. His actual date of birth was probably June 8, 1919, but the studio shaved a few years off that in their "official" bio, placing the year as 1921. No stranger to horses and cattle, that aspect of the job was easy. What he found relatively difficult was that for a "singing cowboy" he did very few songs and the number dropped with each new film.

Hale got top billing in 19 films and had the distinction of being the first of Republic's "B" Western stars to have his film shot in color. That was the 1946 production of *Home on the Range*. His last starring role was in *The Missourians*, in 1950. From that time on he was cast in character parts and occasionally as a heavy, but some of those roles were in decidedly "A" pictures, such as the part of Bale Clinch, in the Texas-size film *Giant*.

Monte Hale was more musician than actor, but ended up acting more than playing his guitar and singing. Although his career in "B" Westerns was short-lived, running only from 1946 to 1950, the 19 films in which he starred were very nicely done considering their low budgets.

Monte Hale never seemed comfortable in front of a camera, but on a stage, in front of a live audience, he was in his element. For such occasions he carried a handsomely engraved Colt .45 SAA. The frame, the 5-1/2-inch barrel and the grip assembly are nickel plated, while the hammer, cylinder and ejector rod housing are plated with gold. The stocks are engraved silver, with his name, three flowers and a Texas star, all of gold, inlaid on each panel. It's a truly distinctive sixgun.

Preferring live audiences with which he could interact, Hale carried this beautifully executed nickel- and gold-plated and lavishly engraved Colt .45 Single Action Army revolver during personal appearances. (Courtesy The Autry Museum of Western Heritage)

William Surrey Hart

SOME HAVE SUGGESTED that William S. Hart's somewhat exotic biography is the stuff of fanciful Hollywood press agentry. That he was born in Newburg, New York is not in dispute, nor is his birthday, December 6, although the year has been called into question. A variety of sources have placed it as 1864, 1865, 1866 or 1870. Sometimes it was given as late as 1890. Most evidence indicates the earliest of those is most likely correct. The reason for the confusion probably has to do with the ever-present age consciousness and discrimination with which Tinseltown has been plagued since actors became film stars and their images very nearly a matter of public property.

The portion of Hart's life history that might seem most suspect among modern film historians is his having been raised among the Lakota Sioux, in South Dakota. It appears to smell too much of Hollywood romanticism to be possible. Remarkably, personal interviews with Hart and, much later, with his son, William S. Hart Jr., who grew up to be a highly respected college professor, indicate that it is nothing less than the unvarnished truth. It also accounts for much of the stoicism that appears to have so instilled his personal character.

It appears that at the tender age of 6 months, Hart's father, who was a miller, moved his family to the plains states in search of work. Staying for a time in several different areas, including Kansas and Wisconsin, the family finally settled in the Dakota Territory, in the area that is now the state of South Dakota, where the lad grew into his teens.

By that time, the nation was not much past its centennial year. Indian wars still flared up, people still relied chiefly on horses for transportation and most of the famous and infamous lawmen and outlaws of the period remained very much alive. A six-shooter continued to be a customary part of the everyday wardrobe of a large segment of local society. Indeed, the West was still a wild place and would remain so for some time to come.

When Hart was in his late teens, his father became afflicted with an eye ailment that was blinding him. The family returned to New York so that he could seek more expert medical treatment than was possible in the hinterlands. It was at about that time that the young Hart determined that he wanted to be an actor. According to his own account, from a newspaper interview done in 1919, his father advised him that if he were to pursue such a career, he should do it right and train on the

London stage. At age 19, he worked his way to Liverpool by ship and walked from there to London. His efforts to get into the theater there were unsuccessful, but he did manage to find enough work to make a living.

When he returned to the United States, Hart began auditioning for roles on Broadway. In the early stages of that effort he was invariably asked where he'd worked before, to which he replied, "London." Directors assumed that he meant the theater, not waiting tables. Hart didn't bother to disabuse them of that assumption. With time, he became quite skilled at his craft, even landing roles in some popular plays of the time that were set in the West. However, his specialty was classical theater and his reputation as a Shakespearian player was outstanding. By the time the 20th century had progressed into

its second decade, William S. Hart was in his 40s and well established in the legitimate theater, making a good living. Then, one day, he stepped into a nickelodeon and his life was changed forever.

The film he saw on the flickering screen was a Western. It upset him. The sets, the costumes, the props, the mannerisms-all were wrong. After all those years in New York, his heart still belonged to the West. He knew he could portray the world that he knew and loved so well with authenticity, but he did nothing about it. Not at first.

What Hart had seen gnawed at him. He knew the West, its land and its people. He was also a highly respected actor, at the height of his craft. Eventually he could stand it no longer and went looking for a movie company. Hollywood was in its infancy. The center of the

This is one of the rare posed publicity stills showing William S. Hart with guns drawn in which both are Colt Single Action Army revolvers.

motion picture industry was still in New York and he had a connection at one of the leading studios in the person of an old friend, Thomas Ince. Early in their careers the two had worked together on the stage. Ince had become a producer and listened with enthusiasm to Hart's proposal that he write and perform in Westerns that would portray the region and its people in a manner true to the spirit of that unique land and culture. In short order, Hart was on his way to California and celluloid immortality.

In 1914 William S. Hart was 49 years old. Even so, he was a lean 6 feet, 2 inches tall and in excellent physical condition. An expert horseman, he and a pinto he called Fritz would become a team. *The Bargain* was the first of 65 movies Hart would do in the next 11 years. In 1925 he was 60 years of age and Westerns were being taken over by showmen like Tom Mix. Stories of the hard reality of the West as Hart portrayed it were being replaced with antics and romantics. It was time for him to retire to

his home, Horseshoe Ranch, in Newhall, California. Upon his death in 1946, the ranch was willed to the people of Los Angeles County and is now a museum and park.

Contemporaries who knew him averred that William S. Hart was as adept with a six-shooter in real life as the characters he played in films. He was the first of the movie cowboys to carry a brace of revolvers on his hips. The sharp-eyed observer will note, however, that while they were both Colts, they were often a mixed pair, with a New Service .45 in his right holster and a Single Action Army in the left. With his large hands, he might have found the double-action revolver much faster to use for repeat shots. Hart was a stickler for authenticity. When the time period in which a photoplay was set predated the SAA, he carried a Colt 1862 Pocket Navy revolver that had been converted to use metallic cartridges. That may have been a concession to convenience, since reloading a percussion revolver is a slow process.

Seen hatless in this publicity still, it is easier to realize that Hart was no longer a young man when he began making Western movies. The creases in his face and puffy eyes are those of a man already past 50.

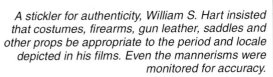

A stickler for authenticity, William S. Hart insisted that costumes, firearms, gun leather, saddles and other props be appropriate to the period and locale depicted in his films. Even the mannerisms were monitored for accuracy.

Although Hart was a skilled shooter, he was not a knowledgeable collector. As mentioned earlier, the revolver he owned that was alleged to have belonged to Billy the Kid was made late in the year The Kid died. His own son suspected it was bogus, too.

His best known revolvers were not actually his, though he bought and paid for them. Hart, as a gift for his son's second birthday, commissioned a pair of SAA .45s, with 7-1/2-inch barrels. Profusely inlaid with silver bands and spirals and with a valentine heart motif, the inlays, not the bare gunmetal, are profusely engraved. The stocks are two-piece ivory, with silver mounts at the top and bottom and the lad's initials, also in silver, appear just below the grip screws on all four plaques. William S. Hart Jr. kept them unfired throughout most of his life, selling them to a private collector only when he was, himself, growing elderly.

"Two-Gun Bill" Hart revolutionized the Western movie, introducing the concept of the "Adult Western." That form of the genre nearly disappeared for a time, but the modern incarnation of it owes its foundation to Hart.

Faded though this photo may be, it's one of the few in which one can determine that the revolver in Hart's right hand is a Colt's New Service, while the one in his left is a Single Action Army Model. The reasons that he chose two distinctly different revolvers, though they were alike in chambering, have never been explained. It likely has to do with the relative ease and speed with which multiple shots can be fired as well as the reloading characteristics of the double-action New Service.

Tim Holt

CHARLES JOHN HOLT III was born into the motion picture industry. His father, Jack Holt, was one of the top Western stars of the silent era. Although the elder Holt's stardom didn't transition into talkies, he evolved into a well-respected character actor and continued working until very near the end of his days. Tim Holt was leading-man handsome in a late adolescent sort of way and retained his youthful appearance throughout his career in movies. Jack Holt's beautiful daughter, Tim's younger sister, Elizabeth Marshall Holt, was one of the most prolific leading ladies in "B" Westerns. In her first outing on screen in a Hopalong Cassidy oater, she was billed as Jacqueline Holt, but the name became Jennifer in subsequent credits.

Born on February 5, 1918, Tim Holt started his own film career early. At age 10 he was cast for a part in *The Red River Valley*. During his early years he lived on the family ranch in southern California. In his teens he attended Culver Military Academy in Indiana where, ironically, his roommate was Hal Roach Jr., who would become one of Hollywood's most important and influential producers.

After graduation in 1936, Holt set out to establish his own Hollywood career, starting with a key role in the film version of the popular radio soap opera, *Stella Dallas,* which starred Barbara Stanwyck. Seen by studio executives as a natural for the Western genre, RKO put him to work with Harry Carey Sr., in *The Law West of Tombstone*. The role of the Cavalry Lieutenant in *Stagecoach* came the following year. From then on he was assured of regular work.

The "B" Westerns began for Tim Holt in 1940. By the time he joined the Army Air Corps and went to war in 1943, he'd done 18 of them. When the hostilities were over, he returned to work. The Westerns continued, but "A" pictures were offered, as well as the "Bs" that provided the bread-and-butter income. Outstanding examples among the former were his roles in *My Darling Clementine* and *Treasure of the Sierra Madre*.

With the coming of television, the days of the "B" Western were numbered. Holt quit doing them in 1952, but appeared in several other sorts of films before finally retiring from the industry in 1959. Tim Holt succumbed to the ravages of a malignant brain tumor on February 15, 1973.

The Holt sixguns are good examples of the differences seen in the silent Westerns and the "B" films of the 1930s through the 1950s. Jack Holt's .45 caliber Bisley is a plain working gun, well-worn and stocked in the original style gutta percha with which most such revolvers were equipped at the factory. Tim's revolvers wear Franzite plastic staghorn stocks and have been nickel-plated to look flashier on screen. The dished out screw holes indicate a poor job of refinishing.

Tim Holt's rather youthful appearance remained with him well into maturity. Unlike some "B" Western leads, his talent as a serious actor was acknowledged by the studios, which led to significant roles in many "A" pictures.

Acting was a family business with the Holts. Tim's father was a silent-era Western star and a respected character actor in talkies. His beautiful younger sister, Elizabeth, was billed as Jennifer Holt and was the most prolific leading lady of the genre.

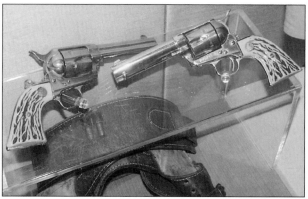

The movie sixguns used by Holt were probably provided by the studio armory. They were badly refinished in nickel plate and stocked with fake staghorn stocks made by Franzite. They look flashy on screen, but without their association with the actor who used them, would engender little collector interest. (Courtesy The Autry Museum of Western Heritage)

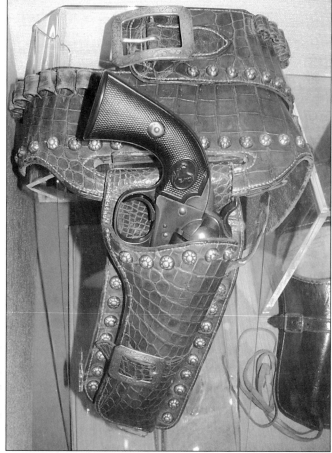

Silent screen Western star Jack Holt used one of the few Colt Bisley variations of the SAA to be seen prominently in the movies. The short-barreled revolver's worn finish and plain, black, gutta percha stocks appear to be original. Of significant interest is that the belt and holster of this drop-loop buscadero rig appear to have been made of alligator leather; a very unusual choice for a Western rig. (Courtesy the Autry Museum of Western Heritage)

Buck Jones

AS IN THE case with many other Western movie stars of his era, the studio biography of Buck Jones is a mixture of fact and purest fiction with a heavy dose of hyperbole added for flavor. As usual, the real story of his early life is relatively mundane. About his death, however, there is an element of true heroism in the finest tradition of Hollywood melodrama.

Jones was born Charles Frederick Gebhart, in Vincennes, Indiana. There is some question about the date because there is no record of a birth certificate. Some sources claim December 4, 1889, but the most widely accepted date has been established as December 12, 1891. The claim that he grew up in Oklahoma seems to have no basis in fact. Rather, he lived in Vincennes and then in Indianapolis until joining the Army at age 16 with his mother's complicity. The lies told to get into the Army may be the source of confusion as to his real birthday.

Young Charles, who was nicknamed "Buck" in childhood, entered the service in January of 1907 and was discharged in December 1909. Part of his hitch was spent in the Philippines, but claims that he served during the Moro Insurrection don't take into consideration that it had been over for eight years by the time he arrived in the Philippines. He served honor-

ably in a cavalry outfit, but without distinction, was released as a private and returned to Indianapolis. For a short time he worked as a test driver at the raceway. The closest he came to actually racing automobiles was much later, in a couple of films.

In less than a year he was back in uniform, stationed with the 6th Cavalry at Fort Des Moines, Iowa. He earned a set of sergeant's stripes, but decided he wanted to get into the budding new field of military aviation. He had to give up his stripes to do it, but got a transfer to an Aviation Signal Corps outfit stationed in Texas City, Texas. His dreams of becoming a pilot came to naught, so at the end of his second enlistment, in October 1913, he put the Army behind him, still just a private. This effectively puts an end to the studio's claim that Buck Jones rode with Pershing against Pancho Villa. That action didn't occur until nearly three years after he'd been discharged.

Immediately following his release from service, Buck got wind that the Miller Brothers 101 Ranch Wild West Show might be hiring. He had no experience as a cowboy, but during his years in the Cavalry he'd learned to ride well and to care for horses. Colonel Joe Miller hired him to do just that. He began his employment with the show by currying horses. It didn't take long before he was performing on horseback in the arena.

While the troupe was playing an engagement in New York, a lovely young lady, Odille "Dell" Osborne, joined the show. Buck was smitten, so when she accepted an offer to sign with a different show in 1915, he followed. They were married soon after and the wedding ceremony was conducted as part of one of the show's performances, with all participants, including the presiding minister on horseback.

The couple produced their own show for a time, then joined Ringling Brothers Circus. When the circus landed in Los Angeles, Dell was pregnant and she and Buck decided the gypsy life of traveling shows should come to an end. The new baby should have a permanent home. He signed on with Universal, doing bit parts and stunts at $5 a day, which was a fair, though by no means extravagant, wage at the time.

Working up slowly and gaining experience as he went, Buck began making better money. Starting with Fox at $40 per week, his rate rose to $150. With his increasing public recognition and the general ill will toward Germany during the World War I period, Buck's obviously teutonic surname was changed to

the all-American name, "Jones." When, in 1919, William Fox, who was running the studio, decided he was in the market for a new Western lead, Buck got the nod. His first starring vehicle, *The Last Straw*, was released in 1920. A hit with the audiences, Buck Jones was suddenly earning a star salary, making $3,500 a week. More than 80 years later that is still a respectable amount. Then, it was practically a king's ransom.

Perhaps it was greed that led him to do it, but in 1928 Buck left Fox to start his own production company. As an independent film maker Buck Jones was a complete failure. Another shot at the Wild West Show circuit was equally disastrous. When the stock market crashed in 1929, he found himself broke and looking to the motion picture studios to restore his career and financial fortunes. This time he went to Columbia, where he did 27 films in just three years. In 1934 he went to Universal and began churning out serials. For the next seven years he moved back and forth between the two studios.

His final film, *Dawn of the Great Divide*, was in the can, but he didn't know it as such, when in 1942 he began touring with a war bond drive. November 28 of that year found him in Boston, for an appearance at the Thanksgiving Day

Buck Jones worked his way up the hard way in Western movies, starting out as a $5 a day bit player and stuntman. By the time he had reached the height of his career, he was earning $3,500 a week.

Parade. That night was spent relaxing at the Coconut Grove nightclub. More than 500 lives were lost in the blaze that swept through the place, including his own. Survivors who witnessed him in action described his deeds that night as having been as heroic as any he'd depicted on film. He saved many lives at the cost of his own helping others to get out of the shabbily built establishment with too few emergency exits.

On screen Buck Jones used many different revolvers, primarily SAA Colts. For personal appearances, a 4-3/4-inch barreled full blue .45 caliber SAA, that's heavily inlaid with silver, represented his cowboy stardom. Ivory stocks that have been exquisitely carved and inlaid with silver to match the rest of the revolver are the highlights that turn this beautiful sixgun into a work of art. The one item he never seemed to change, once it was made for him, was his gunbelt and holster. A drop-loop buscadero rig, crafted by Ed Bolin, it is carved with a lavish floral design and has been edged with lace borders throughout and numerous conchos are inset.

The Colt SAA .45 that Buck Jones carried for personal appearances and live shows is a handsomely adorned work of art. Abundant silver inlays are accented by beautifully carved ivory grips that bear still more silver inlays. His floral carved gunbelt was the creation of master leather craftsman Ed Bolin. (Courtesy The Autry Museum of Western Heritage)

Not especially handsome, at least not in the usual Hollywood way, Jones was successful as a "B" Western hero because he was believable in the role. That was made abundantly clear by the manner of his death-heroically losing his own life to save others in the Coconut Grove fire of 1942.

Lash LaRue

LA RUE ALWAYS DISLIKED the name Alfred, which his parents had given him at birth on June 14, 1917, in Gretna, Louisiana. Nevertheless, he was pretty much stuck with it until his trademark movie gimmick, the use of a bullwhip to fight the bad guys turned him into "Lash" LaRue. The moniker fit and many years later he went so far as to have his name legally changed. His early years were spent in Louisiana, but by the time he was ready for high school his parents had moved to California. He attended St. Johns Military Academy in Los Angeles, and then attended College of the Pacific, with the intention of going into law, but matters took a different direction.

After his schooling, LaRue tried earning a living as a real estate salesman, then as a hairdresser. Nothing seemed to satisfy him. Having studied drama in college, he fancied himself a talented actor and began making the rounds of the Hollywood studios. Warner Brothers gave him an opportunity to demonstrate his abilities, but decided he looked and sounded too much like Humphrey Bogart and they already had the real thing under contract. Ironically, both actors had speech impediments and studied drama in order to overcome the affliction. That may be part of the reason they seemed so similar.

A latecomer to the Western genre, Lash LaRue never quite made the "A" team in the "B" Westerns. Beginning with small parts in 1940, he made his way into several films over the next few years, including a couple of musicals at Universal, starring Deanna Durbin. His breakout role came in 1945, when he played a heavy in Eddie Dean's first film, *Song of Old Wyoming*, from Producer's Releasing Corp. His character is reformed, just in time to get shot at the end of the film. After three Dean films in which he was a featured player, he began appearing in leading roles, starting in 1947's *Law of the Lash*. Unfortunately, the "B" Westerns were declining and LaRue was doing them for one small studio after another. Low budgets and editing shortcuts didn't help. By 1953 the series was over. He continued working in films, sporadically, into the 1960s, but only in character parts. Alcohol and multiple failed marriages took their toll and he ended up broke, out of work and, at one particularly low point, under arrest for vagrancy in Miami, Florida.

Through the 1960s and 1970s, LaRue spent much of his time in and out of monasteries, drying out and getting his head on straight. By the 1980s he discovered the Western movie convention circuit, which brought fans together with the stars of the old "B" oaters.

Until his death in 1996, he made a modest living attending such gatherings. People who met him under those circumstances reported that he was very congenial and among the most popular of the performers who participated in those events.

On screen Lash LaRue wore a black double rig, to match a costume that was liberally studded with small conchos. The nickel-plated, short-barreled Colt SAA revolvers with plastic faux staghorn stocks were unremarkable. What is somewhat interesting is that LaRue appears to have been willing, for a modest fee, to "authenticate" some revolvers about which there is considerable doubt, as having been used by him in his films.

Black Diamond, LaRue's movie mount, looks the part of hero's horse, with all the silver mounted tack. If one didn't know better, you might think the bad guy was riding the good guy's horse. LaRue also used a horse named Rush.

Seen in action on this lobby card, Lash LaRue didn't know one end of a bullwhip from the other when he told producer Robert Tansey that he'd used one since he was a kid. He got badly cut up in an attempt to teach himself. Tansey was amused, not angry, by the subterfuge and its result. Realizing how much LaRue was willing to endure for the role, he hired a real expert, Snowy Baker, to teach his budding star. To his credit, LaRue learned well.

In keeping with the anti-hero image he tried to convey on screen, LaRue dressed all in black for most of his pictures.

Complete descriptions of these revolvers and notarized statements on his letterhead notwithstanding, there remains considerable doubt as to the veracity of LaRue's statements regarding his use of them in his films. (Courtesy the William A. Dascher Collection)

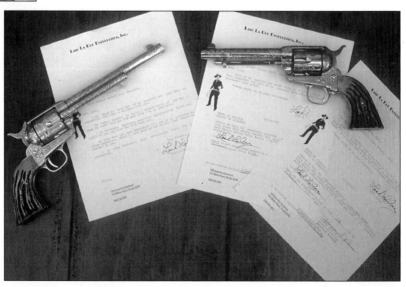

Ken Maynard

KEN MAYNARD'S STUDIO biography has him born in Mission, Texas, on July 21, 1895. He is said to have served as an Army engineer during World War I and went on to become a champion rodeo cowboy before landing in Hollywood. Well, at least the birthday appears to be correct. He and his younger brother Kermit (b. 1897), who was a well respected "B" Western movie performer in his own right, though never a major star, were born in Vevay, Indiana, and raised in nearby Columbus. Ken Maynard did serve in the Army, at Camp (later Fort) Knox. He later worked in several Wild West shows and starred with the Ringling Brothers Circus as a trick rider. No question about it, he was a fine horseman. He may also have ridden in some rodeos, but was never listed on the roles as champion of any major rodeo. Why either he or the studios would lay claim to such honors when it is so easy to check into the records is something of a mystery. How he came to Hollywood in the first place is also unknown, but there are those who claim either Buck Jones or Tom Mix saw him perform with Ringling Brothers and suggested he do so. However it came to be, Maynard arrived in Tinseltown in the early 1920s.

Starting out at Fox, his first films were not Westerns. Though in his first major part he did get to ride, playing the supporting role of Paul Revere in the 1924 film, *Janice Meredith*. Maynard's first Westerns were low-budget silent films, shot in 1925 at the Davis Film Production Company. The following year he moved over to a bigger studio, First National Pictures, that, in the years to come, would evolve into Warner Brothers. There, his career as the lead in Western movies began in earnest. At about the same time he married fellow Hoosier Mary Leeper, who was from South Bend, and acquired Tarzan, the palomino horse he would ride to stardom. By 1929 he was a well-established star and other studios began seeking him out. Universal made him a very lucrative offer, so he moved there, just in time for the talkies to put a big scare into much of the industry. Universal was slow to adapt to the new technology and let Maynard's contract lapse. Just as his star was rising high, he was out of work and The Great Depression was beginning to be felt across the nation.

For the next couple of years Maynard worked at Tiffany Studios, a small outfit already in financial trouble. When they went under in 1932, he moved on to KBS/World Wide. The films he did for both those studios were extremely low-budget affairs and the final products showed it. Nevertheless, he continued to work and earn a living, although the latter studio was also doomed. By 1933 Universal was back on solid ground and, once again, offered Maynard a contract, which included some production control and bigger budgets than he'd had during his time with the minor studios. With his fortunes apparently restored, Maynard seems to have "gone Hollywood." His films began going seriously over budget, which led to loud and profane arguments with his bosses, who refused to renew his contract when it ended in 1934.

At first, his lack of a contract mattered little because he moved almost immediately over to Mascot Studios. They were paying him a huge salary for the time, $10,000 per week, which seems to have given him the impression that they needed him more than he needed them. He began interfering with matters of production with more of the same sort of behavior that had damaged him so severely at Universal. With newcomer Gene Autry waiting in the wings to take over lead Western star status, Mascot didn't need the grief Maynard was giving them anymore.

Maynard signed with Columbia in 1935 and did eight films there over the course of two years. But age was beginning to catch up with him. By the time his contract with Columbia had ended in 1936, he was over 40 and no longer as trim as he once had been. He continued to be argumentative and was drinking to excess. Mary, his wife of 11 years, divorced him.

In spite of his increasingly serious personal problems, Maynard remained popular with his youthful audience. He continued working for lesser studios because his name alone was enough to fill the rows of seats at the Saturday afternoon matinees. His last "B" Western was *Harmony Trail*, which hit the screens in 1944. Maynard's career in films was essentially over, and his formerly lavish lifestyle left him nearly penniless. He'd put nothing back for savings and retirement. Rumor has it that Gene Autry secretly provided him with enough for living expenses for many years. His brother, Kermit, also helped him out, but there's little that can be done for an alcoholic unwilling to reform. For years he lived in a

Most of Ken Maynard's films were well photographed and had plenty of exciting action, so he came across well on screen. As a result, he was one of the most popular of the "B" Western heroes.

Maynard is posed with his screen partner, Tarzan. The actor maintained a stable full of stunt doubles for use in chase scenes or situations that might risk injury to the mount. By all accounts there was a real chemistry between them.

Elaborately tooled in several colors of leather, Ken Maynard's parade outfit is complemented by one of the most profusely decorated gunbelts ever crafted for a "B" Western star. (Courtesy The Autry Museum of Western Heritage)

trailer he'd formerly used on tour. Maynard came to the end of his days on March 30, 1973, destitute and severely ill, at the Motion Picture Home in Woodland Hills, California, the subject of charity.

Ken Maynard's on-screen sixguns were a pair of 5-1/2-inch SAA .45s, nickel-plated and fitted with engraved silver stocks. His initials, in gold, are on the upper forward corner, where factory stock medallions would be placed. In the center of each stock panel is the gold-plated head of a longhorn steer. The gunbelt and holsters that house the revolvers are of hand-carved leather with elaborate silver decoration, as befits a Western hero of the silver screen. It's too bad the real man couldn't fill the boots of the one portrayed on screen.

The engraved silver and gold stocks are the most distinctive feature of Maynard's movie sixguns. The silver work on his floral carved gunbelt and holsters is so profuse that it must have added considerably to the weight of the rig. (Courtesy The Autry Museum of Western Heritage)

Ken Maynard is shown here in a confrontation with veteran heavy Charles King, who at one time or another was probably killed or wounded on film by every "B" Western star in the business. Off screen most people in the film industry had strong feelings about who the real bad guy was.

Steve McQueen

(Josh Randall)

ON THE BIG screen Steve McQueen played all manner of characters, but Western fans remember him best in *The Magnificent Seven* and *Nevada Smith*. It was on the small screen, however, that he gained early recognition. That was in the role of the bounty hunter, Josh Randall, in the television series, *Wanted, Dead or Alive*. Seen on the CBS network from September 1958 until March 1961, it was one of many "Adult Westerns" that dominated television during the period.

A product of Lee Strasberg's Actor's Studio, McQueen's brooding portrayal of the outcast quasi-lawman was in the best tradition of the "method" school of acting. The Josh Randall character provided a useful public service by finding and arresting wanted criminals in a time when the traditional forces of law and order were too few and too far between to be entirely effective. However, he is treated with disdain by the very people who benefit most by his efforts, often regarded as barely a step above the vermin he captures if he can, or kills if he must.

With so many Westerns being produced for television at once, writers were hard pressed to make their series and lead characters dis-

tinctive. One of the most common and effective methods was the use of the "gimmick" gun. Instead of the ubiquitous Single Action Army Colt, the hero of a given series would use something radically different to give himself an advantage in terms of speed or power. There was none more ludicrous than Josh Randall's "mare's leg," but it sure looked neat.

To compound the silliness of the concept, the audience is lied to from the beginning. The claim is that an obviously modified Model 1892 Winchester is firing the .45-70 cartridge. This round is far too big to fit the action. Even if the round could be forced into the action, the rifle would, at best, hold two rounds in the magazine and another in the chamber. There were, to be sure, some Model 1892 rifles made with exceptionally short barrels, particularly for the South American market. However, 12-inch barrels were as short as they got, and more often they were 14 or 15 inches in length.

The stock of the mare's leg is also cut a couple inches past the wrist. The result is that it becomes, essentially, a very clumsy firearm that can only be pointed, not efficiently aimed. On the other hand, the loop lever made it possible to spin-cock the rifle to enhanced dramatic effect. It is obvious to any serious shooter that the mare's leg, as depicted in the series, would have been a handicap, not a help, to its user. Any foe competent with a rifle, shotgun or revolver would probably have put Josh Randall into the hands of the town undertaker in short order, but reality is almost always the loser in such situations. Nevertheless, the series gave a fine young actor an opportunity to demonstrate his talents to a broad audience. In that respect, alone, the mare's leg proved worthwhile.

The practiced slouch, with one shoulder higher than the other, combined with the brooding expression on his face are trademarks common to most of the adherents of Lee Strasberg's "method," as taught at The Actor's Studio. Eventually McQueen found his way as a performer and began innovating instead of imitating; ending up as one of Hollywood's best actors.

Portraying Nevada Smith, the newly orphaned teenager in pursuit of the men who killed his parents, Steve McQueen carries a caplock muzzleloading rifle across his shoulders on this lobby card.

Many of the heroes of the Adult Western television series used a gimmick gun to attract the audience's interest. Steve McQueen's character, Josh Randall, was stuck with one of the worst ideas a scriptwriter ever conceived. While it made for interesting dramatic effect, in the real world the only thing a gun like this would be good for is spare parts. (Courtesy The Autry Museum of Western Heritage)

Tom Mix

BIOGRAPHIES OF MOVIE stars composed by scriptwriters and press agents under the old Hollywood studio system were notorious for hyperbole and outright fabrication. That of Tom Mix is an outstanding example. Mix was touted as a native son of the West, born in a log cabin in El Paso, Texas. Never mind log cabins in El Paso are about as common as adobe homes in New York City, the truth is obviously less romantic. Tom Mix first saw the light of day in 1880 at Mix Run, near the Pennsylvania town of Dubois. Mix's father was a coachman by trade, and the lad grew up riding and training horses. His expert horsemanship was one of the best features of his film performances.

The studios invented a heroic military career for Mix. According to that bio, he had served with distinction during the Spanish-American War, the Boxer Rebellion in China and the Philippine Insurrection. He was also alleged to have fought on both sides during the Boer War in South Africa. The truth is rather mundane, and, in one respect, possibly dishonorable. Mix joined the Army in 1898, serving his entire enlistment far removed from any combat at a military post in the State of Delaware.

To give credit where it is due, his performance must have been outstanding, because it was an age when promotion within the ranks was notoriously slow. In spite of that, he earned First Sergeant's stripes during his four-year hitch. While that is a remarkable record of accomplishment, according to a spokesperson for the Tom Mix Museum, in Dewey, Oklahoma, evidence has recently surfaced to indicate that Mix may have reenlisted in the Army at the end of his term of enlistment and deserted soon after. The allegation is unproved and unlikely to be true, because desertion from military service, even in times of peace, has, until very recently, been treated as a serious crime by the armed forces and no statute of limitations applied. If it were true and made public, it would have caused a scandal for the motion picture studios. Since Mix used his given name as a performer, military authorities would have been quick to identify him and act. For that reason, until proof is provided, this information should be regarded as anecdotal and not definitive.

His law enforcement career was even less noteworthy. Mix served a brief stint as a deputy town marshal when he lived in Dewey. That's it; there was no more. The studio's claims that he had been a sheriff in Colorado, a Texas Ranger and a U.S. Marshal were as much the product of imagination as the scripts the actors followed in his films. The badges and commissions he received from the latter two agencies were purely honorary, based upon the promotional benefits his screen portrayals lent them, not any career history. He was most certainly not a real-life gunfighter, much less a town-taming lawman. The only shooting incident ever recorded in Mix's life involved a 1924 domestic quarrel with his fourth wife, Victoria Forde, during which she shot him in the arm.

Tom Mix left the Army in 1902. By 1904 he had fulfilled a lifelong dream by moving to the Wild West. Oklahoma was still a U.S. Territory and would not be admitted to the Union until November 16, 1907. Settling first in Guthrie, then in Oklahoma City, he found work as a bartender, an athletic coach and a prizefighter. Five years later he was living in Dewey and did some work with the Mulhall and the Miller Brothers 101 Ranch Wild West shows. A movie company spotted him while they were shooting a film in the vicinity. His expertise at handling horses was obvious and they seized the opportunity to hire him as a wrangler for their stock. Stunt work followed; then a few bit parts came his way.

Tall, dark and handsome in the manner so common to Hollywood's leading men, it didn't take long for studio heads to recognize Mix's potential for audience appeal. He soon found himself in leading roles. His flare for showmanship was probably influenced by his work with the Wild West extravaganzas. In a large arena, it required grand gestures, elaborate

The lady seated behind Mix is his lovely daughter, Ruth. She became a popular actress in her own right, appearing in several Westerns and other "B" movies and serials. The horse is Tony Jr. The elder Tony had white stockings only on his rear legs.

costuming and extravagantly decorated saddles, bridles and gun leather for lead players to stand out among the supporting cast. Mix introduced this into his films and audiences, especially children, loved it. While William S. Hart had been the reigning king of the movie cowboys and had made the stories and the characters appear as historically accurate as feasible, Mix made them larger than life. His object was to entertain, not to teach history and the result was that his Hollywood stardom eventually overshadowed that of Hart.

Until Tom Mix came along, horses in Western movies were just that, horses. They were to be ridden from place to place on the lot and, if need be, expendable. Rarely were they anything more than rawboned roman-nosed mus-

tangs and nags. Mix knew something the studio heads didn't; people love horses, especially kids and women. Men appreciate, even admire them, but with kids and women it's love. Large, beautiful and distinctively colored animals that are well-trained stand out as the province of heroes, particularly when adorned with grandly decorated tack. Mix's horse, Tony, was as much a star in the eyes the audience as he was. His fancy costumes, leather and horseflesh would set the tone for Hollywood's Westerns for decades to come.

Mix set another tone, as well; one meant to encourage moral and virtuous behavior on the part of his legions of juvenile fans. His message to them was that good guys, and it was a rare kid who didn't want that role in his cow-

One of S&W's early "Registered Model" .357 Magnums, this revolver may have been carried regularly by Tom Mix in a shoulder holster. For many years people have thought the stocks on it are ivory. Actually, they are wood, painted white.

A brace of Officer's Model Colt .38 Special revolvers, these were sometimes used in movies, but more often used by Mix during shooting exhibitions. The stocks are scrimshawed ivory.

Nickel plated and stocked with genuine mother-of-pearl, this pair of Colt Official Police .38 Special revolvers was frequently worn by Mix in his movies. The metal and the stocks show a lot of wear and scuff marks from hard use during filming.

boy games, didn't smoke, drink or swear. That message was repeated in his films, comic books, radio shows, circuses and rodeos for more than 30 years. The kids listening to his radio broadcasts were also encouraged to grow up, big, strong and healthy by eating Ralston Purina cereal for breakfast. Millions of boxes of that singularly vile food were sold thereby, but most kids felt it worthwhile, because with the box tops and a small amount of money they could send away for "secret message" decoder rings and other premiums. Even though kids didn't really like the stuff, Tom Mix said it was good, and after all, he wouldn't lie, would he?

For all his moralizing, Mix's personal lifestyle was replete with precisely the vices he preached against. Off screen he smoked, drank and swore. He was also guilty of what might be termed a vice peculiarly common to Hollywood. He was married five times. Since none were at the same time he might only have been accused by the pragmatic of "serial polygamy."

Mix's flamboyance took a giant leap when he met Ed Bohlin around 1922. The young Swedish immigrant had a flair for leatherwork, silver and goldsmithing. Bohlin had worked his way to America and settled in Wyoming, where he worked as a cowboy and, eventually, opened a saddle shop. He also performed with a vaudeville troupe that was appearing at the Pantages Theater in Hollywood, where Mix saw him do his act.

This S&W .32 Hand Ejector, with its nickel plating and pearl stocks, has been tastefully engraved. It would be nice to know the uses to which Tom Mix put it, but no information about the revolver is available at the museum.

Not the fancy sort of sixgun normally associated with Tom Mix, this well-worn .45 caliber Colt Bisley was used by him in his last film, The Miracle Rider.

This is a rare Smith & Wesson New Model #3 target revolver, chambered for the .38-44 cartridge. The revolver is set up for the attachment of a shoulder stock. Unfortunately, that highly desirable accessory is missing.

Mix admired and purchased a pair of boots and a jacket that Bohlin had made. Later, Mix convinced Bohlin that he should stay in Hollywood, and make his products for the movie industry. Bohlin's superb craftsmanship and artistry are legendary and most of the cowboy stars became his customers.

By the time motion pictures had been given a voice, Tom Mix was nearly 50 years old. With audible dialogue the technique of screen performance changed. The grandiose gestures required to convey meaning when the screen was mute could be done away with when the actors' words could tell the tale. He didn't make the transition from silent films to "talkies" well. Mix was offered fewer film roles as the decade progressed and, in 1936, he made his last screen appearance in *The Miracle Rider*.

It is difficult to tell from watching his films, but Tom Mix appears to have known something of shooting and had a genuine appreciation for fine firearms. He seems to have begun collecting guns long before it became common practice. There are several that are known to have belonged to him in the museum that honors his memory in Dewey. On film, his six-gun handling looks more like chopping kindling with a hatchet than something one might do while trying to hit a target.

The careful observer will note that Mix often used Single Action Army Colts, the traditional Western movie sixgun, for close-ups, but switched to double-action revolvers for the action scenes. That way he could shoot faster, alternating fire from one hand to another. It's been suggested that he simply didn't have the

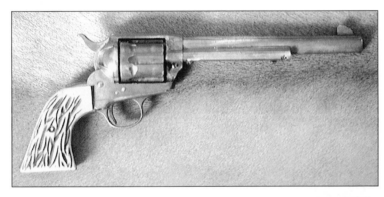

Tom Mix usually reserved SAA Colts like this .38-40 for close-up shots. This one is from the museum collection. He was said to have used double-action revolvers in action scenes, because he lacked the manual dexterity to operate single-actions as rapidly as audiences expected from their cowboy heroes.

Among the double-action revolvers Mix used in his movies and live performances were the Colt Official Police revolvers seen in this promotional still photo.

manual dexterity to use the single-action revolvers as quickly as his audiences would expect. He was one of the original Hollywood two-gun cowboys. Because he usually did his own stunts, he was also one of the first to carry rubber guns in his holsters during fight scenes and when jumping off horses. They didn't hurt as much as the real ones if he fell on one.

There's no provenance to go with any of the guns in the Mix collection. So, how they were acquired and what personal significance many of them may have had is pure speculation. But we do know something about a few of them. There are two matched pairs of nickel-plated, mother-of-pearl stocked, .38 Special Colt Official Police revolvers, with 6-inch barrels. One set, apparently used for personal appearances, has factory medallions inset in the mother-of-pearl stocks. The other pair has plain pearl stocks and are well scarred and scuffed. These seem to have been used hard during actual filming.

A third pair of DA Colts is a set of blued Officer's Model Match revolvers that also bear 6-inch barrels and are fitted with scrimshawed ivory stocks. These seem to have been reserved for trick shooting exhibitions.

A nickel-plated Smith & Wesson .32 caliber Hand Ejector, with a 4-inch barrel, round butt, pearl stocks and excellent scroll engrav-

ing that appears factory original graces the collection. With it are two other S&W's. One is a .38-44 New Model Number 3 target revolver that's in superb condition. It was made for use with a shoulder stock, but that very desirable accessory is missing. There is also one of the very first .357 Magnums, the so called, "Registered Models." The .357 is blued, has a 6-inch barrel and may have been carried by Mix in a shoulder holster for personal protection. On close examination, what appear to be carved ivory stocks are actually wood, painted white, with a red rectangular background painted behind Mix's name to make it stand out.

A Colt Bisley Model .45 with a 4-3/4-inch barrel that he used in his last film, *The Miracle Rider,* is in the museum collection. Its finish is worn to gray metal and its hard rubber stocks are smooth from handling. It's a far cry from the showy sixguns he usually used on screen.

A 7-1/2-inch SAA .45 with mother-of-pearl stocks and a .38-40 of the same length, wearing plastic staghorn-style stocks common to that era, are the only traditional "cowboy-style" six-shooters in the display. There's no indication of what significance they may have had in the actor's life.

A lever-action Marlin .410 gauge shotgun, that looks like a rifle to the casual observer, and several Model 92 Winchesters, one of which is a smoothbore, marked .38 WCF, but

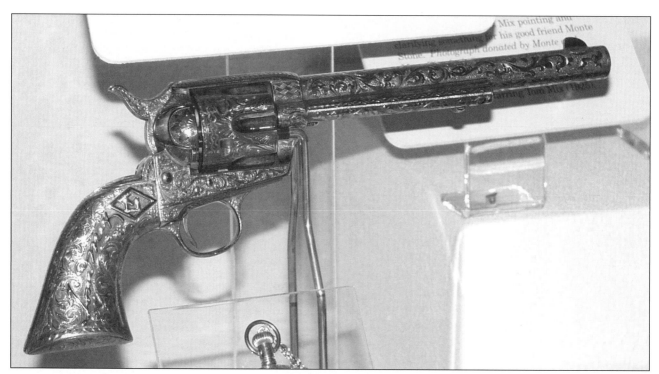

Only the trigger has escaped the hand of the engraver on this (probably) silver-plated .45 caliber revolver owned by Tom Mix. The silver stocks have his name and TM brand inlaid in gold. Ed Bohlin, who did the holster that accompanies it, probably adorned the revolver. (Courtesy The Autry Museum of Western Heritage)

labeled in the display as being .44 caliber, appear to have been among the pieces he used for trick shooting exhibitions on the road. Such firearms were often used in those days, as much for the sake of safety, when shooting in crowded arenas and stadiums, as for the greater likelihood that the shooter would hit what appeared to the audience be a difficult target.

Tom Mix was known to have had a pair of SAA Colts in a fancy, hand-tooled, Bohlin rig that Lou Costello, of the comedy team, Abbott and Costello, owned at the time of his death. That may be what has been displayed at the Autry Museum of Western Heritage. Also in that display is a Remington Model 8 semi-automatic rifle that is one of very few engraved specimens of its kind.

During his lifetime, Mix was known to have given several of his personal guns to friends and associates, but when he died, his attorney, Ivon Parker, received his personal effects, in accordance with the performer's will. Parker ignored the onslaught of requests for these items by collectors and fans. Everything was kept intact until his own death. But at that time, the lawyer's sons and nephews saw the collection in terms of dollar signs. When Mix's belongings were made available for sale, the people of Dewey, Oklahoma, raised the necessary funds to purchase the whole kit and caboodle and placed it in the museum that honors the showman's memory. Today, the collection is owned and controlled by the Oklahoma Historical Society, to which we are indebted for the opportunity to inspect and photograph the collection.

Author's Note: Just before the completion of this book it was learned that 12 of the Tom Mix guns were stolen from the museum in Dewey, on April 13, 2002. It was apparently a smash and grab operation and the thieves managed to get away before the police arrived. Only handguns were taken and those illustrated here are among them. Each is marked with the TM brand. Readers are asked to contact police should they encounter any of them.

Tom Mix's radio show was sponsored by Ralston's cereal. It tasted awful, but millions of boxes were sold when young listeners nagged their mothers for it.

Remington's Model 8 semi-automatic rifle is rarely encountered with engraving of any sort, but this one got the full treatment. Tom Mix commissioned engraving on most of the guns he used for personal appearances and private shooting excursions. (Courtesy The Autry Museum of Western Heritage)

Clayton Moore
(The Lone Ranger)

CLAYTON MOORE WAS neither the first to wear the mask, nor was it the first mask he wore. Yet, just as William Boyd became Hopalong Cassidy in the minds of his fans, Moore personified The Lone Ranger more than just in spirit.

A native of Chicago, Moore was born there on September 14, 1914. The urban environment of his formative years notwithstanding, he knew as a child that he wanted to be in Western movies. In his teens he was a circus performer, doing a trapeze act. He was injured in a fall while working an engagement at the 1934 Chicago World's Fair. This brought an abrupt end to that phase of his career. The following year found him trying unsuccessfully to make it on New York's Broadway stage. Undaunted, he turned his back on The Great White Way and followed the setting sun, arriving in Hollywood in 1938.

Clayton Moore's fortunes turned dramatically for the better in the motion picture industry. Within a year he had churned out 15 chapter serials, one following another at Republic Studios-a new one being put in the can every six weeks, on average. Some had modern settings and others were science fiction, but he did plenty of Westerns, as well. It's hard to think of

him as the bad guy, but he played that part frequently, especially when cast in the Gene Autry and Roy Rogers pictures.

In 1943, with World War II raging, Moore, like many in Hollywood, volunteered for military service, joining the Army Air Corps. When he was discharged in 1945, he returned to work at Republic. From then on he was no longer being cast as the villain in his photoplays. Yet he had worn a mask several times, most notably as *The Crimson Ghost*. It was a masked role in 1949 that proved pivotal. As the lead in *The Ghost of Zorro*, he came to the attention of producer George Trendle, who owned the rights to Fran Striker's creation, *The Lone Ranger*, and was planning to bring the radio and sometime screen-hero's adventures to the newly emerging medium called television.

The first actor to play the role on film was Lee Powell. In 1938 Powell played opposite Victor Daniels, the first Tonto. But Powell joined the Marines and was killed in action in the Pacific in 1944. Moore, when asked by Trendle if he wanted the role replied, "Mr. Trendle, I am the Lone Ranger." And, so he was.

The Lone Ranger was no stranger to audiences. The character had been a staple on radio since January 30, 1933. Brace Beamer, the best known of the Lone Ranger radio voices, played the role for more than 13 years, beginning in 1941. When *The Lone Ranger* first aired on television at 7:30 p.m. on Thursday, September 12, 1949, television sets were still rare and expensive. A child who was lucky enough to be part of a family that owned one was one of the luckiest kids in the neighborhood, because he or she got to watch the show, getting four doses of their hero weekly, while the rest of the neighborhood was limited to just three radio broadcasts, on Monday, Wednesday and Friday. By late 1954, the show was gone from radio, but first-run episodes of the TV series were produced through most of 1957.

Between 1952 and 1954 a salary dispute caused Clayton Moore to be replaced by John Hart. At first, producers believed the switch would go unnoticed by the primarily youthful audience. But there was an uproar. While Hart was a decent man and an entirely adequate performer, as far as the kids were concerned, he simply wasn't the real Lone Ranger. In the end, Moore got his money, Hart went on to other parts, and the kids were happy to have their hero back.

Still, television series have a finite life and this one came to an end after a strong run, shy of eight years by just three days. Even so, Moore continued to play the part in personal appearances and commercials for more than 20 years. The series continues to be seen in reruns to this day.

To ignore Tonto, as played by a Canadian-born member of the Mohawk Nation, Jay Silverheels, would be to miss half the story of The Lone Ranger. However, there is little known about the character's history other

Clayton Moore often made personal appearances as The Lone Ranger to promote charitable causes and commercial enterprises. Posed here with guns drawn, the careful observer will note that his revolvers have no front sights. When they were purchased from a pawnshop, the revolvers had 7-1/2-inch barrels, which were cut to the same length as the ejector rods and nickel plated. The stocks are yellow plastic to simulate ivory.

than that the two met as children when the young John Reid, who would become The Lone Ranger, saved Tonto's life. Tonto returned the favor when he found the scene of a massacre that has left all but one member of a party of Rangers dead. In the story, Tonto is identified as a member of the Potawotamie Nation, which was originally native to the upper Midwest. Presumably, his immediate forebears are among those transported to Indian Territory, the future Oklahoma, but we don't know why he's wandering around Texas when he discovers the friend of his youth.

In 1956, while the television series was still in production, a feature-length movie, simply titled *The Lone Ranger*, was made, and two years later, after the series was shut down, another made it to the big screen. It was called *The Lone Ranger and the Lost City of Gold*.

Moore continued for the next couple of decades to don the costume and play the role for personal appearances and an occasional on-air sales pitch. That came to an abrupt halt in the late 1970s. The Wrather Corporation had acquired the rights to the character and a new feature-length film was being planned. Jack Wrather wanted potential identity problems with the young actor who would assume the role to be minimized, so he obtained an injunction to prevent Clayton Moore from wearing the mask in public. Moore simply began wearing sunglasses

Moore, as The Lone Ranger, is posed here with his horse, Silver, and screen partner, Canadian-born Mohawk Indian, Jay Silverheels. While Moore's gunbelt is strikingly handsome, the one Silverheels wore in his role as Tonto is poorly constructed and appears to have been put together by an amateur.

instead. As long as he didn't call himself "The Lone Ranger" and wore no mask, the courts ruled he could continue his appearances. In the meanwhile, fans let there be no doubt as to their displeasure with Wrather.

In retrospect, things might have been better if Wrather had enlisted the aging Ranger to help with the transition to a younger successor. Unfortunately, Klinton Spilsbury, the star of the 1981 movie, *Legend of the Lone Ranger,* played the role so badly that all his dialogue had to be dubbed. The film was a colossal flop. Spilsbury earned not just one, but two Raspberry Awards for worst actor and worst new actor that year. Meanwhile, either out of conscience or public pressure, Wrather rescinded his order against Moore and the real Lone Ranger got to put his mask back on.

About The Lone Ranger's guns, there's little to tell. They were worn in a beautifully tooled, black, double buscadero rig, with lots of border conchos to accent the "silver bullets" in the cartridge loops. But if it were not for their association with Moore and the character he played, a serious gun collector wouldn't give them a second look. The stocks are plastic, intended to look like ivory. Up close they look like the cheap imitation material of which they're made.

The series was filmed on a very small budget. The sets, location scenes and costumes make that plain. The only props on which significant dollars were spent were the fancy saddle, bridle and breast strap that were worn by Silver. The story behind the revolvers is downright disillusioning. When it came time to arm The Lone Ranger, someone was dispatched to a local pawnshop, where a well-worn pair of used Colt Single Action Army .45s with 7-1/2-inch barrels was purchased. The barrels were promptly cut to match the length of the ejector rods and the sixguns were nickel plated and fitted with their phony stocks. Look closely and you'll see that no one even bothered to replace the front sights.

There's a certain frustrating logic to that. The Lone Ranger nearly always fired from the hip and almost invariably shot the gun from his adversary's hand, without so much as chipping the bad guy's fingernail, let alone drawing blood.

By modern standards, the Lone Ranger as played by Clayton Moore is "high camp." Nevertheless, when the strains of The William Tell Overture are played, millions of hearts beat a little faster and long to "...return with us, now, to those thrilling days of yesteryear. The Lone Ranger rides again. Hi-Yo Silver, awaaayy!"

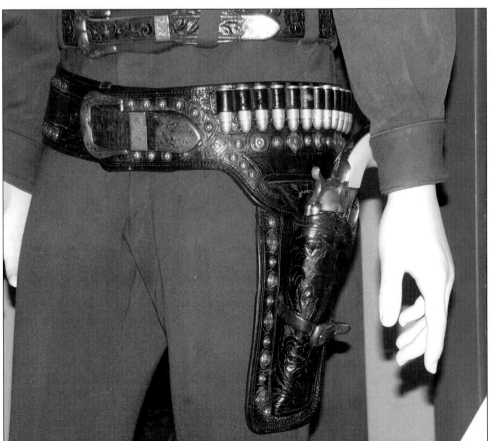

Floral carving, silver conchos and hardware and, of course, "silver bullets" make The Lone Ranger's double buscadero rig one of the most attractive sets of gunleather seen in TV Westerns.

Annie Oakley

BORN IN 1860, Phoebe Anne Oakley Mozee wasn't from the West, as most people imagine her to have been. She was from rural Dark County, Ohio. At the time, that part of Ohio was very sparsely settled, and when we use the term "rural," we really mean back-woods.

Oakley started her shooting career at the tender age of 9 by keeping her nearly desti-tute family supplied with small game for the table. As she matured in her responsibilities and her shooting skills, she earned some extra cash for the family coffers by selling much of the game she hunted to local stores and to markets and restaurants in Cincinnati. While the practice may be frowned upon in many places today, market hunting was considered a perfectly reasonable means of making a liv-ing in the 1870s. Her marksmanship and out-door skills were such that by the age of 15 she'd earned enough to pay off the mortgage on her family's modest home.

Exhibition shooters were popular entertain-ers in the last quarter of the 19th century (and well into the 20th). Among the best known of such marksmen in his day was Frank Butler. During a visit to Cincinnati, a match was arranged between him and the local favorite, the teenage girl, Annie Mozee. She won the contest by a single point. There

were those who said she held back in order not to humiliate the man with whom she became instantly infatuated. Who can say?

Instead of being angry and embarrassed, Butler had nothing but admiration for the young lady's skill. He continued his tour, but began writing Annie regularly. It was clear that he, too, was smitten and, after she grew to suitable age, he married her and made her a part of his act as well as his life.

With a modesty uncharacteristic of that chauvinistic age, not to mention a great sense of good business, Butler made her the star of the show, while he managed the couple's com-mercial interests; in essence becoming "Mister Annie Oakley."

A very attractive woman by the standards of any age, and possessed of an innocent, girl-ish manner, the new Mrs. Butler easily won the hearts of audiences. For stage purposes, her name was changed to that by which she became world-renowned: Annie Oakley. The name, Phoebe Anne Oakley Mozee-Butler, just doesn't seem to have the same pleasant ring to it.

In 1885, while appearing in New Orleans, the couple joined Buffalo Bill's Wild West Show and spent most of the next 15 years touring the United States and Europe. She was very popular with European royalty, thrilling such luminaries as Queen Victoria with her speed, accuracy and endurance with rifle, shotgun and handgun. She once held a German audience enthralled by shooting a cigarette from the lips of the future Kaiser Wilhelm II. How different the history of the early 20th century might have been had her skills failed her at that moment. Actually, she is said to have sent him a letter during World War I asking if he would let her have another try. Curiously, there is no record of her having received a reply.

The aging Sitting Bull, a revered member of the Oglala-Sioux tribe, joined Buffalo Bill for a brief four-month period in the same year as the Butlers. With the Indian wars all but over, he needed to earn money to support his family back on the reservation in South Dakota. It seems the old warrior had a particular affection for Annie and it was he who gave her the nickname by which she would ever after be known, "Little Sure-Shot."

Annie Oakley was partially paralyzed in a train wreck while touring in 1901. With an exemplary display of determination and fortitude, plus multiple surgeries, she recovered sufficiently to resume her career and continued to thrill her audiences and set new records until her retirement in 1920. She died in 1926 having shot an estimated 2 million rounds of ammunition during her career.

More than 70 years have passed and the memory of her remains strong. Her marksmanship skills are the stuff of legend. As well, she was active in charitable works and was well known as a firearms safety and marksmanship instructor. She was quite the lady in every respect.

As an exhibition shooter, Oakley owned and used the firearms of several different well-known makers. Marlin presented at least six different guns to her as tokens of corporate esteem. Among her favorites for trick shooting was the exceptionally accurate .22 caliber

The fact that Annie Oakley was a beautiful woman was certainly not lost on the male members of her audience. However, that was just a bonus. It was her remarkable expertise with rifle, shotgun and pistol that thrilled fans throughout the United States and Europe, who flocked to Buffalo Bill's Wild West Show to witness her skills.

As she grew older, Annie Oakley remained attractive and continued shooting, maintaining her skills and teaching others. She was particularly active in providing marksmanship training to women and children and teaching the principles of firearms safety.

Model 1897 rifle, of which variants and successor models are still made.

Much of Annie Oakley's act involved aerial shooting, for which she usually used a shotgun. Many of her contemporaries used smoothbore rifles for such exhibitions, but she had no need for subterfuge. Her usual choice was a 12-gauge double made by L.C. Smith that, like many of her guns, is engraved. It, along with a pair of gold-plated and profusely engraved Smith & Wessons, one a .44 caliber New Model No. 3 and the other a 1st Model single-shot .22, both with mother-of-pearl stocks, were gifts from her husband that were presented to her around 1900. A similarly decorated J. Stevens No. 37 pistol rounds out the set. While the latter three pistols were too pretty to shoot, a relatively standard nickel-plated New Model No. 3 Target revolver, with mother-of pearl stocks and chambered for the .38-44 target cartridge was actually used in her act.

In 1935 Barbara Stanwyck portrayed Annie Oakley in the biographical film of that name. While, in the usual Hollywood fashion, some liberties were taken with a few of the facts, the film did a reasonably good job of telling the story. In this publicity still, Stanwyck, astride a dummy horse, strikes a pose as if aiming her rifle at a distant aerial target.

Looking every inch the proper Victorian lady, one would hardly suspect that this lovely woman would be one of the most deadly accurate shots who ever lived. Yet, having fired an estimated two million rounds in her lifetime, not one was ever meant to harm another human being.

Centerfire rifle and handgun cartridges were often loaded with shot to be used by exhibition shooters in Wild West Shows, rodeos, fairs and other entertainment venues. The guns in which these rounds were used were often conventional in every other respect, except that they had smooth bores. (Author's Collection)

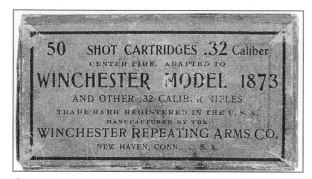

Shot cartridges were made for use in many different chamberings, from .22 rimfire to .45-70. This box contains .32-20s. (Author's Collection)

This trap-grade L.C. Smith side-by-side 12-gauge shotgun was one of Annie Oakley's favorites. The engraving on it includes a likeness of its owner on the left side of the receiver. Its stock and forend are made of exhibition-grade walnut. Having fired an untold quantity of ammunition in its first owner's hands, a century later it remains in excellent condition. (Courtesy The Autry Museum of Western Heritage)

This J. Stevens No. 37 .22 is one of three handguns that were gifts to Annie Oakley from her adoring husband, Frank Butler. All were engraved, gold-plated and stocked with mother-of-pearl. (Courtesy The Autry Museum of Western Heritage)

Around the turn of the 20th century, Oakley began using slide-action .22s, as she's shown doing in this photo, for much of her shooting. They lost nothing in terms of accuracy as compared with the lever-action rifles she used, but were much faster for repeat shots. Following her injuries and recuperation from the 1901 train wreck that nearly ended her career, she may have found their lighter weight more comfortable.

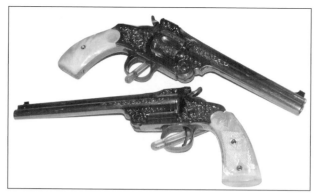

Embellished in the same manner as the J. Stevens .22 are these two Smith & Wessons. One is a .44 caliber New Model No. 3 target revolver. Below it is a First Model single-shot .22. Not surprisingly, these beautiful handguns display no evidence of ever having been fired. (Courtesy The Autry Museum of Western Heritage)

The shot capsules with which these .38-40 cartridges are loaded have thin wooden shells that, from a distance, make them look like conventional lead bullet projectile ammunition. When fired, the thin wood is shattered. Shot sizes for such cartridges were kept very small and the distances to the targets kept relatively short for the sake of safety. If any pellets should stray into the audience, their energy would have dissipated quickly, rendering them harmless. (Author's Collection)

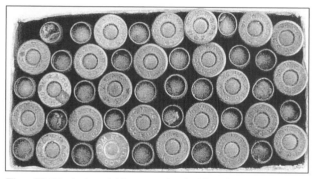

The .32-20 shot cartridges are loaded into longer than conventional cases in order to feed reliably through the action of a repeating rifle. In this instance, the shot is topped with a card wad. Such ammunition was not reserved for trick shooters. Sometimes ordinary shooters used it on small pests, such as birds and rats. (Author's Collection)

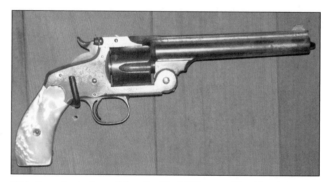

This target version of the Smith & Wesson New Model No. 3 is chambered for the .38-44 cartridge, which was often used for competitive shooting in the latter days of the 19th century. Nickel-plated and pearl-handled, it was used by Annie Oakley in her shows. (Courtesy The Cody Firearms Museum)

Roy Rogers

THE TERM "HERO of the Silver Screen" has been used so much as a part of Hollywood's promotional hyperbole that it has all but lost any real meaning. But if any motion picture star ever deserved to be labeled as such, it is Roy Rogers. No, he never went to war, nor was he a rootin', tootin' lawman, although he did hold a commission as a deputy sheriff for most of his adult life. That was pretty much a courtesy that allowed him to wear his sixguns in public without fear of running afoul of California's often-draconian regulations on the subject.

Roy Rogers was a quiet sort of hero, who lived his life as best he could by the same principles as were espoused in his movies. He bore several personal tragedies in his life with grace. He worked hard at his chosen career and played hard, as well. But he made time for his family and his fans and was especially generous toward underprivileged children. He was a widower with two daughters and a son when he married Dale Evans, who had a grown son of her own by a previous marriage. They had one natural child together, a girl named Robin, who suffered Down Syndrome and repeated illnesses that took her life before her second birthday.

Born Leonard Slye, on November 5, 1911, in Cincinnati, Ohio, his parents were poor, but formed a loving family. They had little money to spend on professional entertainment, so they made their own music at home. When he was just a youngster, they moved to a 10-acre farm in Duck Run. Between his father's job at the U.S. Shoe Company and the farm, they managed to eke out a living. Dropping out of high school in his junior year, the teenaged Leonard, too, went to work at the shoe factory.

In the early years of the Great Depression, Slye, like many others, moved to southern California in search of a better life. Leonard found work picking fruit and driving trucks, but he'd taught himself to play the guitar with some competence, could sing and yodel reasonably well and could call square dances. He wanted to be an entertainer and, with a group of other like-minded young men, formed a band. The group was known by several names before finally becoming The Sons of the Pioneers.

Here, the exact chronology of events becomes somewhat confused. Various biographies differ slightly, but it's clear that over the next few years the band earned popularity with radio audiences and eventually won a contract with Decca Records. Also, there were brief appearances in Charles Starrett and Gene Autry Westerns, during which our principle gained particular notice. These led to a few bit parts and featured roles. One of the most memorable, only for its irony, was as a heavy in a Gene Autry film.

Beginning in 1934, he assumed the stage name Dick Weston. By 1937 he had left The Sons of the Pioneers to concentrate on a career in movies. His first big break was the one he didn't get when he tried out for the starring role in a singing cowboy series at Universal Studios. That led him to Republic Studios, where his name was changed to Roy Rogers. It was at about this time that fate stepped in. Gene Autry was engaged in a salary dispute. The studio suspended him and began promoting Rogers as their new singing cowboy star. From then until 195, he starred in 81 films by Republic. One might think the circumstance would have caused a rift between the two stars, but they were friends and remained so. Autry's quarrel had not been with Rogers, and in a brief time the matter with the studio was resolved.

Before World War II began, most of Roy Rogers' movies had him playing the role of one or another historical character, such as Jesse James or Wild Bill Hickok. Of course the only thing about any of the scripts that was historically accurate was the name of the character Rogers played. All else was fiction of the purest Hollywood sort. When the war began, Gene Autry enlisted in the Army Air Corps, providing an opening at the studio for more lavish musical productions in Rogers' films. The plots tended more to the cops and robbers of the West sort, with a generous sprinkling of Axis spies and saboteurs. From then until he left Republic in 1951 to pursue a career in television, Rogers was the most popular cowboy hero in films, and Republic did all it could to enhance that popularity by dubbing him "King of the Cowboys."

In 1933, while touring with The Sons of the Pioneers, Rogers met his first wife, Grace Arlene Wilkins, in Roswell, New Mexico. Those were lean times and the band often had to feed themselves with small game taken with a shotgun. An idle comment on the air about wishing

This is Roy Rogers, as his fans remember him best, chasing bad guys down the studio back-lot trail, astride Trigger. Rogers made his earliest films as a member of The Sons of the Pioneers, then as a bad guy in a Gene Autry film. Trigger, whose original name was "Golden Cloud," made his first major screen appearance carrying Olivia de Haviland, as the Maid Marian, in the 1938 film, The Adventures of Robin Hood, *which starred Errol Flynn.*

he had a lemon pie brought the young woman to the studio the next evening with two of them. There was an immediate spark between them and for three years they corresponded, with Rogers visiting as often as he could manage. In June of 1936 the couple was wed.

There had been no children by 1940 and the couple chose to adopt their daughter, Cheryl. Shortly after, Arlene became pregnant with their second daughter, Linda Lou. A son, Roy Rogers Jr, followed her four years later. The year before, Rogers legally changed his name to that which millions of fans worldwide had come to know him. A few days after their baby boy's birth Arlene was stricken with a blood clot that prematurely ended her life.

Dale Evans had been playing opposite Rogers for a couple of years before the family had been stricken. In the months that followed, their professional relationship became more personal and, no doubt, Rogers felt that nannies and nurses, however devoted they may have been, were no substitute for a mother for his children. The two were married on New Year's Eve 1947, transforming their professional collaboration into a loving life partnership.

Many of the movies Rogers did during the years immediately following the war had social themes far ahead of their time. Wise use of natural resources was stressed. They included such subjects as land and water conservation and prevention of pollution, promoting ethical hunting and fishing standards, tree farming and replanting to replenish harvested timber, the evils of commercial game poaching, care for orphans and honoring American Indian treaty rights. These were all subjects about which Rogers, as a hunter, fisherman, outdoor sportsman, parent and the grandson of a Choctaw cared deeply.

While not a serious collector, Rogers acquired dozens of firearms during his lifetime. Many were gifts from admirers, others were pieces used in his movies and television shows. As a highly ranked competitive shotgunner, and an

Dale Evans' hands were too small to use a Single Action Army Colt revolver efficiently. When she had to use a gun on screen, she was armed with this much smaller Colt Police Positive revolver. A dummy ejector rod housing affixed to the right side of the barrel gave it the look of a proper Western sixgun. (Courtesy The Roy Rogers and Dale Evans Museum)

Roy Rogers without his sixshooters would be unthinkable, but there were some places where restrictive gun regulations made it illegal for him to do so. For such occasions he used this rig. These revolvers are dummies, incapable of firing a shot. (Courtesy The Autry Museum of Western Heritage)

avid hunter, the guns he used for his pleasure had more to do with those activities. He was also a vocal spokesman for hunter and firearms safety programs and for gun rights issues, often working closely with the NRA. For many of the performers who were his contemporaries, firearms were of little more consequence than any other props used in their movies. Rogers really did know how to use his and thoroughly enjoyed doing so. When the Single Action Shooting Society (SASS), a group that promotes shooting competitions using the guns of the Old West was formed, Rogers became one of its most enthusiastic advocates. For its part, SASS has adopted The Roy Rogers and Dale Evans Happy Trails Childrens' Foundation as its special charity project and profits from some of the annual End of Trail championship match activities are donated to that worthy effort.

Most of the Rogers gun collection is housed in the Roy Rogers and Dale Evans Museum, which can be seen from the highway just off Interstate 15 in Victorville, California. However, one of the more interesting exhibits is in the Autry Museum of Western Heritage, in Los Angeles. During personal appearance tours in such cities as New York and Chicago, and overseas in England and continental Europe, Rogers was usually wearing a pair of sixguns in one of the distinctive brown and black trimmed hand-tooled double rigs that were designed for him and used throughout most of his career. One might suppose that a world famous personality such as he might have gotten special permission from the authorities to bring his guns along in places where such things are normally restricted or prohibited. That may have happened on occasion, but these particular guns are non-firing dummies-strictly for show. Gold-plated and fitted with Hollywood-style plastic imitation stag stocks, it's as impressive looking a rig from a distance as if the guns were the real thing.

The revolver used by Dale Evans in her Queen of the West persona is interesting and indicative of the lengths to which Hollywood's prop masters will go to maintain a Western look and accommodate the needs of a performer. The gun is a Colt Police Positive model, one of the firm's smallest double action revolvers. It's fitted with ivory stocks and has a fake ejector rod housing to make it look similar to the Single Action Army revolvers Rogers carried on screen. Dale Evans was a small woman and one of the larger sixguns like her husband wore would have appeared clumsy in her tiny hands. A Model 1877 Lightning might have been about the right size and would certainly have appeared more authentic, but the long, heavy, double-action trigger stroke might have been too difficult for her to manage efficiently. The "Westernized" Police Positive provided a reasonable solution and few in the audience perceived anything amiss.

Beginning with his starring role at Republic, Rogers carried his sixguns in a double buscadero rig of the typical Hollywood style made by Ed Gilmore of North Hollywood. With lots of conchos and floral carving, the rigs were distinctive for the black border trim around the brown leather. There were several belts and holsters of

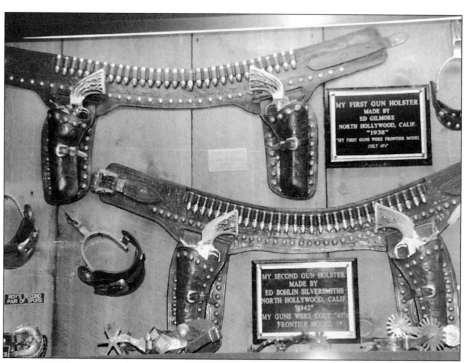

The first and second sixgun rigs Rogers used are nearly identical, but were crafted by Ed Gilmore and Ed Bohlin, respectively. Plastic simulated stag stocks are fitted to his first sixguns and the genuine article, East Indian sambar staghorn, accent the nickel-plated sixguns of the second set. (Courtesy The Roy Rogers and Dale Evans Museum)

nearly identical appearance made by Ed Bolin and by Nudie's Rodeo Tailors. The leather took quite a beating during filming, what with the staged fights, scuffles on the ground and fairly frequent soaking in the studio creeks, lakes and rivers. For that reason, some were used for on-camera action scenes and others for production numbers and personal appearances. The first rig was in especially poor condition and has been lovingly restored to some semblance of its original grandeur by one of the finest craftsmen in the business, Jim Lockwood, of Legends in Leather, in Prescott, Arizona.

The first pair of guns he used was stocked with plastic imitation staghorn. Their blue is worn thin and the case hardened colors have faded. There's a sneaky little secret about them, however. While described as .45s, only one is chambered for that cartridge; the other is a .38-40. That could be problematical if they really were used to bring bad guys to justice, but it makes little or no difference when they are fed with 5-in-1 blanks. By 1942 a pair of revolvers more suited to the heroic image of the Holly-wood-style singing cowboy began appearing on Rogers' hips. These were nickel-plated SAA Colts, with 4-3/4-inch barrels, and had genuine sambar stag stocks. The markings on their barrels have been almost completely polished away by the refinishing, and they, too, are .38-40s.

Nudie made the third rig for Rogers in 1949. It differed slightly from the earlier ones in that the belt had gold trim around the top. The guns got a bit showier, as well. These nickel-plated .45s were stocked with mother-of-pearl with a carved horse head. The one in the right holster has a chip at its heel; the result of the gun having been used at one time as a hammer.

Among the more interesting of the guns he used was a pair of gold-plated .45s with 7-1/2-inch barrels. Stocked with nicely aged simulated ivory, their most significant feature is that they are smoothbores. Made especially for aerial shooting with shot cartridges, they were originally ordered for the Miller Brothers 101 Ranch Wild West Show. Rogers wielded them expertly, powdering thrown targets to the amazement of his watching fans during personal appearances at fairs and rodeos. Most left convinced that he was quite capable of duplicating in real life the feats of marksmanship depicted in his movies.

For his part, Roy Rogers seems always to have thought of himself as Leonard Slye. He is known to have said that, when confronted with a problem, he thought to himself, "What would Roy Rogers do?" There seems no doubt that, however he may have envisioned himself, he truly did become the Roy Rogers his fans imagined him to be.

During Roy Rogers' first few years at Republic Studios, his gunbelt and holsters took a terrible beating during filming and the rig was nearly useless when it was retired. Jim Lockwood, of Legends in Leather in Prescott, Arizona, used his considerable skill to restore the much-abused outfit to a presentable state. The holsters for this set are closed at the bottom. That feature can be hard on a handgun, because dirt and moisture can be trapped causing excessive wear and, possibly, rust. (Courtesy The Roy Rogers and Dale Evans Museum)

Nudie's Rodeo Tailors, of North Hollywood, crafted in 1949 the third rig Roy Rogers used. It featured gold trim, to promote the marketing of Roy Rogers products in an ad campaign called, "Goldmine for '49." The campaign capitalized on the 100th anniversary of the discovery of gold in California. At the same time, Rogers returned to using blued SAA Colts with case hardened colored frames. They were stocked with mother-of-pearl and featured a carved horse's head (presumably representing Trigger). There's a chip missing from the heel of the stock of this revolver, as the result of using its butt as a hammer. (Courtesy The Roy Rogers and Dale Evans Museum)

This publicity still dates from Rogers' early years with Republic Studios. That's his first rig on his hips and the original Trigger. Most male horses used in the movies are gelded, because stallions tend to be dangerous animals. Trigger was a rare exception. As spirited as he was, he was an exceptionally gentle horse and loved being around children. (Courtesy The Roy Rogers and Dale Evans Museum)

The open bottom of the holster and the edge trim indicate that the rig Rogers is wearing in this publicity photo is his third one. The revolver has a 7-1/2-inch barrel, so it isn't one of his usual movie guns, but may be one of the pair of gold-plated smoothbores he used for exhibition shooting. (Courtesy The Roy Rogers and Dale Evans Museum)

George "Gabby" Hayes was Roy Rogers' sidekick in 40 of his films. A veteran of more than 130 motion pictures and a successful career in legitimate theater and vaudeville, Hayes played the bad guy in most of his early roles in Westerns. His screen image notwithstanding, Hayes was an intelligent man and a professional who, when he began doing comic relief took to it seriously and became, arguably, the best of the lot. He and Roy were close friends and the Rogers children thought of him as one of the family. The leather he used and the guns he carried on screen were the antithesis of those Rogers used. (Courtesy The Roy Rogers and Dale Evans Museum)

During his African safari Roy Rogers carried this nickel-plated Smith & Wesson Model 27 .357 Magnum. The Luger, seen above, is one of several pistols that TV sidekick and former member of The Sons of the Pioneers, Pat Brady, gave Rogers. (Courtesy The Roy Rogers and Dale Evans Museum)

This is a pair of "King of the Cowboys" commemoratives. There were several commemorative issues of firearms associated with Roy Rogers and his career. They included rifles, BB guns and several different handgun issues. (Courtesy The Roy Rogers and Dale Evans Museum)

This is the deluxe edition of "The Roy Rogers .45, The Gun That Won The Westerns" commemorative and, as the certificate indicates, bears serial number 00001. Tastefully engraved, with a pattern reminiscent of the style of Cuno Helfricht, it has genuine mother-of-pearl stocks. The United States Historical Society issued this series. (Courtesy The Roy Rogers and Dale Evans Museum)

One of the most attractive pieces in the Roy Rogers collection is this 5-1/2-inch barreled .45 caliber Single Action Army Colt. Fully engraved, it is gold plated and the stocks are sterling silver with gold accents. (Courtesy The Roy Rogers and Dale Evans Museum)

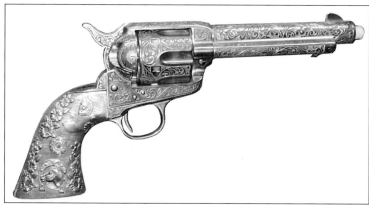

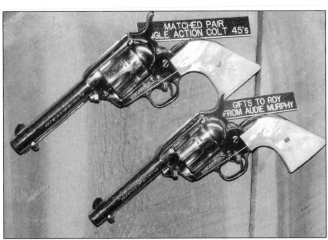

This pair of nickel-plated Second Generation Single Action Army .45 Colt revolvers, with 4-3/4-inch barrels and mother-of-pearl stocks was a gift to Roy Rogers from his friend, Audie Murphy. Murphy was the most decorated American soldier of World War II. His awards included The Medal of Honor. After the war Murphy became an actor and appeared in numerous Westerns. (Courtesy The Roy Rogers and Dale Evans Museum)

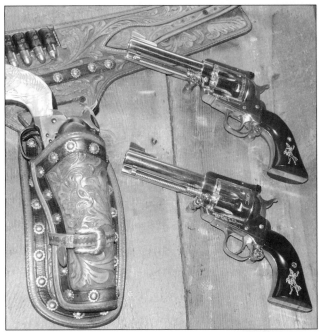

These Ruger Blackhawk revolvers are from a special run made for Buckeye Distributors and fitted with dual cylinders chambered for the .38-40 and 10mm cartridges. As originally issued they were blued, had 6-1/2-inch barrels and goncalo alves stocks. The barrels on these have been shortened to 4-5/8 inches and they've been gold plated. The stocks are black micarta, with a scrimshawed rendition of Roy Rogers mounted on a rearing Trigger. (Courtesy The Roy Rogers and Dale Evans Museum)

Roy Rogers accumulated a great number of firearms during his lifetime but, according to Roy "Dusty" Rogers Jr., he was not truly a gun collector, per se. Most of the guns in his collection were either pieces he used in his work or gifts from friends or from companies that used his name to promote charitable causes in which he was interested. However, he was an avid hunter and a highly ranked competitive shotgunner. Among Rogers' favorites was the Pigeon Grade 12-gauge Winchester Model 12 shotgun seen here, with the luggage tag hanging from its barrel. He bought it from Clark Gable, who was a shooting buddy. (Courtesy The Roy Rogers and Dale Evans Museum)

Here's a star-studded lineup of good guys and bad guys. Although Roy Rogers was their top player throughout most of the 1940s, Republic Studios produced Westerns with numerous other stars. This promotional group photo includes: (standing L to R) Tom Tyler, Ray "Crash" Corrigan, Allan "Rocky" Lane, Monte Hale, George Chesebro (a heavy), Kermit Maynard (he played heroes and villains), (kneeling) Tom Keene, Roy Rogers and William Farnum (a major star of silent films who became one of the finest character players in talkies).

This pair of gold-plated, Single Action Army Colt revolvers would be rare and highly collectible, even if it was not associated with Roy Rogers. Originally ordered for the Miller Brothers 101 Ranch Wild West Show, they have smooth bores for use with shot cartridges in aerial shooting. Rogers used them for that purpose during personal appearances at fairs and rodeos. (Courtesy The Roy Rogers and Dale Evans Museum)

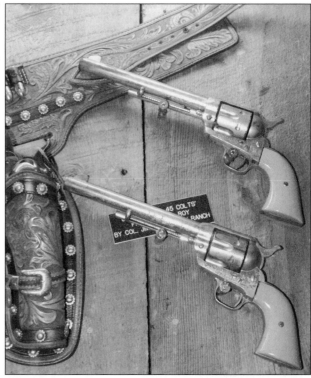

Charles Starrett
(The Durango Kid)

LEAN AND TALL, with the chiseled facial features associated with the leading man in a romance or drawing room comedy, Charles Starrett appears to have been more than content to play the Saturday afternoon matinee Western hero. He seems always to have been drawn to show business. He ran off with a vaudeville show when he was only 13 years of age. His angry father soon caught up with him and shipped the lad off to military school to teach him some discipline and responsibility.

Starrett was born March 28, 1904, in Athol, Massachusetts, the youngest in a family of nine children. He was by no means a child of poverty as so many others in the motion picture business had been before finding success in Hollywood. Instead, he was an heir to the Starrett Precision Tool Company fortune. The firm is still in business and is owned by its founder's descendants after more than 100 years. With his share of the family inheritance, and the money he earned and invested during his motion picture career, he was comfortably well off.

Starrett was a Dartmouth University alumnus and his slot on the varsity football team got him into his first film, a bit part in the Richard Dix football flick, *The Quarterback,*

from Paramount. Stage work followed graduation, first as a student of the American Academy of Dramatic Arts, followed by a stint with a stock company, then in the legitimate theater on Broadway, where a scout once again caused Paramount to take notice of him. He made half a dozen features with them, beginning in 1932, and then began freelancing. Columbia put him under contract in 1935, at $400 per week. That was $50 less than he'd earned at Paramount, but still, quite excellent money for the time.

Columbia started him off in Westerns. He was taking the place of Col. Tim McCoy, but Starrett made it clear to the studio that he wanted other roles, too. He got a few, but was doing so well in the oaters that the studio insisted he continue. Bound by his contract, he went along with the program. Each year the studio raised his salary, which made the matter much more palatable. In the end, he bowed to the inevitable. During the years between 1935 and his retirement from films in 1952, he starred in 131 Westerns at Columbia-a record for the genre.

The turning point for Starrett began in 1940, when what had been planned as a one-off feature, *The Durango Kid,* was released. A major hit, the film was still popular with audiences five years later, when the studio decided to bring the character back in (what else?) *The Return of the Durango Kid*. The masked rider, bane of evil-doers, mounted on a pure white steed (Raider), went on to chase bad guys down through a total of 64 features.

Charles Starrett's Colt SAA sixguns are a bit out of the ordinary for a "B" Western hero, but worthy of note to the serious collector. Sheathed in floral-carved brown leather holsters, with laced back edges, the rig is likely to have been made by the Denver firm of H.H.

Heiser. The revolvers have 5-1/2-inch barrels and are nickel-plated; so far, not so different from the norm. However, rather than the usual ivory, pearl or plastic staghorn, they are stocked with wood and checkered in the rare fleur-des-lis pattern. Moreover, the deep-set inletting of the medallions, and the fact that the medallions on the right face forward, tell us the guns were made between 1911 and 1929. Unfortunately, as is the case with so many Hollywood guns, they appear to have been refinished.

During the 1930s, the musical interludes in Charles Starrett Westerns usually featured The Sons of the Pioneers, with whom he's seen here. They left Columbia Pictures for Republic Studios in the early 1940s, where they resumed working with their old partner and founding member of the group, Roy Rogers.

To see Charles Starrett seated casually on his trusty steed, Raider, as in this publicity still, one would hardly suspect that he was a New England-born, Ivy League college graduate. He might have had a lucrative career in the family tool manufacturing business, but decided early on to make his own way, which he did quite successfully. By the time he retired from the screen he'd starred in 131 Western films. In 64 of those he portrayed the character for which he is best remembered, The Durango Kid.

Charles Starrett's hat, neckerchief, boots, sixguns and holsters, like those of many other Western movie stars, became a sort of uniform. Audiences came to expect to see the same outfit from one picture to the next. (Courtesy The Autry Museum of Western Heritage)

Having started on the legitimate stage, Starrett's intention was to be a serious actor, but the good salary he earned doing oaters caused him to stick with the genre. Eventually he realized that he genuinely enjoyed doing them.

A closer look at the Single Action Army Colts that Starrett used in most of his Durango Kid films reveals rare fleur-de-lis *checkered walnut sstocks with the deep inletted medallions characteristic of manufacture between 1911 and 1929. (Courtesy The Autry Museum of Western Heritage)*

John Wayne

THE MAN WE know as John Wayne was born to the Morrison family and originally named Marion Robert. His middle name was changed early on leaving him with the alliterative moniker, Marion Michael Morrison. Hollywood dubbed him John Wayne. Western movie fans around the world know him simply and fondly as The Duke. That nickname was derived from his dog, an Airedale named Duke that accompanied him as he delivered newspapers in Glendale, California. His family had moved west from Winterset, Iowa, when he was 6. When he passed the local fire station someone would always comment, "Here come Big Duke and Little Duke." No recollection remains as to which of the two was which. Amusingly, Duke was also the name of the horse he rode in the first six Western films he made for Warner Brothers. He never did make his screen name official in court, unlike most film stars, whose given names were changed by the studios. Yet, John Wayne he was, and ever will be.

Many celebrities become controversial, usually for involvement in some form or other of scandal. About John Wayne there was never a breath of scandal, but during the 1960s and 1970s an increasingly liberal element in Hollywood and in the news media tended to be critical of him. As early as the 1940s he had been active and outspoken against the very real attempts by communists to influence the film industry. From then on it was obvious to anyone who cared to notice that Wayne was proudly, even ferociously patriotic. During the Vietnam War, anti-war, even anti-American, feelings were widespread and vocal. Attitudes toward the military were particularly vitriolic. John Wayne was just as vocal in his support of the military and was frequently criticized for it in very personal ways. He dismissed out of hand those who did so, stating with eloquent simplicity, "I've tried to live my life so that my family would love me and my friends respect me. The others can do whatever the hell they please."

Wayne's career began inauspiciously in 1926, as an assistant prop man with Fox Studios. It was a summer job between semesters at The University of Southern California arranged by the football coach, Howard Jones, for his players. There, he was befriended by director John Ford, who thought enough of Wayne to put him on screen in a few small parts. While the young man's acting was crude, he demonstrated a certain presence on screen that made audiences like him. His first lead role came in 1930. The picture was *The Big Trail*, a major film directed by Raul Walsh.

During the 1930s John Wayne paid his dues, slowly improving his craft as an actor, mostly playing feature or leading roles in "B" Westerns. It was in the 1939 classic, *Stagecoach*, that "Star Quality" was first associated with his name. From then until his final appearance in *The Shootist*, in 1976, he was at or near the top of every list of box office favorites.

While critics and fans tend to remember him best in his Western roles, Wayne had no desire to be type-cast in such parts. To that end, he made a point of playing a wide variety of other roles, including seamen, police detectives, even a 19th century diplomat responsible for opening trade with Japan, and a most unlikely historical character, the Mongol leader, Ghengis Khan, in *The Conqueror*. Though he had wanted desperately to serve in the military, through no fault of his own, that was never to be. A football injury to his shoulder made him ineligible. Nevertheless, in his motion pictures he managed to wear the uniform of all branches of the U.S. armed forces in several historical periods. It was the Marine, Sgt. Striker, that he played in 1948's *The Sands of Iwo Jima* for which he was first nominated to receive an Academy Award. But it took 21 years before he earned the gold statuette by playing Marshal Rooster Cogburn in *True Grit*. Many fans believe, also, that he should have won for his role in *The Searchers*.

In his Oscar-winning role as "...the one-eyed fat man," U.S. Marshal Rooster Cogburn, John Wayne played a whiskey-swilling, aging gunfighter. The character had humor, courage and determination, which the title of the film states much more concisely as, True Grit. *That accurately described the character and man who played him.*

Wayne went so far to keep from being pinned down to Western roles as to turn away the lead in what would become a television classic, *Gunsmoke*, suggesting instead that his friend James Arness be pegged for the role of Marshal Matt Dillon. In spite of such efforts, he was still inextricably associated with the Western genre.

A gun collector, shooter and avid hunter, John Wayne knew and appreciated fine firearms. This was often reflected in his films. To be sure, in his "B"-Western days he sported the fancy leather and the flashy guns expected of a cowboy hero, but beginning with his appearance in *Stagecoach,* most of his guns and leather were more workmanlike. Certainly there was a bit of license taken with his frequent use of the loop-levered Model 92 Winchesters, of which there were several. With them he managed to add a bit of panache in otherwise relatively ordinary gunfight scenes. Those carbines may, in some way have also represented something of a lucky charm to him. They were used in the most memorable scenes in several of his best-liked Western features.

In most of his later films he also carried a Colt SAA with a 4-3/4-inch barrel. The gun had

gone gray with age and frequent use. It was distinctive for its worn appearance and old two-piece ivory stocks that had turned golden with time. Wayne carried that revolver in a simple holster on a wide gunbelt, high and tight, behind his right hip. In the thirteenth cartridge loop from the end on the right side of the belt he usually placed a .45-70 cartridge. That has been the subject of much speculation and several different explanations. The best one is probably that it was a technique used by some in the Old West who might encounter a prolonged gunfight to alert them they were down to their last couple of rounds for the six-shooter and it was time to get out of the area.

While John Wayne was thoroughly familiar with the 19th century firearms used in the Westerns he made, when it came to off-screen use for his hunting activities, his choices were very much up-to-date. In saying that, the reader must bear in mind that he passed away more than 20 years ago and his peak years afield ended more than a decade before. That said, his upland game and waterfowling chores were addressed with a couple of Browning shotguns, a Citori over/under and an Auto-5, respectively. For

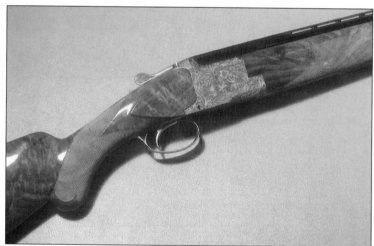

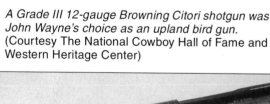

A Grade III 12-gauge Browning Citori shotgun was John Wayne's choice as an upland bird gun. (Courtesy The National Cowboy Hall of Fame and Western Heritage Center)

Wayne's waterfowl gun was this 12-gauge Browning Auto-5. Although it's had excellent care, it shows evidence of many seasons of regular use in a duck blind. (Courtesy The National Cowboy Hall of Fame and Western Heritage Center)

medium and large game he favored a Weatherby .300 Magnum, a rifle he liked so well that he actually endorsed it in the company's early advertising. All three of these guns show the effects of extensive use, but have had excellent care and maintenance.

While there are many pieces among the items in The Duke's personal gun collection that may interest collectors, the elaborately engraved, gold-inlaid and ivory-stocked revolvers that he used in his last movie, *The Shootist*, are among the most handsome. They were presented to him in 1955 by the Great Western Company, which made very close copies of the classic Colt SAA revolvers. Gun buffs cringed at the end of the final shootout. Ron Howard picked one of the revolvers up and used it to stop the final adversary, the bartender, from blasting the fatally wounded Wayne. Then, disgusted by having just been forced to kill a man, threw the gun across the room as Wayne nodded approval and died. But just as actors have stunt doubles, so to do some props. The sixgun Howard threw was actually a Ruger Blackhawk that had been modified to look like the fancy GW revolvers.

Over the course of his lifetime, The Duke became an American icon and a symbol of all that is right, just and good about his country. On May 22, 1979, to seek official recognition of that, just before his passing, Irish-born Maureen O'Hara and English-born Elizabeth Taylor appeared before a Congressional Committee to ask that a Congressional Gold Medal be struck to honor their good friend John Wayne. O'Hara, a frequent co-star, spoke simply but passionately of the man she loved so dearly.

"It is my great honor to be here," she said. "I beg you to strike a medal for Duke; to order the President to strike it. And I feel it should say just one thing, 'John Wayne - American.'"

On the following day, May 23rd, the order for the medal was issued. Wayne died a few days later, on June 11, 1979. The medal was presented to his family at the Capitol in Washington, D.C., on March 6, 1980.

John Wayne was a modest man. He once stated that his epitaph should read, in Spanish, "Feo, fuerte y formal." He wanted to be remembered as having been ugly, strong and dignified.

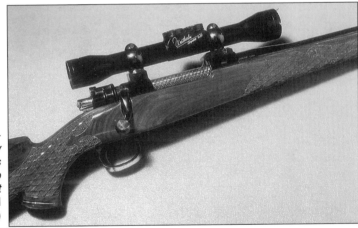

Early Weatherby rifles were built on fine quality German-made Mauser actions that were commercially produced for sporting use. John Wayne used this .300 Weatherby Magnum extensively and thought so much of it that he lent his name to the endorsement of the product. (Courtesy The National Cowboy Hall of Fame and Western Heritage Center)

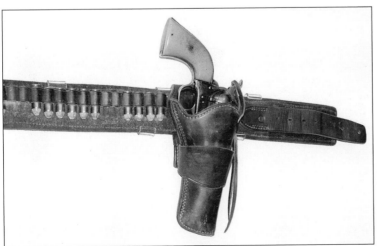

Made in 1893, the Duke's ivory-handled Single Action Army Colt .45 has had a lot of use over the years. Very little of its original finish remains, and that only in the most protected areas. It became familiar to moviegoers the world over, because he used it in most of the Westerns he did during the last two decades of his life. (Courtesy The National Cowboy Hall of Fame and Western Heritage Center)

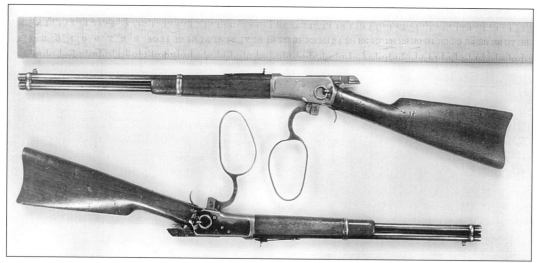

There may have been as many as half a dozen large-loop lever carbines used by Wayne in his movies over the course of his career. Their barrels were shortened to prevent him hitting himself in the shoulder with the front sight as the rifle was spun. In the process, the muzzles were crudely crowned. Since they only fired blanks, that didn't matter at all. In order for the cartridge to feed into the chamber, a thin, but strong, wire was used to guide the round into it. Otherwise, it would rise too high and catch on the upper edge of the chamber, locking the lever in mid spin. That could lead to a wrist, hand or shoulder injury. (Courtesy The National Cowboy Hall of Fame and Western Heritage Center)

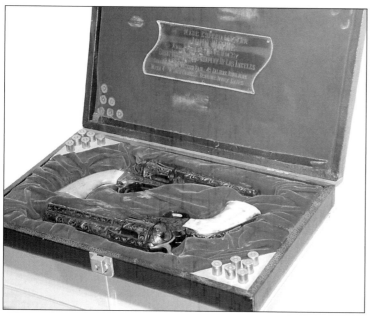

Fully engraved, stocked with smooth, one-piece ivory and resting in a red velvet-lined case, these single-action .45s with 4-3/4-inch barrels, made by Great Western, were presented to John Wayne in 1955. They are certainly the finest revolvers the firm ever produced. These are the sixguns The Duke used in his final film, The Shootist. (Courtesy The National Cowboy Hall of Fame and Western Heritage Center)

This handsome Single Action Army .45 caliber Colt revolver was commissioned to commemorate his epic motion picture, The Alamo, which Wayne produced and in which he played the role of Davy Crockett. It has a 5-1/2-inch barrel, is gold-plated, superbly engraved and accented with finely carved ivory stocks. (Courtesy The National Cowboy Hall of Fame and Western Heritage Center)

How'd They Do That?

MAKING WESTERN MOVIES and television shows can be dangerous work. Saloon brawls, falling horses, fires, gunfights, runaway stagecoaches and wagons, falls from buildings and cliffs, simulating gunshot wounds and ricochets, are among the myriad hazards faced by performers, extras and production personnel alike. Injuries are not costly in terms of production delays, but are personal tragedies to those directly involved. Thus, for both humane and economic reasons, safety becomes a primary concern in any action sequence.

In the early days of Hollywood it was accepted practice to trip horses to make them fall. That they often broke their legs, their necks or were otherwise seriously injured was regarded by many studios as part of the price of doing business. Fight sequences frequently looked phony on film. If they didn't, it was the result of actual blows being struck. That wasn't especially healthy for the participants. Expert marksmen were sometimes employed to place near miss shots with live ammunition close enough to the actors to add drama and realism. All that began to change in the 1930s and by the 1940s property masters, stunt coordinators, Foley artists and

special effects wizards were simulating violent action that looked real, but with minimal risk to man and beast.

Horses, for example, were trained to fall on command, but it was done so that the animal dropped into soft sand, coming up unhurt. A bottle smashed over an actor's head might cause a concussion, or even death. So bottles made of a secret formula, the key ingredient of which is sugar, look real and break into pieces harmlessly. The panes of glass through which actors fall or are pushed are made of the same stuff, shattering realistically, but harmlessly, with no danger of cuts, because the edges are actually rounded.

Republic Studios was among the pioneers in the staging of on-screen fights. Where before the actors or their stand-ins simply did mock battle, such scenes came to be choreographed, blow by simulated blow and tumble by exciting tumble. Techniques were developed for throwing punches that actually missed, but between the optical illusion created by the camera's angle and the reaction of the individual supposedly being hit, the audience could be made to believe what the eye saw was real. Once the film was processed, during the editing phase Foley artists could add the sound effects that blended auditory realism with the visual.

In most instances the firearms used in the old "B" Western movies were real. Many that were kept in the studio arsenals of that time would today be classified as valuable antiques. Unfortunately, frequent handling and neglect following the use of blackpowder blanks wore the finish and corroded the bores of many. Sixty years ago, they were just old guns, but by the 1960s and 1970s the studios and the rental agencies came to realize that the better ones were worth a great deal of money and began selling them to collectors and replacing them with authentic-looking replicas.

Firearms safety on motion picture sets becomes an almost fanatical matter. Live ammunition of any kind is absolutely prohibited anywhere near the set, except in extraordinary circumstances. Even though no projectile is involved, blank ammunition is also carefully controlled, because it, too, can be dangerous. There is sufficient energy from the fired blank cartridge to do serious injury or cause death with nothing more than expanding gases and the paper wad used to contain the powder. For that reason, if you watch carefully, and use a bit of visual geometry, you will see that the actors are usually pointing their guns a bit wide of their cinematic adversaries.

Another major consideration is noise. Full-power blanks are just as loud as the real thing and unprotected exposure can cause serious hearing damage. Moreover, such noise can frighten horses, making them shy away from the source or, possibly, become uncontrollable. Half a ton of scared animal presents a danger all its own. Modern shooters are careful to wear hearing protection when on the firing line, but our heroes would look pretty silly wearing the muffs usually used, and their hats wouldn't fit too well over them. Moreover, their horses ears stuffed with cotton would look pretty strange, as well. Depending upon the needs in terms of sound and muzzle flash, blanks are made up in a variety of ways. All

A bullet striking a rock, then whizzing off in some random direction, is called a ricochet. It's accompanied by a high-pitched whistling sound. A small explosive squib load provides the visual impression, while a special effects rifle like this is used to simulate the sound, so that it all comes together as a POW...YAAaaannnnnggg. On the screen the player simply cringes slightly at the "near miss." (Courtesy The Autry Museum of Western Heritage)

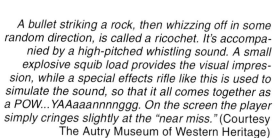

Expert archers are relatively rare, and even the best among them sometimes have bad days. For that reason, when the script calls for an arrow to strike a specific spot it's fired not with a bow, but a gun. The gun used is a pneumatic device like this one that propels the arrow with sufficient velocity to lodge it in the target. It's fired from very close range, but just off camera, to be sure the arrow hits its mark, without endangering the actor. (Courtesy The Autry Museum of Western Heritage)

that's really necessary, for example, is for the special effects people to make up quarter power blanks, so that the puff of smoke from the gun being fired looks right on film, but it's no more loud than ordinary conversation. The sound can be added during editing, while our hero can shoot between the ears of his galloping steed without worry about being bucked from the saddle.

In the old days of moviemaking, gunshot wounds were all but antiseptic. The blank cartridge would fire and the victim would clutch at his body and fall down. There was often no attempt to show blood. There might not even be a hole in the person's shirt. Modern audiences require more realism. To that end, special effects artists use squibs, small

explosive charges under the performer's shirt. The "shooting victim" wears protection under it to avoid harm. The charges are wired to a board and when the shots go off, the charges are ignited, simulating bullet strikes. These usually include copious amounts of simulated blood to add realism. In some instances, the appearance of reality is downright gruesome.

And, what about the Indians? Arrows whizzing about with near misses present a problem all their own. Few archers have the skill to place shots next to a person's head with absolute assurance there will be no injury. The trick here is to use a rifle. In this instance, a pneumatic rifle fired from very close range, but just off camera.

Simulated glass can be crystal clear or made in any color desired. It is easily molded into sheets, bottles, lamps, beer mugs or any other object. When dropped or struck it shatters easily, but harmlessly. Its edges are rounded to prevent cuts. The secret formula with which it's made uses sugar as its primary ingredient, so it can even be safely eaten, and tastes good as well. (Courtesy The Autry Museum of Western Heritage)

This is a squib shirt. Cuts in it are masked to keep them from being seen. Beneath it a player wears padding to prevent injury by the squibs as they are activated. When the action on screen calls for the performer to be shot, tiny explosives with simulated blood are set off remotely to make it look as though bullets are actually striking him. (Courtesy The Autry Museum of Western Heritage)

Making the action look genuine, while protecting cast and crew in the process, is an exacting task requiring careful planning, the mind of a scientist and the heart of an artist. They call it, "movie magic." And, as always, don't try this at home.

Blank cartridges can be made to provide as much or as little muzzle flash and explosive sound as desired. In the Westerns the most commonly used blanks are known as the 5 in 1. Based on the .38-40 cartridge, they can be used in rifles chambered for the .38-40 and .44-40 rounds and in revolvers for those rounds and the .45 Colt cartridge, as well. Thus, two rifle chamberings and three for revolvers, served by one blank cartridge, equal 5 in 1. (Courtesy The Autry Museum of Western Heritage.

THE ARMS LIBRARY

A Glossary of the Construction, Decoration and Use of Arms and Armor in All Countries and in All Times. By George Cameron Stone., Dover Publishing, New York 1999. Softcover. $39.95

An exhaustive study of arms and armor in all countries through recorded history - from the stone age up to the second world war. With over 4500 Black & White Illustrations. This Dover edition is an unabridged republication of the work originally published in 1934 by the Southworth Press, Portland MA. A new Introduction has been specially prepared for this edition.

Accoutrements of the United States Infantry, Riflemen, and Dragoons 1834-1839. by R.T. Huntington, Historical Arms Series No. 20. Canada: Museum Restoration. 58 pp. illus. Softcover. $8.95

Although the 1841 edition of the U.S. Ordnance Manual provides ample information on the equipment that was in use during the 1840s, it is evident that the patterns of equipment that it describes were not introduced until 1838 or 1839. This guide is intended to fill this gap in our knowledge by providing an overview of what we now know about the accoutrements that were issued to the regular infantryman, rifleman, and dragoon, in the 1830's with excursions into earlier and later years.

Age of the Gunfighter; Men and Weapons on the Frontier 1840-1900, by Joseph G. Rosa, University of Oklahoma Press, Norman, OK, 1999. 192 pp., illustrated. Paper covers. $21.95

Stories of gunfighters and their encounters and detailed descriptions of virtually every firearm used in the old West.

Air Guns, by Eldon G. Wolff, Duckett's Publishing Co., Tempe, AZ, 1997. 204 pp., illus Paper covers. $35.00

Historical reference covering many makers, European and American guns, canes and more.

Allied and Enemy Aircraft: May 1918; Not to be Taken from the Front Lines, Historical Arms Series No. 27. Canada: Museum Restoration. Softcover. $8.95

The basis for this title is a very rare identification manual published by the French government in 1918 that illustrated 60 aircraft with three or more views: French, English American, German, Italian, and Belgian, which might have been seen over the trenches of France. Each is describe in a text translated from the original French. This is probably the most complete collection of illustrations of WW1 aircraft which has survived.

American Beauty; The Prewar Colt National Match Government Model Pistol, by Timothy J. Mullin, Collector Grade Publications, Cobourg, Ontario, Canada. 72 pp., illustrated. $34.95

Includes over 150 serial numbers, and 20 spectacular color photos of factory engraved guns and other authenticated upgrades, including rare "double-carved" ivory grips.

The American Military Saddle, 1776-1945, by R. Stephen Dorsey & Kenneth L. McPheeters, Collector's Library, Eugene, OR, 1999. 400 pp., illustrated. $59.95

The most complete coverage of the subject ever writeen on the American Military Saddle. Nearly 1000 actual photos and official drawings, from the major public and private collections in the U.S. and Great Britain.

American Police Collectibles; Dark Lanterns and Other Curious Devices, by Matthew G. Forte, Turn of the Century Publishers, Upper Montclair, NJ, 1999. 248 pp., illustrated. $24.95

For collectors of police memorabilia (handcuffs, police dark lanterns, mechanical and chain nippers, rattles, billy clubs and nightsticks) and police historians.

Ammunition; Small Arms, Grenades, and Projected Munitions, by Greenhill Publishing. 144 pp., Illustrated. $22.95 The best concise guide to modern ammunition available today. Covers ammo for small arms, grenades, and projected munitions. 144 pp., Illustrated. As NEW – Hardcover.

Antique Guns, the Collector's Guide, 2nd Edition, edited by John Traister, Stoeger Publishing Co., So. Hackensack, NJ, 1994. 320 pp., illus. Paper covers. $19.95

Covers a vast spectrum of pre-1900 firearms: those manufactured by U.S. gunmakers as well as Canadian, French, German, Belgian, Spanish and other foreign firms.

Arming the Glorious Cause; Weapons of the Second War for Independence, by James B. Whisker, Daniel D. Hartzler and Larry W. Tantz, Old Bedford Village Press, Bedford, PA., 1998. 175 pp., illustrated. $45.00

A photographic study of Confederate weapons.

Arms & Accoutrements of the Mounted Police 1873-1973, by Roger F. Phillips and Donald J. Klancher, Museum Restoration Service, Ont., Canada, 1982. 224 pp., illus. $49.95

A definitive history of the revolvers, rifles, machine guns, cannons, ammunition, swords, etc. used by the NWMP, the RNWMP and the RCMP during the first 100 years of the Force.

Arms and Armor In Antiquity and The Middle Ages. By Charles Boutell, Combined Books Inc., PA 1996. 296 pp., w/ b/w illus. Also a descriptive Notice of Modern Weapons. Translated from the French of M.P. Lacombe, and with a preface, notes, and one additional chapter on Arms and Armour in England. $14.95

Arms and Armor in the Art Institute of Chicago. By Waltler J. Karcheski, Bulfinch, New York 1999. 128 pp., 103 color photos, 12 black & white illustrations. $50.00

The George F. Harding Collection of arms and armor is the most visited installation at the Art Institute of Chicago - a testament to the enduring appeal of swords, muskets and the other paraphernalia of medieval and early modern war. Organized both chronologically and by type of weapon, this book captures the best of this astonishing collection in 115 striking photographs - most in color - accompanied by illuminating text. Here are intricately filigreed breastplates and ivory-handled crossbows, samurai katana and Toledo-steel scimitars, elaborately decorated maces and beautifully carved flintlocks - a treat for anyone who has ever been beguiled by arms, armor and the age of chivalry.

Arms and Armor in Colonial America 1526-1783 by Harold Peterson, Dover Publishing, New York, 2000. 350 pages with over 300 illustrations, index, bibliography & appendix. Softcover. $29.95

Over 200 years of firearms, ammunition, equipment & edged weapons.

Arms and Armor: The Cleveland Museum of Art. By Stephen N. Fliegel, Abrams, New York, 1998. 172 color photos, 17 halftones. 181 pages. $49.50

Intense look at the culture of the warrior and hunter, with an intriguing discussion of the decorative arts found on weapons and armor, set against the background of political and social history. Also provides information on the evolution of armor, together with manufacture and decoration, and weapons as technology and art.

Arms and Equipment of the Civil War, by Jack Coggins, Barnes & Noble, Rockleight, N.J., 1999. 160 pp., illustrated. $12.98

This unique encyclopedia provides a new perspective on the war. It provides lively explanations of how ingenious new weapons spelled victory or defeat for both sides. Aided by more than 500 illustrations and on-the-scene comments by Union and Confederate soldiers.

Arms Makers of Colonial America, by James B. Whisker, Selinsgrove, PA:, 1992: Susquehanna University Press. 1st edition. 217 pages, illustrated. $45.00

A comprehensively documented historial survey of the broad spectrum of arms makers in America who were active before 1783.

Arms Makers of Maryland, by Daniel D. Hartzler, George Shumway, York, PA, 1975. 200 pp., illus. $50.00

A thorough study of the gunsmiths of Maryland who worked during the late 18th and early 19th centuries.

Arms Makers of Pennsylvania, by James B. Whisker, Selinsgrove, PA, Susquehanna Univ. Press, 1990. 1st edition. 218 pages, illustrated in black and white and color. $45.00

Concentrates primarily on the cottage industry gunsmiths & gun makers who worked in the Keystone State from it's early years through 1900.

Arms Makers of Western Pennsylvania, by James B. Whisker, Old Bedford Village Press. 1st edition. This deluxe hard bound edition has 176 pages, $45.00

Printed on fine coated paper, with many large photographs, and detailed text describing the period, lives, tools, and artistry of the Arms Makers of Western Pennsylvania.

Arsenal Of Freedom: The Springfield Armory 1890-1948, by Lt. Col. William Brophy, Andrew Mowbray, Inc., Lincoln, RI,1997. 20 pgs. of photos. 400 pages. As new - Softcover. $29.95

A year by year account drawn from offical records. Packed with reports, charts, tables, line drawings, and 20 page photo section.

Artistic Ingredients of the Longrifle, by George Shumway Publisher, 1989 102 pp., with 94 illus. $20.00

After a brief review of Pennsylvania-German folk art and architecture, to establish the artistic enviroment in which the longrifle was made, the author demonstrates that the sophisticated rococo decoration on the many of the finer longrifles is comparable to the best rococo work of Philadelphia cabinet makers and silversmiths.

The Art of Gun Engraving, by Claude Gaier and Pietro Sabatti, Knickerbocker Press, N.Y., 1999. 160 pp., illustrated. $34.95

The richness and detail lavished on early firearms represents a craftmanship nearly vanished. Beginning with crossbows in the 100's, hunting scenes, portraits, or mythological themes are intricately depicted within a few square inches of etched metal. The full-color photos contained herein recaptures this lost art with exquisite detail.

Astra Automatic Pistols, by Leonardo M. Antaris, FIRAC Publishing Co., Sterling, CO, 1989. 248 pp., illus. $55.00

Charts, tables, serial ranges, etc. The definitive work on Astra pistols.

Basic Documents on U.S. Martial Arms, commentary by Col. B. R. Lewis, reissue by Ray Riling, Phila., PA, 1956 and 1960. *Rifle Musket Model 1855.*

The first issue rifle of musket caliber, a muzzle loader equipped with the Maynard Primer, 32 pp. *Rifle Musket Model 1863.* The typical Union muzzle-loader of the Civil War, 26 pp. *Breech-Loading Rifle Musket Model 1866.* The first of our 50-caliber breechloading rifles, 12 pp. *Remington Navy Rifle Model 1870.* A commercial type breech-loader made at Springfield, 16 pp. *Lee Straight Pull Navy Rifle Model 1895.* A magazine cartridge arm of 6mm caliber. 23 pp. *Breech-Loading Arms* (five models) 27 pp. *Ward-Burton Rifle Musket 1871-16* pp. Each $10.00.

Battle Weapons of the American Revolution, by George C. Neuman, Scurlock Publishing Co., Texarkana, TX, 2001. 400 pp. Illus. Softcovers. $34.95

The most extensive photographic collection of Revolutionary War weapons ever in one volume. More than 1,600 photos of over 500 muskets, rifles, swords, bayonets, knives and other arms used by both sides in America's War for Independence.

The Bedford County Rifle and Its Makers, by George Shumway. 40pp. illustrated, Softcover. $10.00

The authors study of the graceful and distinctive muzzle-loading rifles made in Bedford County, Pennsylvania. Stands as a milestone on the long path to the understanding of America's longrifles.

Behold the Longrifle Again, by James B. Whisker, Old Bedford Village Press, Bedford, PA, 1997. 176 pp., illus. $45.00

Excellent reference work for the collector profusely illustrated with photographs of some of the finest Kentucky rifles showing front and back profiles and overall view.

The Belgian Rattlesnake; The Lewis Automatic Machine Gun, by William M. Easterly, Collector Grade Publications, Cobourg, Ontario, Canada, 1998. 584 pp., illustrated. $79.95

The most complete account ever published on the life and times of Colonel Isaac Newton Lewis and his crowning invention, the Lewis Automatic machine gun.

Beretta Automatic Pistols, by J.B. Wood, Stackpole Books, Harrisburg, PA, 1985. 192 pp., illus. $24.95

Only English-language book devoted to the Beretta line. Includes all important models.

The Big Guns, Civil War Siege, Seacoast, and Naval Cannon, by Edwin Olmstead, Wayne E. Stark, and Spencer C. Tucker, Museum Restoration Service, Bloomfield, Ontario, Canada, 1997. 360 pp., illustrated. $80.00

This book is designed to identify and record the heavy guns available to both sides by the end of the Civil War.

Birmingham Gunmakers, by Douglas Tate, Safari Press, Inc., Huntington Beach, CA, 1997. 300 pp., illus. $50.00

An invaluable book for anybody interested in the fine sporting arms crafted in this famous British gunmakers' city.

Blue Book of Gun Values, 22nd Edition, edited by S.P. Fjestad, Blue Book Publications, Inc. Minneapolis, MN 2001. $34.95

This new 22nd Edition simply contains more firearms values and information than any other single publication. Expanded to over 1,600 pages featuring over 100,000 firearms prices, the new Blue Book of Gun Values also contains over ¾ million words of text – no other book is even close! Most of the information contained in this publication is simply not available anywhere else, for any price!

Blue Book of Modern Black Powder Values, by Dennis Adler, Blue Book Publications, Inc. Minneapolis, MN 2000. 200 pp., illustrated. 41 color photos. Softcover. $14.95

This new title contains more up-to-date black powder values and related information than any other single publication. With 120 pages, this new book will keep you up to date on modern black powder models and prices, including most makes & models introduced this year! .

The Blunderbuss 1500-1900, by James D. Forman, Historical Arms Series No. 32. Canada: Museum Restoration, 1994. An excellent and authoritative booklet giving tons of information on the Blunderbuss, a very neglected subject. 40 pages, illustrated. Softcover. $8.95

Boarders Away I: With Steel-Edged Weapons & Polearms, by William Gilkerson, Andrew Mowbray, Inc. Publishers, Lincoln, RI, 1993. 331 pages. $48.00

Contains the essential 24 page chapter 'War at Sea' which sets the historical and practical context for the arms discussed. Includeds chapters on, Early Naval Weapons, Boarding Axes, Cutlasses, Officers Fighting Swords and Dirks, and weapons at hand of Random Mayhem.

Boarders Away, Volume II: Firearms of the Age of Fighting Sail, by William Gilkerson, Andrew Mowbray, Inc. Publishers, Lincoln, RI, 1993. 331 pp., illus. $65.00

Covers the pistols, muskets, combustibles and small cannon used aboard American and European fighting ships, 1626-1826.

The Book of Colt Firearms, by R. L. Wilson, Blue Book Publications, Inc, Minneapolis, MN, 1993. 616 pp., illus. $158.00

A complete Colt library in a single volume. In over 1,250.000 words, over 1,250 black and white and 67 color photographs, this mammoth work tells the Colt story from 1832 throught the present.

Boothroyd's Revised Directory of British Gunmakers, by Geoffrey Boothroyd, Long Beach, CA: Safari Press, 2000. Revised edition. 412pp, photos. $39.95

Over a 30 year period Geoffrey Boothroyd has accumulated information on just about every sporting gun maker that ever has existed in the British Isles from 1850 onward. In this magnificent reference work he has placed all the gun makers he has found over the years (over 1000 entries) in an alphabetical listing with as much information as he has been able to unearth. One of the best reference sources on all British makers (including Wales, Scotland and Ireland) in which you can find data on the most obscure as well as the most famous. Contains starting date of the business, addresses, proprietors, what they made and how long they operated with other interesting details for the collector of fine British guns.

Boston's Gun Bible, by Boston T. Party, Ignacio, CO: Javelin Press, August 2000. Expanded Edition.Softcover. $28.00

This mammoth guide for gun owners everywhere is a completely updated and expanded edition (more than 500 new pages!) of Boston T. Party's classic Boston on Guns and Courage. Pulling no punches, Boston gives new advice on which shoulder weapons and handguns to buy and why before exploring such topics as why you should consider not getting a concealed carry permit, what guns and gear will likely be outlawed next, how to spend within your budget, why you should go to a quality defensive shooting academy now, which guns and gadgets are inferior and why, how to stay off illegal government gun registration lists, how to spot an undercover agent trying to entrap law-abiding gun owners and much more.

Breech-Loading Carbines of the United States Civil War Period, by Brig. Gen. John Pitman, Armory Publications, Tacoma, WA, 1987. 94 pp., illus. $29.95

The first in a series of previously unpublished manuscripts originated by the late Brigadier General John Putnam. Exploded drawings showing parts actual size follow each sectioned illustration.

The Breech-Loading Single-Shot Rifle, by Major Ned H. Roberts and Kenneth L. Waters, Wolfe Publishing Co., Prescott, AZ, 1995. 333 pp., illus. $28.50

A comprehensive and complete history of the evolution of the Schutzen and single-shot rifle.

The Bren Gun Saga, by Thomas B. Dugelby, Collector Grade Publications, Cobourg, Ontario, Canada, 1999, revised and expanded edition. 406 pp., illustrated. $65.95

A modern, definitive book on the Bren in this revised expanded edition, which in terms of numbers of pages and illustrations is nearly twice the size of the original.

British Board of Ordnance Small Arms Contractors 1689-1840, by De Witt Bailey, Rhyl, England: W. S. Curtis, 2000. 150 pp. $18.00

Thirty years of research in the Archives of the Ordnance Board in London has identified more than 600 of these suppliers. The names of many can be found marking the regulation firearms of the period. In the study, the contractors are identified both alphabetically and under a combination of their date period together with their specialist trade.

The British Enfield Rifles, Volume 1, The SMLE Mk I and Mk III Rifles, by Charles R. Stratton, North Cape Pub. Tustin, CA, 1997. 150 pp., illus. Paper covers. $16.95

A systematic and thorough examination on a part-by-part basis of the famous British battle rifle that endured for nearly 70 years as the British Army's number one battle rifle.

British Enfield Rifles, Volume 2, No.4 and No.5 Rifles, by Charles R. Stratton, North Cape Publications, Tustin, CA, 1999. 150 pp., illustrated. Paper covers. $16.95

The historical background for the development of both rifles describing each variation and an explanation of all the "marks", "numbers" and codes found on most parts.

British Enfield Rifles, Volume 4, The Pattern 1914 and U. S. Model 1917 Rifles, by Charles R. Stratton, North Cape Publications, Tustin, CA, 2000. Paper covers. $16.95

One of the lease know American and British collectible military rifles is analyzed on a part by part basis. All markings and codes, refurbishment procedures and WW 2 upgrade are included as are the varios sniper rifle versions.

The British Falling Block Breechloading Rifle from 1865, by Jonathan Kirton, Tom Rowe Books, Maynardsville, TN, 2nd edition, 1997. 380 pp., illus. $70.00

Expanded 2nd edition of a comprehensive work on the British falling block rifle.

British Gun Engraving, by Douglas Tate, Safari Press, Inc., Huntington Beach, CA, 1999. 240 pp., illustrated. Limited, signed and numbered edition, in a slipcase. $80.00

A historic and photographic record of the last two centuries.

British Service Rifles and Carbines 1888-1900, by Alan M. Petrillo, Excaliber Publications, Latham, NY, 1994. 72 pp., illus, Paper covers. $11.95

A complete review of the Lee-Metford and Lee-Enfield rifles and carbines.

British Single Shot Rifles, Volume 1, Alexander Henry, by Wal Winfer, Tom Rowe, Maynardsville, TN, 1998, 200 pp., illus. $50.00

Detailed Study of the single shot rifles made by Henry. Illustrated with hundreds of photographs and drawings.

British Single Shot Rifles Volume 2, George Gibbs, by Wal Winfer, Tom Rowe, Maynardsville, TN, 1998. 177 pp., illus. $50.00

Detailed study of the Farquharson as made by Gibbs. Hundreds of photos.

British Single Shot Rifles, Volume 3, Jeffery, by Wal Winfer, Rowe Publications, Rochester, N.Y., 1999. 260 pp., illustrated. $60.00

The Farquharsan as made by Jeffery and his competitors, Holland & Holland, Bland, Westley, Manton, etc. Large section on the development of nitro cartridges including the .600.

British Single Shot Rifles, Vol. 4; Westley Richards, by Wal Winfer, Rowe Publications, Rochester, N.Y., 2000. 265 pages, illustrated, photos. $60.00

In his 4th volume Winfer covers a detailed study of the Westley Richards single shot rifles, including Monkey Tails, Improved Martini, 1872,1873, 1878,1881, 1897 Falling Blocks. He also covers Westley Richards Cartridges, History and Reloading information.

British Small Arms Ammunition, 1864-1938 (Other than .303 inch), by Peter Labbett, Armory Publications, Seattle, WA. 1993, 358 pages, illus. Four-color dust jacket. $79.00

A study of British military rifle, handgun, machine gun, and aiming tube ammunition through 1 inch from 1864 to 1938. Photo-illustrated including the firearms that chambered the cartridges.

The British Soldier's Firearms from Smoothbore to Rifled Arms, 1850-1864, by Dr. C.H. Roads, R&R Books, Livonia, NY, 1994. 332 pp., illus. $49.00

A reprint of the classic text covering the development of British military hand and shoulder firearms in the crucial years between 1850 and 1864.

British Sporting Guns & Rifles, compiled by George Hoyem, Armory Publications, Coeur d'Alene, ID, 1997. 1024 pp., illus. In two volumes. $250.00
Eighteen old sporting firearms trade catalogs and a rare book reproduced with their color covers in a limited, signed and numbered edition.

Browning Dates of Manufacture, compiled by George Madis, Art and Reference House, Brownsboro, TX, 1989. 48 pp. $10.00
Gives the date codes and product codes for all models from 1824 to the present.

Browning Sporting Arms of Distinction 1903-1992, by Matt Eastman, Matt Eastman Publications, Fitzgerald, GA, 1995. 450 pp., illus. $49.95
The most recognized publication on Browning sporting arms; covers all models.

Buffalo Bill's Wild West: An American Legend, by R.L. Wilson and Greg Martine, Random House, N.Y., 1999. 3,167 pp., illustrated. $60.00
Over 225 color plates and 160 black-and-white illustrations, with in-depth text and captions, the colorful arms, posters, photos, costumes, saddles, accoutrement are brought to life.

Bullard Arms, by G. Scott Jamieson, The Boston Mills Press, Ontario, Canada, 1989. 244 pp., illus. $35.00
The story of a mechanical genius whose rifles and cartridges were the equal to any made in America in the 1880s.

Burning Powder, compiled by Major D.B. Wesson, Wolfe Publishing Company, Prescott, AZ, 1992. 110 pp. Soft cover. $10.95
A rare booklet from 1932 for Smith & Wesson collectors.

The Burnside Breech Loading Carbines, by Edward A. Hull, Andrew Mowbray, Inc., Lincoln, RI, 1986. 95 pp., illus. $16.00
No. 1 in the "Man at Arms Monograph Series." A model-by-model historical/technical examination of one of the most widely used cavalry weapons of the American Civil War based upon important and previously unpublished research.

Camouflage Uniforms of European and NATO Armies; 1945 to the Present, by J. F. Borsarello, Atglen, PA: Schiffer Publications. Over 290 color and b/w photographs, 120 pages. Softcover. $29.95
This full-color book covers nearly all of the NATO, and other European armies' camouflaged uniforms, and not only shows and explains the many patterns, but also their efficacy of design. Described and illustrated are the variety of materials tested in over forty different armies, and includes the history of obsolete trial tests from 1945 to the present time. More than two hundred patterns have been manufactured since World War II using various landscapes and seasonal colors for their look. The Vietnam and Gulf Wars, African or South American events, as well as recent Yugoslavian independence wars have been used as experimental terrains to test a variety of patterns. This book provides a superb reference for the historian, reenactor, designer, and modeler.

Camouflage Uniforms of the Waffen-SS A Photographic Reference, by Michael Beaver, Schiffer Publishing, Atglen, PA. Over 1,000 color and b/w photographs and illustrations, 296 pages. $69.95
Finally a book that unveils the shroud of mystery surrounding Waffen-SS camouflage clothing. Illustrated here, both in full color and in contemporary black and white photographs, this unparalleled look at Waffen-SS combat troops and their camouflage clothing will benefit both the historian and collector.

Canadian Gunsmiths from 1608: A Checklist of Tradesmen, by John Belton, Historical Arms Series No. 29. Canada: Museum Restoration, 1992. 40 pp., 17 illustrations. Softcover. $8.95
This Checklist is a greatly expanded version of HAS No. 14, listing the names, occupation, location, and dates of more than 1,500 men and women who worked as gunmakers, gunsmiths, armorers, gun merchants, gun patent holders, and a few other gun related trades. A collection of contemporary gunsmiths' letterhead have been provided to add color and depth to the study.

Cap Guns, by James Dundas, Schiffer Publishing, Atglen, PA, 1996. 160 pp., illus. Paper covers. $29.95
Over 600 full-color photos of cap guns and gun accessories with a current value guide.

Carbines of the Civil War, by John D. McAulay, Pioneer Press, Union City, TN, 1981. 123 pp., illus. Paper covers. $12.95
A guide for the student and collector of the colorful arms used by the Federal cavalry.

Carbines of the U.S. Cavalry 1861-1905, by John D. McAulay, Andrew Mowbray Publishers, Lincoln, RI, 1996. $35.00
Covers the crucial use of carbines from the beginning of the Civil War to the end of the cavalry carbine era in 1905.

Cartridge Carbines of the British Army, by Alan M. Petrillo, Excalibur Publications, Latham, NY, 1998. 72 pp., illustrated. Paper covers. $11.95
Begins with the Snider-Enfield which was the first regulation cartridge carbine introduced in 1866 and ends with the .303 caliber No.5, Mark 1 Enfield.

Cartridge Catalogues, compiled by George Hoyem, Armory Publications, Coeur d'Alene, ID., 1997. 504 pp., illus. $125.00
Fourteen old ammunition makers' and designers' catalogs reproduced with their color covers in a limited, signed and numbered edition. Completely revised edition of the general purpose reference work for which collectors, police, scientists and laymen reach first for answers to cartridge identification questions. Available October, 1996.

Cartridge Reloading Tools of the Past, by R.H. Chamberlain and Tom Quigley, Tom Quigley, Castle Rock, WA, 1998. 167 pp., illustrated. Paper covers. $25.00
A detailed treatment of the extensive Winchester and Ideal lines of handloading tools and bulletmolds plus Remington, Marlin, Ballard, Browning and many others.

Cartridges for Collectors, by Fred Datig, Pioneer Press, Union City, TN, 1999. In three volumes of 176 pp. each. Vol.1 (Centerfire); Vol.2 (Rimfire and Misc.) types;
Vol.3 (Additional Rimfire, Centerfire, and Plastic.). All illustrations are shown in full-scale drawings. Volume 1, softcover only, $19.95. Volumes 2 & 3, Hardcover $19.95

Civil War Arms Makers and Their Contracts, edited by Stuart C. Mowbray and Jennifer Heroux, Andrew Mowbray Publishing, Lincoln, RI, 1998. 595 pp. $39.50
A facsimile reprint of the Report by the Commissioner of Ordnance and Ordnance Stores, 1862.

Civil War Arms Purchases and Deliveries, edited by Stuart C. Mowbray, Andrew Mowbray Publishing, Lincoln, RI, 1998. 300pp., illus. $39.50
A facsimile reprint of the master list of Civil War weapons purchases and deliveries including Small Arms, Cannon, Ordnance and Projectiles.

Civil War Breech Loading Rifles, by John D. McAulay, Andrew Mowbray, Inc., Lincoln, RI, 1991. 144 pp., illus. Paper covers. $15.00
All the major breech-loading rifles of the Civil War and most, if not all, of the obscure types are detailed, illustrated and set in their historical context.

Civil War Cartridge Boxes of the Union Infantryman, by Paul Johnson, Andrew Mowbray, Inc., Lincoln, RI, 1998. 352 pp., illustrated. $45.00
There were four patterns of infantry cartridge boxes used by Union forces during the Civil War. The author describes the development and subsequent pattern changes to these cartridge boxes.

Civil War Commanders, by Dean Thomas, Thomas Publications, Gettysburg, PA. 1998. 72 pp., illustrated, photos. Paper Covers. $9.95
138 photographs and capsule biographies of Union and Confederate officers. A convenient personalities reference guide.

Civil War Firearms, by Joseph G. Bilby, Combined Books, Conshohocken, PA, 1996. 252 pp., illus. $34.95
A unique work combining background data on each firearm including its battlefield use, and a guide to collecting and firing surviving relics and modern reproductions.

Civil War Guns, by William B. Edwards, Thomas Publications, Gettysburg, PA, 1997. 444 pp., illus. $40.00
The complete story of Federal and Confederate small arms; design, manufacture, identifications, procurement issue, employment, effectiveness, and postwar disposal by the recognized expert.

Civil War Infantryman: In Camp, On the March, And in Battle, by Dean Thomas, Thomas Publications, Gettysburg, PA. 1998. 72 pages, illustrated, Softcovers. $12.95
Uses first-hand accounts to shed some light on the "common soldier" of the Civil War from enlistment to muster-out, including camp, marching, rations, equipment, fighting, and more.

Civil War Pistols, by John D. McAulay, Andrew Mowbray Inc., Lincoln, RI, 1992. 166 pp., illus. $38.50
A survey of the handguns used during the American Civil War.

Civil War Sharps Carbines and Rifles, by Earl J. Coates and John D. McAulay, Thomas Publications, Gettysburg, PA, 1996. 108 pp., illus. Paper covers. $12.95
Traces the history and development of the firearms including short histories of specific serial numbers and the soldiers who received them.

Civil War Small Arms of the U.S. Navy and Marine Corps, by John D. McAulay, Mowbray Publishing, Lincoln, RI, 1999. 186 pp., illustrated. $39.00
The first reliable and comprehensive guide to the firearms and edged weapons of the Civil War Navy and Marine Corps.

The W.F. Cody Buffalo Bill Collector's Guide with Values, by James W. Wojtowicz, Collector Books, Paducah, KY, 1998. 271 pp., illustrated. $24.95
A profusion of colorful collectibles including lithographs, programs, photographs, books, medals, sheet music, guns, etc. and today's values.

Col. Burton's Spiller & Burr Revolver, by Matthew W. Norman, Mercer University Press, Macon, GA, 1997. 152 pp., illus. $22.95
A remarkable archival research project on the arm together with a comprehensive story of the establishment and running of the factory.

Collector's Guide to Colt .45 Service Pistols Models of 1911 and 1911A1, Enlarged and revised edition. Clawson Publications, Fort Wayne, IN, 1998. 130 pp., illustrated. $45.00
From 1911 to the end of production in 1945 with complete military identification including all contractors.

A Collector's Guide to United States Combat Shotguns, by Bruce N. Canfield, Andrew Mowbray Inc., Lincoln, RI, 1992. 184 pp., illus. Paper covers. $24.00
This book provides full coverage of combat shotguns, from the earliest examples right up to the Gulf War and beyond.

A Collector's Guide to Winchester in the Service, by Bruce N. Canfield, Andrew Mowbray, Inc., Lincoln, RI, 1991. 192 pp., illus. Paper covers. $22.00
The firearms produced by Winchester for the national defense. From Hotchkiss to the M14, each firearm is examined and illustrated.

A Collector's Guide to the '03 Springfield, by Bruce N. Canfield, Andrew Mowbray Inc., Lincoln, RI, 1989. 160 pp., illus. Paper covers. $22.00
A comprehensive guide follows the '03 through its unparalleled tenure of service. Covers all of the interesting variations, modifications and accessories of this highly collectible military rifle.

Collector's Illustrated Encyclopedia of the American Revolution, by George C. Neumann and Frank J. Kravic, Rebel Publishing Co., Inc., Texarkana, TX, 1989. 286 pp., illus. $36.95
A showcase of more than 2,300 artifacts made, worn, and used by those who fought in the War for Independence.

Colonial Frontier Guns, by T.M. Hamilton, Pioneer Press, Union City, TN, 1988. 176 pp., illus. Paper covers. $17.50

A complete study of early flint muskets of this country.

Colt: An American Legend, by R.L. Wilson, Artabras, New York, 1997. 406 pages, fully illustrated, most in color. $60.00

A reprint of the commemorative album celebrates 150 years of the guns of Samuel Colt and the manufacturing empire he built, with expert discussion of every model ever produced, the innovations of each model and variants, updated model and serial number charts and magnificent photographic showcases of the weapons.

The Colt Armory, by Ellsworth Grant, Man-at-Arms Bookshelf, Lincoln, RI, 1996. 232 pp., illus. $35.00

A history of Colt's Manufacturing Company.

Colt Blackpowder Reproductions & Replica: A Collector's and Shooter's Guide, by Dennis Miller, Blue Book Publications, Minneapolis, MN, 1999. 288 pp., illustrated. Paper covers. $29.95

The first book on this important subject, and a must for the investor, collector, and shooter.

Colt Heritage, by R.L. Wilson, Simon & Schuster, 1979. 358 pp., illus. $75.00

The official history of Colt firearms 1836 to the present.

Colt Memorabilia Price Guide, by John Ogle, Krause Publications, Iola, WI, 1998. 256 pp., illus. Paper covers. $29.95

The first book ever compiled about the vast array of non-gun merchandise produced by Sam Colt's companies, and other companies using the Colt name.

The Colt Model 1905 Automatic Pistol, by John Potocki, Andrew Mowbray Publishing, Lincoln, RI, 1998. 191 pp., illus. $28.00

Covers all aspects of the Colt Model 1905 Automatic Pistol, from its invention by the legendary John Browning to its numerous production variations.

Colt Peacemaker British Model, by Keith Cochran, Cochran Publishing Co., Rapid City, SD, 1989. 160 pp., illus. $35.00

Covers those revolvers Colt squeezed in while completing a large order of revolvers for the U.S. Cavalry in early 1874, to those magnificent cased target revolvers used in the pistol competitions at Bisley Commons in the 1890s.

Colt Peacemaker Encyclopedia, by Keith Cochran, Keith Cochran, Rapid City, SD, 1986. 434 pp., illus. $65.00

A must book for the Peacemaker collector.

Colt Peacemaker Encyclopedia, Volume 2, by Keith Cochran, Cochran Publishing Co., SD, 1992. 416 pp., illus. $60.00

Included in this volume are extensive notes on engraved, inscribed, historical and noted revolvers, as well as those revolvers used by outlaws, lawmen, movie and television stars.

Colt Percussion Accoutrements 1834-1873, by Robin Rapley, Robin Rapley, Newport Beach, CA, 1994. 432 pp., illus. Paper covers. $39.95

The complete collector's guide to the identification of Colt percussion accoutrements; including Colt conversions and their values.

Colt Pocket Hammerless Pistols, by Dr. John W. Brunner, Phillips Publications, Williamstown, NJ, 1998. 212 pp., illustrated. $59.95

You will never again have to question a .25, .32 or .380 with this well illustrated, definitive reference guide at hand.

Colt Revolvers and the Tower of London, by Joseph G. Rosa, Royal Armouries of the Tower of London, London, England, 1988. 72 pp., illus. Soft covers. $15.00

Details the story of Colt in London through the early cartridge period.

Colt Rifles and Muskets from 1847-1870, by Herbert Houze, Krause Publications, Iola, WI, 1996. 192 pp., illus. $34.95

Discover previously unknown Colt models along with an extensive list of production figures for all models.

Colt's SAA Post War Models, by George Garton, The Gun Room Press, Highland Park, NJ, 1995. 166 pp., illus. $39.95

Complete facts on the post-war Single Action Army revolvers. Information on calibers, production numbers and variations taken from factory records.

Colt Single Action Army Revolvers: The Legend, the Romance and the Rivals, by "Doc" O'Meara, Krause Publications, Iola, WI, 2000. 160 pp., illustrated with 250 photos in b&w and a 16 page color section. $34.95

Production figures, serial numbers by year, and rarities.

Colt Single Action Army Revolvers and Alterations, by C. Kenneth Moore, Mowbray Publishers, Lincoln, RI, 1999. 112 pp., illustrated. $35.00

A comprehensive history of the revolvers that collectors call "Artillery Models." These are the most historical of all S.A.A. Colts, and this new book covers all the details.

Colt Single Action Army Revolvers and the London Agency, by C. Kenneth Moore, Andrew Mowbray Publishers, Lincoln, RI, 1990. 144 pp., illus. $35.00

Drawing on vast documentary sources, this work chronicles the relationship between the London Agency and the Hartford home office.

The Colt U.S. General Officers' Pistols, by Horace Greeley IV, Andrew Mowbray Inc., Lincoln, RI, 1990. 199 pp., illus. $38.00

These unique weapons, issued as a badge of rank to General Officers in the U.S. Army from WWII onward, remain highly personal artifacts of the military leaders who carried them. Includes serial numbers and dates of issue.

Colts from the William M. Locke Collection, by Frank Sellers, Andrew Mowbray Publishers, Lincoln, RI, 1996. 192 pp., illus. $55.00

This important book illustrates all of the famous Locke Colts, with captions by arms authority Frank Sellers.

Colt's Dates of Manufacture 1837-1978, by R.L. Wilson, published by Maurie Albert, Coburg, Australia; N.A. distributor I.D.S.A. Books, Hamilton, OH, 1983. 61 pp. $6.00

An invaluable pocket guide to the dates of manufacture of Colt firearms up to 1978.

Colt's 100th Anniversary Firearms Manual 1836-1936: A Century of Achievement, Wolfe Publishing Co., Prescott, AZ, 1992. 100 pp., illus. Paper covers. $12.95

Originally published by the Colt Patent Firearms Co., this booklet covers the history, manufacturing procedures and the guns of the first 100 years of the genius of Samuel Colt.

Colt's Pocket '49: Its Evolution Including the Baby Dragoon and Wells Fargo, by Robert Jordan and Darrow Watt, privately printed, Loma Mar, CA 2000. 304 pages, with 984 color photos, illus. Beautifully bound in a deep blue leather like case. $125.00

Detailed information on all models and covers engraving, cases, accoutrements, holsters, fakes, and much more. Included is a summary booklet containing information such as serial numbers, production ranges & identifing photos. This book is a masterpiece on its subject.

Complete Guide to all United States Military Medals 1939 to Present, by Colonel Frank C. Foster, Medals of America Press, Fountain Inn, SC, 2000. 121 pp.,illustrated, photos. $29.95

Complete criteria for every Army, Navy, Marines, Air Force, Coast Guard, and Merchant Marine awards since 1939. All decorations, service medals, and ribbons shown in full-color and accompanied by dates and campaigns as well as detailed descriptions on proper wear and display.

Complete Guide to the M1 Garand and the M1 Carbine, by Bruce N. Canfield, 2nd printing, Andrew Mowbray Inc., Lincoln, RI, 1999. 296 pp., illus. $39.50

Expanded and updated coverage of both the M1 Garand and the M1 Carbine, with more than twice as much information as the author's previous book on this topic.

The Complete Guide to U.S. Infantry Weapons of the First War, by Bruce Canfield, Andrew Mowbray, Publisher, Lincoln, RI, 2000. 304 pp., illus. $39.95

The definitive study of the U.S. Infantry weapons used in WW1.

The Complete Guide to U.S. Infantry Weapons of World War Two, by Bruce Canfield, Andrew Mowbray, Publisher, Lincoln, RI, 1995. 303 pp., illus. $39.95

A definitive work on the weapons used by the United States Armed Forces in WWII.

A Concise Guide to the Artillery at Gettysburg, by Gregory Coco, Thomas Publications, Gettysburg, PA, 1998. 96 pp., illus. Paper Covers. $10.00

Coco's tenth book on Gettysburg is a beginner's guide to artillery and its use at the battle. It covers the artillery batteries describing the types of cannons, shells, fuses, etc.using interesting narrative and human interest stories.

Cooey Firearms, Made in Canada 1919-1979, by John A. Belton, Museum Restoration, Canada, 1998. 36pp., with 46 illus. Paper Covers. $8.95

More than 6 million rifles and at least 67 models, were made by this small Canadian riflemaker. They have been identified from the first 'Cooey Canuck' through the last variations made by the 'Winchester-Cooey'. Each is desciled and most are illustrated in this first book on The Cooey.

Cowboy Collectibles and Western Memorabilia, by Bob Bell and Edward Vebell, Schiffer Publishing, Atglen, PA, 1992. 160 pp., illus. Paper covers. $29.95

The exciting era of the cowboy and the wild west collectibles including rifles, pistols, gun rigs, etc.

Cowboy Culture: The Last Frontier of American Antiques, by Michael Friedman, Schiffer Publishing, Ltd., West Chester, PA, 1992. 300 pp., illustrated.

Covers the artful aspects of the old west, the antiques and collectibles. Illustrated with clear color plates of over 1,000 items such as spurs, boots, guns, saddles etc.

Cowboy and Gunfighter Collectible, by Bill Mackin, Mountain Press Publishing Co., Missoula, MT, 1995. 178 pp., illus. Paper covers. $25.00

A photographic encyclopedia with price guide and makers' index.

Cowboys and the Trappings of the Old West, by William Manns and Elizabeth Clair Flood, Zon International Publishing Co., Santa Fe, NM, 1997, 1st edition. 224 pp., illustrated. $45.00

A pictorial celebration of the cowboys dress and trappings.

Cowboy Hero Cap Pistols, by Rudy D'Angelo, Antique Trader Books, Dubuque, IA, 1998. 196 pp., illus. Paper covers. $34.95

Aimed at collectors of cap pistols created and named for famous film and television cowboy heros, this in-depth guide hits all the marks. Current values are given.

Custom Firearms Engraving, by Tom Turpin, Krause Publications, Iola, WI, 1999. 208 pp., illustrated. $49.95

Over 200 four-color photos with more than 75 master engravers profiled. Engravers Directory with addresses in the U.S. and abroad.

The Decorations, Medals, Ribbons, Badges and Insignia of the United States Army; World War 2 to Present, by Col. Frank C. Foster, Medals of America Press, Fountain Inn, SC. 2001. 145 pages, illustrated. $29.95

The most complete guide to United States Army medals, ribbons, rank, insignia nad patches from WWII to the present day. Each medal and insignia shown in full color. Includes listing of respective criteria and campaigns.

The Decorations, Medals, Ribbons, Badges and Insignia of the United States Navy; World War 2 to Present, by James G. Thompson, Medals of America Press, Fountain Inn, SC. 2000. 123 pages, illustrated. $29.95

The most complete guide to United States Army medals, ribbons, rank, insignia nad patches from WWII to the present day. Each medal and insignia shown in full color. Includes listing of respective criteria and campaigns.

The Derringer in America, Volume 1, The Percussion Period, by R.L. Wilson and L.D. Eberhart, Andrew Mowbray Inc., Lincoln, RI, 1985. 271 pp., illus. $48.00

A long awaited book on the American percussion deringer.

The Derringer in America, Volume 2, The Cartridge Period, by L.D. Eberhart and R.L. Wilson, Andrew Mowbray Inc., Publishers, Lincoln, RI, 1993. 284 pp., illus. $65.00

Comprehensive coverage of cartridge deringers organized alphabetically by maker. Includes all types of deringers known by the authors to have been offered to the American market.

The Devil's Paintbrush: Sir Hiram Maxim's Gun, by Dolf Goldsmith, 3rd Edition, expanded and revised, Collector Grade Publications, Toronto, Canada, 2000. 384 pp., illus. $79.95

The classic work on the world's first true automatic machine gun.

Dr. Josephus Requa Civil War Dentist and the Billinghurst-Requa Volley Gun, by John M. Hyson, Jr., & Margaret Requa DeFrancisco, Museum Restoration Service, Bloomfield, Ont., Canada, 1999. 36 pp., illus. Paper covers. $8.95

The story of the inventor of the first practical rapid-fire gun to be used during the American Civil War.

The Duck Stamp Story, by Eric Jay Dolin and Bob Dumaine, Krause Publications, Iola, WI, 2000. 208 pp., illustrated with color throughout. Paper covers. $29.95; Hardbound. $49.95.

Detailed information on the value and rarity of every federal duck stamp. Outstanding art and illustrations.

The Dutch Luger (Parabellum) A Complete History, by Bas J. Martens and Guus de Vries, Ironside International Publishers, Inc., Alexandria, VA, 1995. 268 pp., illus. $49.95.

The history of the Luger in the Netherlands. An extensive description of the Dutch pistol and trials and the different models of the Luger in the Dutch service.

The Eagle on U.S. Firearms, by John W. Jordan, Pioneer Press, Union City, TN, 1992. 140 pp., illus. Paper covers. $17.50.

Stylized eagles have been stamped on government owned or manufactured firearms in the U.S. since the beginning of our country. This book lists and illustrates these various eagles in an informative and refreshing manner.

Encyclopedia of Rifles & Handguns; A Comprehensive Guide to Firearms, edited by Sean Connolly, Chartwell Books, Inc., Edison, NJ., 1996. 160 pp., illustrated. $26.00.

A lavishly illustrated book providing a comprehensive history of military and civilian personal firepower.

Eprouvettes: A Comprehensive Study of Early Devices for the Testing of Gunpowder, by R.T.W. Kempers, Royal Armouries Museum, Leeds, England, 1999. 352 pp., illustrated with 240 black & white and 28 color plates. $125.00.

The first comprehensive study of eprouvettes ever attempted in a single volume.

European Firearms in Swedish Castles, by Kaa Wennberg, Bohuslaningens Boktryckeri AB, Uddevalla, Sweden, 1986. 156 pp., illus. $50.00.

The famous collection of Count Keller, the Ettersburg Castle collection, and others. English text.

European Sporting Cartridges, Part 1, by W.B. Dixon, Armory Publications, Inc., Coeur d'Alene, ID, 1997. 250 pp., illus. $63.00

Photographs and drawings of over 550 centerfire cartridge case types in 1,300 illustrations produced in German and Austria from 1875 to 1995.

European Sporting Cartridges, Part 2, by W.B. Dixon, Armory Publications, Inc., Coeur d'Alene, ID, 2000. 240 pp., illus. $63.00

An illustrated history of centerfire hunting and target cartridges produced in Czechoslovakia, Switzerland, Norway, Sweden, Finland, Russia, Italy, Denmark, Belguim from 1875 to 1998. Adds 50 specimens to volume 1 (Germany-Austria). Also, illustrates 40 small arms magazine experiments during the late 19th Century, and includes the English-Language export ammunition catalogue of Kovo (Povaszke Strojarne), Prague, Czeck. from the, 1930's.

Fifteen Years in the Hawken Lode, by John D. Baird, The Gun Room Press, Highland Park, NJ, 1976. 120 pp., illus. $24.95.

A collection of thoughts and observations gained from many years of intensive study of the guns from the shop of the Hawken brothers.

'51 Colt Navies, by Nathan L. Swayze, The Gun Room Press, Highland Park, NJ, 1993. 243 pp., illus. $59.95.

The Model 1851 Colt Navy, its variations and markings.

Fighting Iron, by Art Gogan, Andrew Mowbray, Inc., Lincoln, R.I., 1999. 176 pp., illustrated. $28.00.

It doesn't matter whether you collect guns, swords, bayonets or accoutrement—sooner or later you realize that it all comes down to the metal. If you don't understand the metal you don't understand your collection.

Fine Colts, The Dr. Joseph A. Murphy Collection, by R.L. Wilson, Sheffield Marketing Associates, Inc., Doylestown, PA, 1999. 258 pp., illustrated. Limited edition signed and numbered. $99.00.

This lavish new work covers exquisite, deluxe and rare Colt arms from Paterson and other percussion revolvers to the cartridge period and up through modern times.

Firearms, by Derek Avery, Desert Publications, El Dorado, AR, 1999. 95 pp., illustrated. $9.95

The firearms included in this book are by necessity only a selection, but nevertheless one that represents the best and most famous weapons seen since the Second World War.

Firearms and Tackle Memorabilia, by John Delph, Schiffer Publishing, Ltd., West Chester, PA, 1991. 124 pp., illus. $39.95.

A collector's guide to signs and posters, calendars, trade cards, boxes, envelopes, and other highly sought after memorabilia. With a value guide.

Firearms of the American West 1803-1865, Volume 1, by Louis A. Garavaglia and Charles Worman, University of Colorado Press, Niwot, CO, 1998. 402 pp., illustrated. $59.95.

Traces the development and uses of firearms on the frontier during this period.

Firearms of the American West 1866-1894, by Louis A. Garavaglia and Charles G. Worman, University of Colorado Press, Niwot, CO, 1998. 416 pp., illus. $59.95.

A monumental work that offers both technical information on all of the important firearms used in the West during this period and a highly entertaining history of how they were used, who used them, and why.

Firearms from Europe, by David Noe, Larry W. Yantz, Dr. James B. Whisker, Rowe Publications, Rochester, N.Y., 1999. 192 pp., illustrated. $45.00.

A history and description of firearms imported during the American Civil War by the United States of America and the Confederate States of America.

Firepower from Abroad, by Wiley Sword, Andrew Mowbray Publishing, Lincoln, R.I., 2000. 120 pp., illustrated. $23.00.

The Confederate Enfield and the LeMat revolver and how they reached the Confederate market.

Flayderman's Guide to Antique American Firearms and Their Values, 7th Edition, edited by Norm Flayderman, DBI books, a division of Krause Publications, Iola, WI, 1998. 656 pp., illus. Paper covers. $32.95.

A completely updated and new edition with more than 3,600 models and variants extensively described with all marks and specifications necessary for quick identification.

The FN-FAL Rifle, et al, by Duncan Long, Paladin Press, Boulder, CO, 1999. 144 pp., illustrated. Paper covers. $18.95.

Detailed descriptions of the basic models produced by Fabrique Nationale and the myriad variants that evolved as a result of the firearms universal acceptance.

The .45-70 Springfield, by Joe Poyer and Craig Riesch, North Cape Publications, Tustin, CA, 1996. 150 pp., illus. Paper covers. $16.95.

A revised and expanded second edition of a best-selling reference work organized by serial number and date of production to aid the collector in identifying popular "Trapdoor" rifles and carbines.

The French 1935 Pistols, by Eugene Medlin and Colin Doane, Eugene Medlin, El Paso, TX, 1995. 172 pp., illus. Paper covers. $25.95.

The development and identification of successive models, fakes and variants, holsters and accessories, and serial numbers by dates of production.

Freund & Bro. Pioneer Gunmakers to the West, by F.J. Pablo Balentine, Graphic Publishers, Newport Beach, CA, 1997. 380 pp., illustrated $69.95.

The story of Frank W. and George Freund, skilled German gunsmiths who plied their trade on the Western American frontier during the final three decades of the nineteenth century.

From the Kingdom of Lilliput: The Miniature Firearms of David Kucer, by K. Corey Keeble and **The Making of Miniatures,** by David Kucer, Museum Restoration Service, Ontario, Canada, 1994. 51 pp., illus, $25.00.

An overview of the subject of miniatures in general combined with an outline by the artist himself on the way he makes a miniature firearm.

Frontier Pistols and Revolvers, by Dominique Venner, Book Sales Inc., Edison, N.J., 1998. 144 pp., illus. $19.95.

Colt, Smith & Wesson, Remington and other early-brand revolvers which tamed the American frontier are shown amid vintage photographs, etchings and paintings to evoke the wild West.

The Fusil de Tulole in New France, 1691-1741, by Russel Bouchard, Museum Restorations Service, Bloomfield, Ontario, Canada, 1997. 36 pp., illus. Paper covers. $8.95

The development of the company and the identification of their arms.

Game Guns & Rifles: Percussion to Hammerless Ejector in Britain, by Richard Akehurst, Trafalgar Square, N. Pomfret, VT, 1993. 192 pp., illus. $39.95.

Long considered a classic this important reprint covers the period of British gunmaking between 1830-1900.

The Gas Trap Garand, by Billy Pyle, Collector Grade Publications, Cobourg, Ontario, Canada, 1999 316 pp., illustrated. $59.95.

The in-depth story of all, the initial 80 Model Shop rifles made under the personal supervision of John Garand himself in 1934 and 1935, and the first 50,000 plus production "gas trap" M1's manufactured at Springfield Armory between August, 1937 and August, 1940.

George Schreyer, Sr. and Jr., Gunmakers of Hanover, Pennsylvania, by George Shumway, George Shumway Publishers, York, PA, 1990. 160pp., illus. $50.00.

This monograph is a detailed photographic study of almost all known surviving long rifles and smoothbore guns made by highly regarded gunsmiths George Schreyer, Sr. and Jr.

The German Assault Rifle 1935-1945, by Peter R. Senich, Paladin Press, Boulder, CO, 1987. 328 pp., illus. $60.00.

A complete review of machine carbines, machine pistols and assault rifles employed by Hitler's Wehrmacht during WWII.

The German K98k Rifle, 1934-1945: The Backbone of the Wehrmacht, by Richard D. Law, Collector Grade Publications, Toronto, Canada, 1993. 336 pp., illus. $69.95.

The most comprehensive study ever published on the 14,000,000 bolt-action K98k rifles produced in Germany between 1934 and 1945.

German Machine Guns, by Daniel D. Musgrave, revised edition, Ironside International Publishers, Inc. Alexandria, VA, 1992. 586 pp., 650 illus. $49.95.

The most definitive book ever written on German machineguns. Covers the introduction and development of machineguns in Germany from 1899 to the rearmament period after WWII.

German Military Rifles and Machine Pistols, 1871-1945, by Hans Dieter Gotz, Schiffer Publishing Co., West Chester, PA, 1990. 245 pp., illus. $35.00.

This book portrays in words and pictures the development of the modern German weapons and their ammunition including the scarcely known experimental types.

The German MP40 Maschinenpistole, by Frank Iannamico, Moose Lake Publishing, Harmony, ME, 1999. 185 pp., illustrated. Paper covers. $19.95.

The history, development and use of this famous gun of World War 2.

German 7.9mm Military Ammunition, by Daniel W. Kent, Daniel W. Kent, Ann Arbor, MI, 1991. 244 pp., illus. $35.00.

The long-awaited revised edition of a classic among books devoted to ammunition.

The Golden Age of Remington, by Robert W.D. Ball, Krause publications, Iola, WI, 1995. 194 pp., illus. $29.95.

For Remington collectors or firearms historians, this book provides a pictorial history of Remington through World War I. Includes value guide.

The Government Models, by William H.D. Goddard, Andrew Mowbray Publishing, Lincoln, RI, 1998. 296 pp., illustrated. $58.50.

The most authoritative source on the development of the Colt model of 1911.

Grasshoppers and Butterflies, by Adrian B. Caruana, Museum Restoration Service, Alexandria, Bay, N.Y., 1999. 32 pp., illustrated. Paper covers. $8.95.

No.39 in the Historical Arms Series. The light 3 pounders of Pattison and Townsend.

The Greener Story, by Graham Greener, Quiller Press, London, England, 2000. 256 pp., illustrated with 32 pages of color photos. $64.50.

W.W. Greener, his family history, inventions, guns, patents, and more.

A Guide to American Trade Catalogs 1744-1900, by Lawrence B. Romaine, Dover Publications, New York, NY. 422 pp., illus. Paper covers. $12.95

A Guide to Ballard Breechloaders, by George J. Layman, Pioneer Press, Union City, TN, 1997. 261 pp., illus. Paper covers. $19.95

Documents the saga of this fine rifle from the first models made by Ball & Williams of Worchester, to its production by the Marlin Firearms Co, to the cessation of 19th century manufacture in 1891, and finally to the modern reproductions made in the 1990's.

A Guide to the Maynard Breechloader, by George J. Layman, George J. Layman, Ayer, MA, 1993. 125 pp., illus. Paper covers. $11.95.

The first book dedicated entirely to the Maynard family of breech-loading firearms. Coverage of the arms is given from the 1850s through the 1880s.

A Guide to U. S. Army Dress Helmets 1872-1904, by Kasal and Moore, North Cape Publications, 2000. 88 pp., illus. Paper covers. $15.95

This thorough study provides a complete description of the Model 1872 & 1881 dress helmets worn by the U.S. Army. Including all componets from bodies to plates to plumes & shoulder cords and tells how to differentiate the originals from reproductions. Extensively illustrated with photographs, '8 pages in full color' of complete helmets and their components.

Gun Collecting, by Geoffrey Boothroyd, Sportsman's Press, London, 1989. 208 pp., illus. $29.95.

The most comprehensive list of 19th century British gunmakers and gunsmiths ever published.

Gunmakers of London 1350-1850, by Howard L. Blackmore, George Shumway Publisher, York, PA, 1986. 222 pp., illus. $35.00.

A listing of all the known workmen of gun making in the first 500 years, plus a history of the guilds, cutlers, armourers, founders, blacksmiths, etc. 260 gunmarks are illustrated.

Gunmakers of London Supplement 1350-1850, by Howard L. Blackmore, Museum Restoration Service, Alexandria Bay, NY, 1999. 156 pp., illustrated. $60.00.

Begins with an introductory chapter on "foreighn" gunmakers followed by records of all the new information found about previously unidentified armourers, gunmakers and gunsmiths.

The Guns that Won the West: Firearms of the American Frontier, 1865-1898, by John Walter, Stackpole Books, Inc., Mechanicsburg, PA.,1999. 256 pp., illustrated. $34.95.

Here is the story of the wide range of firearms from pistols to rifles used by plainsmen and settlers, gamblers, native Americans and the U.S. Army.

Gunsmiths of Illinois, by Curtis L. Johnson, George Shumway Publishers, York, PA, 1995. 160 pp., illus. $50.00.

Genealogical information is provided for nearly one thousand gunsmiths. Contains hundreds of illustrations of rifles and other guns, of handmade origin, from Illinois.

The Gunsmiths of Manhattan, 1625-1900: A Checklist of Tradesmen, by Michael H. Lewis, Museum Restoration Service, Bloomfield, Ont., Canada, 1991. 40 pp., illus. Paper covers. $8.95.

This listing of more than 700 men in the arms trade in New York City prior to about the end of the 19th century will provide a guide for identification and further research.

The Guns of Dagenham: Lanchester, Patchett, Sterling, by Peter Laidler and David Howroyd, Collector Grade Publications, Inc., Cobourg, Ont., Canada, 1995. 310 pp., illus. $39.95.

An in-depth history of the small arms made by the Sterling Company of Dagenham, Essex, England, from 1940 until Sterling was purchased by British Aerospace in 1989 and closed.

Guns of the Western Indian War, by R. Stephen Dorsey, Collector's Library, Eugene, OR, 1997. 220 pp., illus. Paper covers. $30.00.

The full story of the guns and ammunition that made western history in the turbulent period of 1865-1890.

Gun Powder Cans & Kegs, by Ted & David Bacyk and Tom Rowe, Rowe Publications, Rochester, NY, 1999. 150 pp., illus. $65.00.

The first book devoted to powder tins and kegs. All cans and kegs in full color. With a price guide and rarity scale.

The Guns of Remington: Historic Firearms Spanning Two Centuries, compiled by Howard M. Madaus, Biplane Productions, Publisher, in co-operation with Buffalo Bill Historical Center, Cody, WY, 1998. 352 pp., illustrated with over 800 color photos. $79.95.

A complete catalog of the firearms in the exhibition, "It Never Failed Me: The Arms & Art of Remington Arms Company" at the Buffalo Bill Historical Center, Cody, Wyoming.

Gun Tools, Their History and Identification by James B. Shaffer, Lee A. Rutledge and R. Stephen Dorsey, Collector's Library, Eugene, OR, 1992. 375 pp., illus. $30.00.

Written history of foreign and domestic gun tools from the flintlock period to WWII.

Gun Tools, Their History and Identifications, Volume 2, by Stephen Dorsey and James B. Shaffer, Collectors' Library, Eugene, OR, 1997. 396 pp., illus. Paper covers. $30.00.

Gun tools from the Royal Armouries Museum in England, Pattern Room, Royal Ordnance Reference Collection in Nottingham and from major private collections.

Gunsmiths of the Carolinas 1660-1870, by Daniel D. Hartzler and James B. Whisker, Old Bedford Village Press, Bedford, PA, 1998. 176 pp., illustrated. $40.00.

This deluxe hard bound edition of 176 pages is printed on fine coated paper, with about 90 pages of large photographs of fine longrifles from the Carolinas, and about 90 pages of detailed research on the gunsmiths who created the highly prized and highly collectable longrifles. Dedicated to serious students of original Kentucky rifles, who may seldom encounter fine longrifles from the Carolinas.

Gunsmiths of Maryland, by Daniel D. Hartzler and James B. Whisker, Old Bedford Village Press, Bedford, PA, 1998. 208 pp., illustrated. $45.00.

Covers firelock Colonial period through the breech-loading patent models. Featuring longrifles.

Gunsmiths of Virginia, by Daniel D. Hartzler and James B. Whisker, Old Bedford Village Press, Bedford, PA, 1992. 206 pp., illustrated. $45.00.

A photographic study of American longrifles.

Gunsmiths of West Virginia, by Daniel D. Hartzler and James B. Whisker, Old Bedford Village Press, Bedford, PA, 1998. 176 pp., illustrated. $40.00.

A photographic study of American longrifles.

Gunsmiths of York County, Pennsylvania, by Daniel D. Hartzler and James B. Whisker, Old Bedford Village Press, Bedford, PA, 1998. 160 pp., illustrated. $40.00.

160 pages of photographs and research notes on the longrifles and gunsmiths of York County, Pennsylvania. Many longrifle collectors and gun builders have noticed that York County style rifles tend to be more formal in artistic decoration than some other schools of style. Patriotic themes, and folk art were popular design elements.

Hall's Military Breechloaders, by Peter A. Schmidt, Andrew Mowbray Publishers, Lincoln, RI, 1996. 232 pp., illus. $55.00.

The whole story behind these bold and innovative firearms.

The Handgun, by Geoffrey Boothroyd, David and Charles, North Pomfret, VT, 1989. 566 pp., illus. $60.00.

Every chapter deals with an important period in handgun history from the 14th century to the present.

Handgun of Military Rifle Marks 1866-1950, by Richard A. Hoffman and Noel P. Schott, Mapleleaf Militaria Publishing, St. Louis, MO, 1999, second edition. 60 pp., illustrated. Paper covers. $20.00.

An illustrated guide to identifying military rifle and marks.

Handguns & Rifles: The Finest Weapons from Around the World, by Ian Hogg, Random House Value Publishing, Inc., N.Y., 1999. 128 pp., illustrated. $18.98.

The serious gun collector will welcome this fully illustrated examination of international handguns and rifles. Each entry covers the history of the weapon, what purpose it serves, and its advantages and disadvantages.

The Hawken Rifle: Its Place in History, by Charles E. Hanson, Jr., The Fur Press, Chadron, NE, 1979. 104 pp., illus. Paper covers. $15.00.
A definitive work on this famous rifle.

Hawken Rifles, The Mountain Man's Choice, by John D. Baird, The Gun Room Press, Highland Park, NJ, 1976. 95 pp., illus. $29.95.
Covers the rifles developed for the Western fur trade. Numerous specimens are described and shown in photographs.

High Standard: A Collector's Guide to the Hamden & Hartford Target Pistols, by Tom Dance, Andrew Mowbray, Inc., Lincoln, RI, 1991. 192 pp., illus. Paper covers. $24.00.
From Citation to Supermatic, all of the production models and specials made from 1951 to 1984 are covered according to model number or series.

Historic Pistols: The American Martial Flintlock 1760-1845, by Samuel E. Smith & Edwin W. Bitter, The Gun Room Press, Highland Park, NJ, 1986. 353 pp., illus. $45.00.
Covers over 70 makers and 163 models of American martial arms.

Historical Hartford Hardware, by William W. Dalrymple, Colt Collector Press, Rapid City, SD, 1976. 42 pp., illus. Paper covers. $10.00.
Historically associated Colt revolvers.

The History and Development of Small Arms Ammunition, Volume 2, by George A. Hoyem, Armory Publications, Oceanside, CA, 1991. 303 pp., illus. $65.00.
Covers the blackpowder military centerfire rifle, carbine, machine gun and volley gun ammunition used in 28 nations and dominions, together with the firearms that chambered them.

The History and Development of Small Arms Ammunition, Volume 4, by George A. Hoyem, Armory Publications, Seattle, WA, 1998. 200 pp., illustrated $65.00.
A comprehensive book on American black powder and early smokeless rifle cartridges.

The History of Colt Firearms, by Dean Boorman, Lyons Press, New York, NY, 2001. 144 pp., illus. $29.95
Discover the fascinating story of the world's most famous revolver, complete with more than 150 stunning full-color photographs.

History of Modern U.S. Military Small Arms Ammunition. Volume 1, 1880-1939, revised by F.W. Hackley, W.H. Woodin and E.L. Scranton, Thomas Publications, Gettysburg, PA, 1998. 328 pp., illus. $49.95.
This revised edition incorporates all publicly available information concerning military small arms ammunition for the period 1880 through 1939 in a single volume.

History of Modern U.S. Military Small Arms Ammunition. Volume 2, 1940-1945 by F.W. Hackley, W.H. Woodin and E.L. Scranton. Gun Room Press, Highland Park, NJ. 300 + pages, illustrated. $39.95
Based on decades of original research conducted at the National Archives, numerous military, public and private museums and libraries, as well as individual collections, this edition incorporates all publicly available information concerning military small arms ammunition for the period 1940 through 1945.

The History of Winchester Rifles, by Dean Boorman, Lyons Press, New York, NY, 2001. 144 pp., illus. $29.95
A captivating and wonderfully photographed history of one of the most legendary names in gun lore. 150 full-color photos.

The History of Winchester Firearms 1866-1992, sixth edition, updated, expanded, and revised by Thomas Henshaw, New Win Publishing, Clinton, NJ, 1993. 280 pp., illus. $27.95.
This classic is the standard reference for all collectors and others seeking the facts about any Winchester firearm, old or new.

History of Winchester Repeating Arms Company, by Herbert G. Houze, Krause Publications, Iola, WI, 1994. 800 pp., illus. $50.00.
The complete Winchester history from 1856-1981.

Honour Bound: The Chauchat Machine Rifle, by Gerard Demaison and Yves Buffetaut, Collector Grade Publications, Inc., Cobourg, Ont., Canada, 1995. $39.95.
The story of the CSRG (Chauchat) machine rifle, the most manufactured automatic weapon of World War One.

Hopkins & Allen Revolvers & Pistols, by Charles E. Carder, Avil Onze Publishing, Delphos, OH, 1998, illustrated. Paper covers. $24.95.
Covers over 165 photos, graphics and patent drawings.

How to Buy and Sell Used Guns, by John Traister, Stoeger Publishing Co., So. Hackensack, NJ, 1984. 192 pp., illus. Paper covers. $10.95.
A new guide to buying and selling guns.

Hunting Weapons From the Middle Ages to the Twentieth Century, by Howard L. Blackmore, Dover Publications, Meneola, NY, 2000. 480 pp., illustrated. Paper covers. $16.95.
Dealing mainly with the different classes of weapons used in sport—swords, spears, crossbows, guns, and rifles—from the Middle Ages until the present day.

Identification Manual on the .303 British Service Cartridge, No. 1-Ball Ammunition, by B.A. Temple, I.D.S.A. Books, Piqua, OH, 1986. 84 pp., 57 illus. $12.50

Identification Manual on the .303 British Service Cartridge, No. 2-Blank Ammunition, by B.A. Temple, I.D.S.A. Books, Piqua, OH, 1986. 95 pp., 59 illus. $12.50

Identification Manual on the .303 British Service Cartridge, No. 3-Special Purpose Ammunition, by B.A. Temple, I.D.S.A. Books, Piqua, OH, 1987. 82 pp., 49 illus. $12.50

Identification Manual on the .303 British Service Cartridge, No. 4-Dummy Cartridges Henry 1869-c.1900, by B.A. Temple, I.D.S.A. Books, Piqua, OH, 1988. 84 pp., 70 illus. $12.50

Identification Manual on the .303 British Service Cartridge, No. 5-Dummy Cartridges (2), by B.A. Temple, I.D.S.A. Books, Piqua, OH, 1994. 78 pp. $12.50

The Illustrated Book of Guns, by David Miller, Salamander Books, N.Y., N.Y., 2000. 304 pp., illustrated in color. $34.95.
An illustrated directory of over 1,000 military and sporting firearms.

The Illustrated Encyclopedia of Civil War Collectibles, by Chuck Lawliss, Henry Holt and Co., New York, NY, 1997. 316 pp., illus. Paper covers. $22.95.
A comprehensive guide to Union and Confederate arms, equipment, uniforms, and other memorabilia.

Illustrations of United States Military Arms 1776-1903 and Their Inspector's Marks, compiled by Turner Kirkland, Pioneer Press, Union City, TN, 1988. 37 pp., illus. Paper covers. $7.00.
Reprinted from the 1949 Bannerman catalog. Valuable information for both the advanced and beginning collector.

Indian War Cartridge Pouches, Boxes and Carbine Boots, by R. Stephen Dorsey, Collector's Library, Eugene, OR, 1993. 156 pp., illus. Paper covers. $20.00.
The key reference work to the cartridge pouches, boxes, carbine sockets and boots of the Indian War period 1865-1890.

An Introduction to the Civil War Small Arms, by Earl J. Coates and Dean S. Thomas, Thomas Publishing Co., Gettysburg, PA, 1990. 96 pp., illus. Paper covers. $10.00.
The small arms carried by the individual soldier during the Civil War.

Japanese Rifles of World War Two, by Duncan O. McCollum, Excalibur Publications, Latham, NY, 1996. 64 pp., illus. Paper covers. $18.95.
A sweeping view of the rifles and carbines that made up Japan's arsenal during the conflict.

Kalashnikov Arms, compiled by Alexei Nedelin, Design Military Parade, Ltd., Moscow, Russia, 1997. 240 pp., illus. $49.95.
Weapons versions stored in the St. Petersburg Military Historical Museum of Artillery, Engineer Troops and Communications and in the Izhmash JSC.

Kalashnikov "Machine Pistols, Assault Rifles, and Machine Guns, 1945 to the Present", by John Walter, Paladin Press, Boulder, CO, 1999, hardcover, photos, illus., 146 pp. $22.95
This exhaustive work published by Greenhill Military Manuals features a gun-by-gun directory of Kalashnikov variants. Technical specifications and illustrations are provided throughout, along with details of sights, bayonets, markings and ammunition. A must for the serious collector and historian.

The Kentucky Pistol, by Roy Chandler and James Whisker, Old Bedford Village Press, Bedford, PA, 1997. 225 pp., illus. $60.00
A photographic study of Kentucky pistols from famous collections.

The Kentucky Rifle, by Captain John G.W. Dillin, George Shumway Publisher, York, PA, 1993. 221 pp., illus. $50.00.
This well-known book was the first attempt to tell the story of the American longrifle. This edition retains the original text and illustrations with supplemental footnotes provided by Dr. George Shumway.

Know Your Broomhandle Mausers, by R.J. Berger, Blacksmith Corp., Southport, CT, 1985. 96 pp., illus. Paper covers. $12.95.
An interesting story on the big Mauser pistol and its variations.

Krag Rifles, by William S. Brophy, The Gun Room Press, Highland Park, NJ, 1980. 200 pp., illus. $35.00.
The first comprehensive work detailing the evolution and various models, both military and civilian.

The Krieghoff Parabellum, by Randall Gibson, Midland, TX, 1988. 279 pp., illus. $40.00.
A comprehensive text pertaining to the Lugers manufactured by H. Krieghoff Waffenfabrik.

Las Pistolas Espanolas Tipo "Mauser," by Artemio Mortera Perez, Quiron Ediciones, Valladolid, Spain, 1998. 71 pp., illustrated. Paper covers. $34.95.
This book covers in detail Spanish machine pistols and C96 copies made in Spain. Covers all Astra "Mauser" pistol series and the complete line of Beistegui C96 type pistols. Spanish text.

Law Enforcement Memorabilia Price and Identification Guide, by Monty McCord, DBI Books a division of Krause Publications, Inc. Iola, WI, 1999. 208 pp., illustrated. Paper covers. $19.95.
An invaluable reference to the growing wave of law enforcement collectors. Hundreds of items are covered from miniature vehicles to clothes, patches, and restraints.

Legendary Sporting Guns, by Eric Joly, Abbeville Press, New York, N.Y., 1999. 228 pp., illustrated. $65.00.
A survey of hunting through the ages and relates how many different types of firearms were created and refined for use afield.

Legends and Reality of the AK, by Val Shilin and Charlie Cutshaw, Paladen Press, Boulder, CO, 2000. 192 pp., illustrated. Paper covers. $35.00.
A behind-the-scenes look at history, design and impact of the Kalashnikov family of weapons.

LeMat, the Man, the Gun, by Valmore J. Forgett and Alain F. and Marie-Antoinette Serpette, Navy Arms Co., Ridgefield, NJ, 1996. 218 pp., illus. $49.95.
The first definitive study of the Confederate revolvers invention, development and delivery by Francois Alexandre LeMat.

Les Pistolets Automatiques Francaise 1890-1990, by Jean Huon, Combined Books, Inc., Conshohocken, PA, 1997. 160 pp., illus. French text. $34.95
French automatic pistols from the earliest experiments through the World Wars and Indo-China to modern security forces.

Levine's Guide to Knives And Their Values, 4th Edition, by Bernard Levine, DBI Books, a division of Krause Publications, Iola, WI, 1997. 512 pp., illus. Paper covers. $27.95
All the basic tools for identifying, valuing and collecting folding and fixed blade knives.

The Light 6-Pounder Battalion Gun of 1776, by Adrian Caruana, Museum Restoration Service, Bloomfield, Ontario, Canada, 2001. 76 pp., illus. Paper covers. $8.95

The London Gun Trade, 1850-1920, by Joyce E. Gooding, Museum Restoration Service, Bloomfield, Ontario, Canada, 2001. 48 pp., illus. Paper covers. $8.95
Names, dates and locations of London gunmakers working between 1850 and 1920 are listed. Compiled from the original Kelly's Post Office Directories of the City of London.

The London Gunmakers and the English Duelling Pistol, 1770-1830, by Keith R. Dill, Museum Restoration Service, Bloomfield, Ontario, Canada, 1997. 36 pp., illus. Paper covers. $8.95
Ten gunmakers made London one of the major gunmaking centers of the world. This book examines how the design and construction of their pistols contributed to that reputation and how these characteristics may be used to date flintlock arms.

Longrifles of North Carolina, by John Bivens, George Shumway Publisher, York, PA, 1988. 256 pp., illus. $50.00.
Covers art and evolution of the rifle, immigration and trade movements. Committee of Safety gunsmiths, characteristics of the North Carolina rifle.

Longrifles of Pennsylvania, Volume 1, Jefferson, Clarion & Elk Counties, by Russel H. Harringer, George Shumway Publisher, York, PA, 1984. 200 pp., illus. $50.00.
First in series that will treat in great detail the longrifles and gunsmiths of Pennsylvania.

The Luger Handbook, by Aarron Davis, Krause Publications, Iola, WI, 1997. 112 pp., illus. Paper covers. $9.95
Quick reference to classify Luger models and variations with complete details including proofmarks.

Lugers at Random, by Charles Kenyon, Jr., Handgun Press, Glenview, IL, 1990. 420 pp., illus. $59.95.
A new printing of this classic, comprehensive reference for all Luger collectors.

The Luger Story, by John Walter, Stackpole Books, Mechanicsburg, PA, 2001. 256 pp., illus. Paper Covers $29.95.
The standard history of the world's most famous handgun.

M1 Carbine, by Larry Ruth, Gun room Press, Highland Park, NJ, 1987. 291 pp., illus. Paper $19.95.
The origin, development, manufacture and use of this famous carbine of World War II.

The M1 Carbine: Owner's Guide, by Scott A. Duff, Scott A. Duff, Export, PA, 1997. 126 pp., illus. Paper covers. $19.95.
This book answers the questions M1 owners most often ask concerning maintenance activities not encounted by military users.

The M1 Garand: Owner's Guide, by Scott A. Duff, Scott A. Duff, Export, PA, 1998. 132 pp., illus. Paper covers. $19.95.
This book answers the questions M1 owners most often ask concerning maintenance activities not encounted by military users.

The M1 Garand Serial Numbers and Data Sheets, by Scott A. Duff, Export, PA, 1995. 101 pp., illus. Paper covers. $11.95.
Provides the reader with serial numbers related to dates of manufacture and a large sampling of data sheets to aid in identification or restoration.

The M1 Garand 1936 to 1957, by Joe Poyer and Craig Riesch, North Cape Publications, Tustin, CA, 1996. 216 pp., illus. Paper covers. $19.95.
Describes the entire range of M1 Garand production in text and quick-scan charts.

The M1 Garand: Post World War, by Scott A. Duff, Scott A. Duff, Export, PA, 1990. 139 pp., illus. Soft covers. $19.95.
A detailed account of the activities at Springfield Armory through this period. International Harvester, H&R, Korean War production and quantities delivered. Serial numbers.

The M1 Garand: World War 2, by Scott A. Duff, Scott A. Duff, Export, PA, 1993. 210 pp., illus. Paper covers. $39.95.
The most comprehensive study available to the collector and historian on the M1 Garand of World War II.

Maine Made Guns and Their Makers, by Dwight B. Demeritt Jr., Maine State Museum, Augusta, ME, 1998. 209 pp., illustrated. $55.00.
An authoritative, biographical study of Maine gunsmiths.

Marlin Firearms: A History of the Guns and the Company That Made Them, by Lt. Col. William S. Brophy, USAR, Ret., Stackpole Books, Harrisburg, PA, 1989. 672 pp., illus. $75.00.
The definitive book on the Marlin Firearms Co. and their products.

Martini-Henry .450 Rifles & Carbines, by Dennis Lewis, Excalibur Publications, Latham, NY, 1996. 72 pp., illus. Paper covers. $11.95.
The stories of the rifles and carbines that were the mainstay of the British soldier through the Victorian wars.

Mauser Bolt Rifles, by Ludwig Olson, F. Brownell & Son, Inc., Montezuma, IA, 1999. 364 pp., illus. $59.95.
The most complete, detailed, authoritative and comprehensive work ever done on Mauser bolt rifles. Completely revised deluxe 3rd edition.

Mauser Military Rifles of the World, 2nd Edition, by Robert Ball, Krause Publications, Iola, WI, 2000. 304 pp., illustrated with 1,000 b&w photos and a 48 page color section. $44.95.
This 2nd edition brings more than 100 new photos of these historic rifles and the wars in which they were carried.

Mauser Smallbores Sporting, Target and Training Rifles, by Jon Speed, Collector Grade Publications, Cobourg, Ontario, Canada 1998. 349 pp., illustrated. $67.50.
A history of all the smallbore sporting, target and training rifles produced by the legendary Mauser-Werke of Obendorf Am Neckar.

Military Holsters of World War 2, by Eugene J. Bender, Rowe Publications, Rochester, NY, 1998. 200 pp., illustrated. $45.00.
A revised edition with a new price guide of the most definitive book on this subject.

Military Pistols of Japan, by Fred L. Honeycutt, Jr., Julin Books, Palm Beach Gardens, FL, 1997. 168 pp., illus. $42.00.
Covers every aspect of military pistol production in Japan through WWII.

The Military Remington Rolling Block Rifle, by George Layman, Pioneer Press, TN, 1998. 146 pp., illus. Paper covers. $24.95.
A standard reference for those with an interest in the Remington rolling block family of firearms.

Military Rifles of Japan, 5th Edition, by F.L. Honeycutt, Julin Books, Lake Park, FL, 1999. 208 pp., illus. $42.00.
A new revised and updated edition. Includes the early Murata-period markings, etc.

Military Small Arms Data Book, by Ian V. Hogg, Stackpole Books, Mechanicsburg, PA, 1999. $44.95. 336 pp., illustrated.
Data on more than 1,500 weapons. Covers a vast range of weapons from pistols to anti-tank rifles. Essential data, 1870-2000, in one volume.

Modern Beretta Firearms, by Gene Gangarosa, Jr., Stoeger Publishing Co., So. Hackensack, NJ, 1994. 288 pp., illus. Paper covers. $16.95.
Traces all models of modern Beretta pistols, rifles, machine guns and combat shotguns.

Modern Gun Values, The Gun Digest Book of, 10th Edition, by the Editors of Gun Digest, DBI Books, a division of Krause Publications, Iola, WI., 1996. 560 pp., illus. Paper covers. $21.95.
Greatly updated and expanded edition describing and valuing over 7,000 firearms manufactured from 1900 to 1996. The standard for valuing modern firearms.

Modern Gun Identification & Value Guide, 13th Edition, by Russell and Steve Quertermous, Collector Books, Paducah, KY, 1998. 504 pp., illus. Paper covers. $14.95.
Features current values for over 2,500 models of rifles, shotguns and handguns, with over 1,800 illustrations.

More Single Shot Rifles, by James C. Grant, The Gun Room Press, Highland Park, NJ, 1976. 324 pp., illus. $35.00.
Details the guns made by Frank Wesson, Milt Farrow, Holden, Borchardt, Stevens, Remington, Winchester, Ballard and Peabody-Martini.

Mortimer, the Gunmakers, 1753-1923, by H. Lee Munson, Andrew Mowbray Inc., Lincoln, RI, 1992. 320 pp., illus. $65.00.
Seen through a single, dominant, English gunmaking dynasty this fascinating study provides a window into the classical era of firearms artistry.

The Mosin-Nagant Rifle, by Terence W. Lapin, North Cape Publications, Tustin, CA, 1998. 30 pp., illustrated. Paper covers. $19.95.
The first ever complete book on the Mosin-Nagant rifle written in English. Covers every variation.

The Navy Luger, by Joachim Gortz and John Walter, Handgun Press, Glenview, IL, 1988. 128 pp., illus. $24.95.
The 9mm Pistole 1904 and the Imperial German Navy. A concise illustrated history.

The New World of Russian Small Arms and Ammunition, by Charlie Cutshaw, Paladin Press, Boulder, CO, 1998. 160 pp., illustrated. $42.95.
Detailed descriptions, specifications and first-class illustrations of the AN-94, PSS silent pistol, Bizon SMG, Saifa-12 tactical shotgun, the GP-25 grenade launcher and more cutting edge Russian weapons.

The Number 5 Jungle Carbine, by Alan M. Petrillo, Excalibur Publications, Latham, NY, 1994. 32 pp., illus. Paper covers. $7.95.
A comprehensive treatment of the rifle that collectors have come to call the "Jungle Carbine"—the Lee-Enfield Number 5, Mark 1.

The '03 Era: When Smokeless Revolutionized U.S. Riflery, by Clark S. Campbell, Collector Grade Publications, Inc., Ontario, Canada, 1994. 334 pp., illus. $44.50.
A much-expanded version of Campbell's *The '03 Springfields*, representing forty years of in-depth research into "all things '03."

Observations on Colt's Second Contract, November 2, 1847, by G. Maxwell Longfield and David T. Basnett, Museum Restoration Service, Bloomfield, Ontario, Canada, 1997. 36 pp., illus. Paper covers. $6.95.
This study traces the history and the construction of the Second Model Colt Dragoon supplied in 1848 to the U.S. Cavalry.

Official Guide to Gunmarks, 3rd Edition, by Robert H. Balderson, House of Collectibles, New York, NY, 1996. 367 pp., illus. Paper covers. $15.00.
Identifies manufacturers' marks that appear on American and foreign pistols, rifles and shotguns.

Official Price Guide to Gun Collecting, by R.L. Wilson, Ballantine/House of Collectibles, New York, NY, 1998. 450 pp., illus. Paper covers. $21.50.
Covers more than 30,000 prices from Colt revolvers to Winchester rifles and shotguns to German Lugers and British sporting rifles and game guns.

Official Price Guide to Military Collectibles, 6th Edition, by Richard J. Austin, Random House, Inc., New York, NY, 1998. 200 pp., illus. Paper cover. $20.00.

Covers weapons and other collectibles from wars of the distant and recent past. More than 4,000 prices are listed. Illustrated with 400 black & white photos plus a full-color insert.

The Official Soviet SVD Manual, by Major James F. Gebhardt (Ret.) Paladin Press, Boulder, CO, 1999. 112 pp., illustrated. Paper covers. $15.00.

Operating instructions for the 7.62mm Dragunov, the first Russian rifle developed from scratch specifically for sniping.

Old Gunsights: A Collector's Guide, 1850 to 2000, by Nicholas Stroebel, Krause Publications, Iola, WI, 1998. 320 pp., illus. Paper covers. $29.95

An in-depth and comprehensive examination of old gunsights and the rifles on which they were used to get accurate feel for prices in this expanding market.

Old Rifle scopes, by Nicholas Stroebel, Krause Publications, Iola, WI, 2000. 400 pp., illustrated. Paper covers. $31.95.

This comprehensive collector's guide takes aim at more than 120 scope makers and 60 mount makers and features photos and current market values for 300 scopes and mounts manufactured from 1950-1985.

The P-08 Parabellum Luger Automatic Pistol, edited by J. David McFarland, Desert Publications, Cornville, AZ, 1982. 20 pp., illus. Paper covers. $11.95.

Covers every facet of the Luger, plus a listing of all known Luger models.

Packing Iron, by Richard C. Rattenbury, Zon International Publishing, Millwood, NY, 1993. 216 pp., illus. $45.00.

The best book yet produced on pistol holsters and rifle scabbards. Over 300 variations of holster and scabbards are illustrated in large, clear plates.

Parabellum: A Technical History of Swiss Lugers, by Vittorio Bobba, Priuli & Verlucca, Editori, Torino, Italy, 1996. Italian and English text. Illustrated. $100.00.

Patents for Inventions, Class 119 (Small Arms), 1855-1930. British Patent Office, Armory Publications, Oceanside, CA, 1993. 7 volume set. $250.00.

Contains 7980 abridged patent descriptions and their sectioned line drawings, plus a 37-page alphabetical index of the patentees.

Pattern Dates for British Ordnance Small Arms, 1718-1783, by DeWitt Bailey, Thomas Publications, Gettysburg, PA, 1997. 116 pp., illus. Paper covers. $20.00

The weapons discussed in this work are those carried by troops sent to North America between 1737 and 1783, or shipped to them as replacement arms while in America.

The Pitman Notes on U.S. Martial Small Arms and Ammunition, 1776-1933, Volume 2, Revolvers and Automatic Pistols, by Brig. Gen. John Pitman, Thomas Publications, Gettysburg, PA, 1990. 192 pp., illus. $29.95.

A most important primary source of information on United States military small arms and ammunition.

The Plains Rifle, by Charles Hanson, Gun Room Press, Highland Park, NJ, 1989. 169 pp., illus. $35.00.

All rifles that were made with the plainsman in mind, including pistols.

Powder and Ball Small Arms, by Martin Pegler, Windrow & Green, London, 1998. 128 pp., illus. $39.95.

Part of the new "Live Firing Classic Weapons" series featuring full color photos of experienced shooters dressed in authentic costumes handling, loading and firing historic weapons.

The Powder Flask Book, by Ray Riling, R&R Books, Livonia, NY, 1993. 514 pp., illus. $69.95.

The complete book on flasks of the 19th century. Exactly scaled pictures of 1,600 flasks are illustrated.

Proud Promise: French Autoloading Rifles, 1898-1979, by Jean Huon, Collector Grade Publications, Inc., Cobourg, Ont., Canada, 1995. 216 pp., illus. $39.95.

The author has finally set the record straight about the importance of French contributions to modern arms design.

E. C. Prudhomme's Gun Engraving Review, by E. C. Prudhomme, R&R Books, Livonia, NY, 1994. 164 pp., illus. $60.00.

As a source for engravers and collectors, this book is an indispensable guide to styles and techniques of the world's foremost engravers.

Purdey Gun and Rifle Makers: The Definitive History, by Donald Dallas, Quiller Press, London, 2000. 245 pp., illus. Color throughout. $100.00

A limited edition of 3,000 copies. Signed and Numbered. With a PURDEY book plate.

Reloading Tools, Sights and Telescopes for Single Shot Rifles, by Gerald O. Kelver, Brighton, CO, 1982. 163 pp., illus. Paper covers. $13.95.

A listing of most of the famous makers of reloading tools, sights and telescopes with a brief description of the products they manufactured.

The Remington-Lee Rifle, by Eugene F. Myszkowski, Excalibur Publications, Latham, NY, 1995. 100 pp., illus. Paper covers. $22.50.

Features detailed descriptions, including serial number ranges, of each model from the first Lee Magazine Rifle produced for the U.S. Navy to the last Remington-Lee Small Bores shipped to the Cuban Rural Guard.

Revolvers of the British Services 1854-1954, by W.H.J. Chamberlain and A.W.F. Taylerson, Museum Restoration Service, Ottawa, Canada, 1989. 80 pp., illus. $27.50.

Covers the types issued among many of the United Kingdom's naval, land or air services.

Rhode Island Arms Makers & Gunsmiths, by William O. Archibald, Andrew Mowbray, Inc., Lincoln, RI, 1990. 108 pp., illus. $16.50.

A serious and informative study of an important area of American arms making.

Rifles of the World, by Oliver Achard, Chartwell Books, Inc., Edison, NJ, 141 pp., illus. $24.95.

A unique insight into the world of long guns, not just rifles, but also shotguns, carbines and all the usual multi-barreled guns that once were so popular with European hunters, especially in Germany and Austria.

The Rock Island '03, by C.S. Ferris, C.S. Ferris, Arvada, CO, 1993. 58 pp., illus. Paper covers. $12.50.

A monograph of interest to the collector or historian concentrating on the U.S. M1903 rifle made by the less publicized of our two producing facilities.

Round Ball to Rimfire, Vol. 1, by Dean Thomas, Thomas Publications, Gettysburg, PA, 1997. 144 pp., illus. $40.00.

The first of a two-volume set of the most complete history and guide for all small arms ammunition used in the Civil War. The information includes data from research and development to the arsenals that created it.

Ruger and his Guns, by R.L. Wilson, Simon & Schuster, New York, NY, 1996. 358 pp., illus. $65.00.

A history of the man, the company and their firearms.

Russell M. Catron and His Pistols, by Warren H. Buxton, Ucross Books, Los Alamos, NM, 1998. 224 pp., illustrated. Paper covers. $49.50.

An unknown American firearms inventor and manufacturer of the mid twentieth century. Military, commerical, ammunition.

The SAFN-49 and The FAL, by Joe Poyer and Dr. Richard Feirman, North Cape Publications, Tustin, CA, 1998. 160 pp., illus. Paper covers. $14.95.

The first complete overview of the SAFN-49 battle rifle, from its pre-World War 2 beginnings to its military service in countries as diverse as the Belgian Congo and Argentina. The FAL was "light" version of the SAFN-49 and it became the Free World's most adopted battle rifle.

Sam Colt's Own Record 1847, by John Parsons, Wolfe Publishing Co., Prescott, AZ, 1992. 167 pp., illus. $24.50.

Chronologically presented, the correspondence published here completes the account of the manufacture, in 1847, of the Walker Model Colt revolver.

J. P. Sauer & Sohn, Sauer "Dein Waffenkamerad" Volume 2, by Cate & Krause, Walsworth Publishing, Chattanooga, TN, 2000. 440 pp., illus. $79.00.

A historical study of Sauer automatic pistols. This new volume includes a great deal of new knowledge that has surfaced about the firm J.P. Sauer. You will find new photos, documentation, serial number ranges and historial facts which will expand the knowledge and interest in the oldest and best of the German firearms companies.

Scottish Firearms, by Claude Blair and Robert Woosnam-Savage, Museum Restoration Service, Bloomfield, Ont., Canada, 1995. 52 pp., illus. Paper covers. $8.95.

This revision of the first book devoted entirely to Scottish firearms is supplemented by a register of surviving Scottish long guns.

The Scottish Pistol, by Martin Kelvin. Fairleigh Dickinson University Press, Dist. By Associated University Presses, Cranbury, NJ, 1997. 256 pp., illus. $49.50.

The Scottish pistol, its history, manufacture and design.

Sharps Firearms, by Frank Seller, Frank M. Seller, Denver, CO, 1998. 358 pp., illus. $55.00.

Traces the development of Sharps firearms with full range of guns made including all martial variations.

Simeon North: First Official Pistol Maker of the United States, by S. North and R. North, The Gun Room Press, Highland Park, NJ, 1972. 207 pp., illus. $15.95.

Reprint of the rare first edition.

The SKS Carbine, by Steve Kehaya and Joe Poyer, North Cape Publications, Tustin, CA, 1997. 150 pp., illus. Paper covers. $16.95.

The first comprehensive examination of a major historical firearm used through the Vietnam conflict to the diamond fields of Angola.

The SKS Type 45 Carbines, by Duncan Long, Desert Publications, El Dorado, AZ, 1992. 110 pp., illus. Paper covers. $19.95

Covers the history and practical aspects of operating, maintaining and modifying this abundantly available rifle.

Smith & Wesson 1857-1945, by Robert J. Neal and Roy G. Jinks, R&R Books, Livonia, NY, 1996. 434 pp., illus. $50.00.

The bible for all existing and aspiring Smith & Wesson collectors.

Sniper Variations of the German K98k Rifle, by Richard D. Law, Collector Grade Publications, Ontario, Canada, 1997. 240 pp., illus. $47.50.

Volume 2 of "Backbone of the Wehrmacht" the author's in-depth study of the German K98k rifle. This volume concentrates on the telescopic-sighted rifle of choice for most German snipers during World War 2.

Southern Derringers of the Mississippi Valley, by Turner Kirkland, Pioneer Press, Tenn., 1971. 80 pp., illus., paper covers. $4.00.

A guide for the collector, and a much-needed study.

Soviet Russian Postwar Military Pistols and Cartridges, by Fred A. Datig, Handgun Press, Glenview, IL, 1988. 152 pp., illus. $29.95.

Thoroughly researched, this definitive sourcebook covers the development and adoption of the Makarov, Stechkin and the new PSM pistols. Also included in this source book is coverage on Russian clandestine weapons and pistol cartridges.

Soviet Russian Tokarev "TT" Pistols and Cartridges 1929-1953, by Fred Datig, Graphic Publishers, Santa Ana, CA, 1993. 168 pp., illus. $39.95.

Details of rare arms and their accessories are shown in hundreds of photos. It also contains a complete bibliography and index.

Soviet Small-Arms and Ammunition, by David Bolotin, Handgun Press, Glenview, IL, 1996. 264 pp., illus. $49.95.
  An authoritative and complete book on Soviet small arms.

Sporting Collectibles, by Jim and Vivian Karsnitz, Schiffer Publishing Ltd., West Chester, PA, 1992. 160 pp., illus. Paper covers. $29.95.
  The fascinating world of hunting related collectibles presented in an informative text.

The Springfield 1903 Rifles, by Lt. Col. William S. Brophy, USAR, Ret., Stackpole Books Inc., Harrisburg, PA, 1985. 608 pp., illus. $75.00.
  The illustrated, documented story of the design, development, and production of all the models, appendages, and accessories.

Springfield Armory Shoulder Weapons 1795-1968, by Robert W.D. Ball, Antique Trader Books, Dubuque, IA, 1998. 264 pp., illus. $34.95.
  This book documents the 255 basic models of rifles, including test and trial rifles, produced by the Springfield Armory. It features the entire history of rifles and carbines manufactured at the Armory, the development of each weapon with specific operating characteristics and procedures.

Springfield Model 1903 Service Rifle Production and Alteration, 1905-1910, by C.S. Ferris and John Beard, Arvada, CO, 1995. 66 pp., illus. Paper covers. $12.50.
  A highly recommended work for any serious student of the Springfield Model 1903 rifle.

Springfield Shoulder Arms 1795-1865, by Claud E. Fuller, S. & S. Firearms, Glendale, NY, 1996. 76 pp., illus. Paper covers. $17.95.
  Exact reprint of the scarce 1930 edition of one of the most definitive works on Springfield flintlock and percussion muskets ever published.

Standard Catalog of Firearms, 11ᵗʰ Edition, by Ned Schwing, Krause Publications, Iola, WI, 2001.1328 Pages, illustrated. 6,000+ b&w photos plus a 16-page color section. Paper covers. $32.95.
  This is the largest, most comprehensive and best-selling firearm book of all time! And this year's edition is a blockbuster for both shooters and firearm collectors. More than 12,000 firearms are listed and priced in up to six grades of condition. That's almost 80,000 prices! Gun enthusiasts will love the new full-color section of photos highlighting the finest firearms sold at auction this past year –including the new record for an American historical firearm: $684,000!

Standard Catalog of Winchester, 1ˢᵗ Edition, edited by David D. Kowalski, Krause Publications, Iola, WI, 2000. 704 pp., illustrated with 2,000 B&W photos and 75 color photos. Paper covers. $39.95.
  This book identifies and values more than 5,000 collectibles, including firearms, cartridges shotshells, fishing tackle, sporting goods and tools manufactured by Winchester Repeating Arms Co

Steel Canvas: The Art of American Arms, by R.L. Wilson, Random House, NY, 1995, 384 pp., illus. $65.00.
  Presented here for the first time is the breathtaking panorama of America's extraordinary engravers and embellishers of arms, from the 1700s to modern times.

Stevens Pistols & Pocket Rifles, by K.L. Cope, Museum Restoration Service, Alexandria Bay, NY, 1992. 114 pp., illus. $24.50.
  This is the story of the guns and the man who designed them and the company which he founded to make them.

A Study of Colt Conversions and Other Percussion Revolvers, by R. Bruce McDowell, Krause Publications, Iola, WI, 1997. 464 pp., illus. $39.95.
  The ultimate reference detailing Colt revolvers that have been converted from percussion to cartridge.

The Sumptuous Flaske, by Herbert G. Houze, Andrew Mowbray, Inc., Lincoln, RI, 1989. 158 pp., illus. Soft covers. $35.00.
  Catalog of a recent show at the Buffalo Bill Historical Center bringing together some of the finest European and American powder flasks of the 16th to 19th centuries.

The Swedish Mauser Rifles, by Steve Kehaya and Joe Poyer, North Cape Publications, Tustin, CA, 1999. 267 pp., illustrated. Paper covers. $19.95.
  Every known variation of the Swedish Mauser carbine and rifle is described including all match and target rifles and all sniper fersions. Includes serial number and production data.

Televisions Cowboys, Gunfighters & Cap Pistols, by Rudy A. D'Angelo, Antique Trader Books, Norfolk, VA, 1999. 287 pp., illustrated in color and black and white. Paper covers. $31.95.
  Over 850 beautifully photographed color and black and white images of cap guns, actors, and the characters they portrayed in the "Golden Age of TV Westerns. With accurate descriptions and current values.

Thompson: The American Legend, by Tracie L. Hill, Collector Grade Publications, Ontario, Canada, 1996. 584 pp., illus. $85.00.
  The story of the first American submachine gun. All models are featured and discussed.

Toys That Shoot and Other Neat Stuff, by James Dundas, Schiffer Books, Atglen, PA, 1999. 112 pp., illustrated. Paper covers. $24.95.
  Shooting toys from the twentieth century, especially 1920's to 1960's, in over 420 color photographs of BB guns, cap shooters, marble shooters, squirt guns and more. Complete with a price guide.

The Trapdoor Springfield, by M.D. Waite and B.D. Ernst, The Gun Room Press, Highland Park, NJ, 1983. 250 pp., illus. $39.95.
  The first comprehensive book on the famous standard military rifle of the 1873-92 period.

Treasures of the Moscow Kremlin: Arsenal of the Russian Tsars, A Royal Armories and the Moscow Kremlin exhibition. HM Tower of London 13, June 1998 to 11 September, 1998. BAS Printers, Over Wallop, Hampshire, England. xxii plus 192 pp. over 180 color illustrations. Text in English and Russian. $65.00.
  For this exhibition catalog each of the 94 objects on display are photographed and described in detail to provide a most informative record of this important exhibition.

U.S. Breech-Loading Rifles and Carbines, Cal. 45, by Gen. John Pitman, Thomas Publications, Gettysburg, PA, 1992. 192 pp., illus. $29.95.
  The third volume in the Pitman Notes on U.S. Martial Small Arms and Ammunition, 1776-1933. This book centers on the "Trapdoor Springfield" models.

U.S. Handguns of World War 2: The Secondary Pistols and Revolvers, by Charles W. Pate, Andrew Mowbray, Inc., Lincoln, RI, 1998. 515 pp., illus. $39.00.
  This indispensable new book covers all of the American military handguns of World War 2 except for the M1911A1 Colt automatic.

United States Martial Flintlocks, by Robert M. Reilly, Mowbray Publishing Co., Lincoln, RI, 1997. 264 pp., illus. $40.00.
  A comprehensive history of American flintlock longarms and handguns (mostly military) c. 1775 to c. 1840.

U.S. Martial Single Shot Pistols, by Daniel D. Hartzler and James B. Whisker, Old Bedford Village Pess, Bedford, PA, 1998. 128 pp., illus. $45.00.
  A photographic chronicle of military and semi-martial pistols supplied to the U.S. Government and the several States.

U.S. Military Arms Dates of Manufacture from 1795, by George Madis, David Madis, Dallas, TX, 1989. 64 pp. Soft covers. $6.00.
  Lists all U.S. military arms of collector interest alphabetically, covering about 250 models.

U.S. Military Small Arms 1816-1865, by Robert M. Reilly, The Gun Room Press, Highland Park, NJ, 1983. 270 pp., illus. $39.95.
  Covers every known type of primary and secondary martial firearms used by Federal forces.

U.S. M1 Carbines: Wartime Production, by Craig Riesch, North Cape Publications, Tustin, CA, 1994. 72 pp., illus. Paper covers. $16.95.
  Presents only verifiable and accurate information. Each part of the M1 Carbine is discussed fully in its own section; including markings and finishes.

U.S. Naval Handguns, 1808-1911, by Fredrick R. Winter, Andrew Mowbray Publishers, Lincoln, RI, 1990. 128 pp., illus. $26.00.
  The story of U.S. Naval Handguns spans an entire century—included are sections on each of the important naval handguns within the period.

Walther: A German Legend, by Manfred Kersten, Safari Press, Inc., Huntington Beach, CA. 400 pp., illustrated. $85.00.
  This comprehensive book covers, in rich detail, all aspects of the company and its guns, including an illustrious and rich history, the WW2 years, all the pistols (models 1 through 9), the P-38, P-88, the long guns, .22 rifles, centerfires, Wehrmacht guns, and even a gun that could shoot around a corner.

Walther Pistols: Models 1 Through P99, Factory Variations and Copies, by Dieter H. Marschall, Ucross Books, Los Alamos, NM. 2000. 140 pages, with 140 b & w illustrations, index. Paper Covers. $19.95.
  This is the English translation, revised and updated, of the highly successful and widely acclaimed German language edition. This book provides the collector with a reference guide and overview of the entire line of the Walther military, police, and self-defense pistols from the very first to the very latest. Models 1-9, PP, PPK, MP, AP, HP, P.38, P1, P4, P38K, P5, P88, P99 and the Manurhin models. Variations, where issued, serial ranges, calibers, marks, proofs, logos, and design aspects in an astonishing quantity and variety are crammed into this very well researched and highly regarded work.

The Walther Handgun Story: A Collector's and Shooter's Guide, by Gene Gangarosa, Steiger Publications, 1999. 300., illustrated. Paper covers. $21.95.
  Covers the entire history of the Walther empire. Illustrated with over 250 photos.

Walther P-38 Pistol, by Maj. George Nonte, Desert Publications, Cornville, AZ, 1982. 100 pp., illus. Paper covers. $11.95.
  Complete volume on one of the most famous handguns to come out of WWII. All models covered.

Walther Models PP & PPK, 1929-1945 – Volume 1, by James L. Rankin, Coral Gables, FL, 1974. 142 pp., illus. $40.00
  Complete coverage on the subject as to finish, proofmarks and Nazi Party inscriptions.

Walther Volume II, Engraved, Presentation and Standard Models, by James L. Rankin, J.L. Rankin, Coral Gables, FL, 1977. 112 pp., illus. $40.00.
  The new Walther book on embellished versions and standard models. Has 88 photographs, including many color plates.

Walther, Volume III, 1908-1980, by James L. Rankin, Coral Gables, FL, 1981. 226 pp., illus. $40.00.
  Covers all models of Walther handguns from 1908 to date, includes holsters, grips and magazines.

Winchester: An American Legend, by R.L. Wilson, Random House, New York, NY, 1991. 403 pp., illus. $65.00.
  The official history of Winchester firearms from 1849 to the present.

Winchester Bolt Action Military & Sporting Rifles 1877 to 1937, by Herbert G. Houze, Andrew Mowbray Publishing, Lincoln, RI, 1998. 295 pp., illus. $45.00.
  Winchester was the first American arms maker to commercially manufacture a bolt action repeating rifle, and this book tells the exciting story of these Winchester bolt actions.

The Winchester Book, by George Madis, David Madis Gun Book Distributor, Dallas, TX, 1986. 650 pp., illus. $49.50.
  A new, revised 25th anniversary edition of this classic book on Winchester firearms. Complete serial ranges have been added.

Winchester Dates of Manufacture 1849-1984, by George Madis, Art & Reference House, Brownsboro, TX, 1984. 59 pp. $9.95.
A most useful work, compiled from records of the Winchester factory.

Winchester Engraving, by R.L. Wilson, Beinfeld Books, Springs, CA, 1989. 500 pp., illus. $135.00.
A classic reference work of value to all arms collectors.

The Winchester Handbook, by George Madis, Art & Reference House, Lancaster, TX, 1982. 287 pp., illus. $24.95.
The complete line of Winchester guns, with dates of manufacture, serial numbers, etc.

The Winchester-Lee Rifle, by Eugene Myszkowski, Excalibur Publications, Tucson, AZ 2000. 96 pp., illustrated. Paper Covers. $22.95
The development of the Lee Straight Pull, the cartridge and the approval for military use. Covers details of the inventor and memorabilia of Winchester-Lee related material.

Winchester Lever Action Repeating Firearms, Vol. 1, The Models of 1866, 1873 and 1876, by Arthur Pirkle, North Cape Publications, Tustin, CA, 1995. 112 pp., illus. Paper covers. $19.95.
Complete, part-by-part description, including dimensions, finishes, markings and variations throughout the production run of these fine, collectible guns.

Winchester Lever Action Repeating Rifles, Vol. 2, The Models of 1886 and 1892, by Arthur Pirkle, North Cape Publications, Tustin, CA, 1996. 150 pp., illus. Paper covers. $19.95.
Describes each model on a part-by-part basis by serial number range complete with finishes, markings and changes.

Winchester Lever Action Repeating Rifles, Volume 3, The Model of 1894, by Arthur Pirkle, North Cape Publications, Tustin, CA, 1998. 150 pp., illus. Paper covers. $19.95.
The first book ever to provide a detailed description of the Model 1894 rifle and carbine.

The Winchester Lever Legacy, by Clyde "Snooky" Williamson, Buffalo Press, Zachary, LA, 1988. 664 pp., illustrated. $75.00
A book on reloading for the different calibers of the Winchester lever action rifle.

The Winchester Model 94: The First 100 Years, by Robert C. Renneberg, Krause Publications, Iola, WI, 1991. 208 pp., illus. $34.95.
Covers the design and evolution from the early years up to the many different editions that exist today.

Winchester Rarities, by Webster, Krause Publications, Iola, WI, 2000. 208 pp., with over 800 color photos, illus. $49.95.
This book details the rarest of the rare; the one-of-a-kind items and the advertising pieces from years gone by. With nearly 800 full color photos and detailed pricing provided by experts in the field, this book gives collectors and enthusiasts everything they need.

Winchester Shotguns and Shotshells, by Ronald W. Stadt, Krause Publications, Iola, WI, 1995. 256 pp., illus. $34.95.
The definitive book on collectible Winchester shotguns and shotshells manufactured through 1961.

The Winchester Single-Shot- Volume 1; A History and Analysis, by John Campbell, Andrew Mowbray, Inc., Lincoln RI, 1995. 272 pp., illus. $55.00.
Covers every important aspect of this highly-collectible firearm.

The Winchester Single-Shot- Volume 2; Old Secrets and New Discoveries, by John Campbell, Andrew Mowbray, Inc., Lincoln RI, 2000. 280 pp., illus. $55.00.
An exciting follow-up to the classic first volume.

Winchester Slide-Action Rifles, Volume 1: Model 1890 & 1906, by Ned Schwing, Krause Publications, Iola, WI, 1992. 352 pp., illus. $39.95.
First book length treatment of models 1890 & 1906 with over 50 charts and tables showing significant new information about caliber style and rarity.

Winchester Slide-Action Rifles, Volume 2: Model 61 & Model 62, by Ned Schwing, Krause Publications, Iola, WI, 1993. 256 pp., illus. $34.95.
A complete historic look into the Model 61 and the Model 62. These favorite slide-action guns receive a thorough presentation which takes you to the factory to explore receivers, barrels, markings, stocks, stampings and engraving in complete detail.

Winchester's North West Mounted Police Carbines and other Model 1876 Data, by Lewis E. Yearout, The author, Great Falls, MT, 1999. 224 pp., illustrated. Paper covers. $38.00
An impressive accumulation of the facts on the Model 1876, with particular empasis on those purchased for the North West Mounted Police.

Worldwide Webley and the Harrington and Richardson Connection, by Stephen Cuthbertson, Ballista Publishing and Distributing Ltd., Gabriola Island, Canada, 1999. 259 pp., illus. $50.00
A masterpiece of scholarship. Over 350 photographs plus 75 original documents, patent drawings, and advertisements accompany the text.

Index

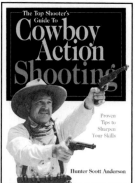
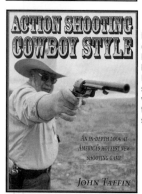

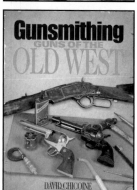
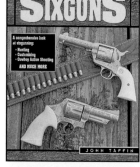

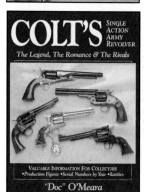

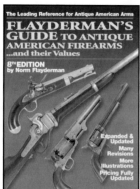
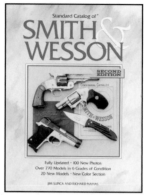

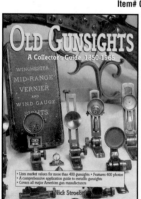
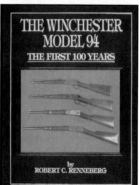

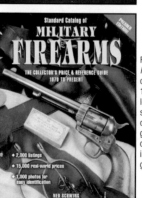
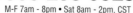